HEALTH INSURANCE IN DEVELOPING COUNTRIES
THE SOCIAL SECURITY APPROACH

HEALTH INSURANCE IN DEVELOPING COUNTRIES
THE SOCIAL SECURITY APPROACH

Aviva Ron   Brian Abel-Smith
Giovanni Tamburi

INTERNATIONAL LABOUR OFFICE   GENEVA

Copyright © International Labour Organisation 1990
First published 1990
Reprinted 1993

Publications of the International Labour Office enjoy copyright under Protocol 2 of the Universal Copyright Convention. Nevertheless, short excerpts from them may be reproduced without authorisation, on condition that the source is indicated. For rights of reproduction or translation, application should be made to the Publications Branch (Rights and Permissions), International Labour Office, CH-1211 Geneva 22, Switzerland. The International Labour Office welcomes such applications.

Ron, A., Abel-Smith, B., and Tamburi, G.
Health insurance in developing countries: The social security approach
Geneva, International Labour Office, 1990
/Health insurance/, /Health policy/, /Health service/s, /Developing country/s. 02.03.2
ISBN 92-2-106475-1

ILO Cataloguing in Publication Data

The designations employed in ILO publications, which are in conformity with United Nations practice, and the presentation of material therein do not imply the expression of any opinion whatsoever on the part of the International Labour Office concerning the legal status of any country, area or territory or of its authorities, or concerning the delimitation of its frontiers.
The responsibility for opinions expressed in signed articles, studies and other contributions rests solely with their authors, and publication does not constitute an endorsement by the International Labour Office of the opinions expressed in them.
Reference to names of firms and commercial products and processes does not imply their endorsement by the International Labour Office, and any failure to mention a particular firm, commercial product or process is not a sign of disapproval.

ILO publications can be obtained through major booksellers or ILO local offices in many countries, or direct from ILO Publications, International Labour Office, CH-1211 Geneva 22, Switzerland. A catalogue or list of new publications will be sent free of charge from the above address.

Printed in Switzerland

FOREWORD

People must be healthy in order to contribute to social and economic development: development goals cannot be achieved without a healthy population.

In 1978 the historic International Conference on Primary Health Care in Alma-Ata (USSR) charted a new course for health policy. Comprehensive goals for Health for All by the Year 2000 were set in the Strategy agreed in 1981.

Developing countries have fully endorsed both the goals and the policies set out in Alma-Ata; they are making considerable efforts to find the resources and create the conditions required to meet them.

However, the economic situation—often unfavourable—together with financial, administrative and political constraints, has made progress slow and uneven. As of today, few countries have been able to mobilise all the financial and human resources needed to meet desired targets in the health sector in the anticipated period of time.

How to finance health plans and how to make the best use of resources have both become critical issues. The various strategies and options available to governments in order to mobilise resources for health have been outlined in several international meetings, such as the Technical Discussions held during the 40th World Health Assembly in 1987. Emphasis was laid on the considerable potential of social security programmes directed towards the provision of health services. These programmes, generally organised according to compulsory health insurance criteria, have a long history. Their adaptation to Third World conditions is more recent, except in Latin America where they have attained substantial social relevance and population coverage.

Among the international agencies of the United Nations family, technical competence for social security matters, including health insurance, is attributed to the International Labour Organisation (ILO). Standard setting, research, technical co-operation, training and the dissemination of information on social security have been carried out in the ILO for over 50 years. ILO expertise in planning, implementing and financing health insurance schemes has been put at the disposal of a large number of developing countries and the international financial institutions. Systems of delivering basic health care, financing concepts and legislation that suit the conditions of developing countries have been tested and applied. On many occasions, activities have been undertaken jointly with the WHO, since both agencies share common objectives and concerns, with the added focus of reaching Health for All.

An appraisal of the current situation shows that senior officials of Ministries of Health and of other Ministries dealing with economic and social planning in developing countries have seldom had the opportunity to review all the available information and technical background material on social security. This contrasts with the desire now expressed by health policy planners and administrators to explore the potential role of social security as a means of broadening the access of the population to primary health care and related health facilities and services.

The compulsory health insurance approach has, at times, been examined with some hesitation in Ministries of Health, or viewed narrowly as a para-fiscal device, rather than for its potential as a comprehensive health care programme. Inadequate understanding of the concept has often resulted in its being regarded as a threat, as if health insurance within the social security framework would take health care out of the domain of the Ministry of Health. There is therefore a need for clarification and increased understanding of the positive aspects of social security, as well as its potential shortcomings, in the light of actual experience.

The experience gained by the ILO indicates that social security health insurance programmes can take a variety of forms, particularly with regard to the institutional framework, the organisation of the delivery of health services, relations with the medical profession, and financing. There is no standard model that can satisfy the needs of all developing countries.

Thus, it seemed to the ILO that a new effort was required to stimulate serious consideration of the health insurance option. Furthermore, it appeared that the effort should concentrate on bringing about an understanding of the rich and diverse experience of social security health care programmes in a large geographical region, such as Asia and Oceania. The technical issues and factors influencing the development of such programmes needed also to be better understood.

For this purpose, an Asian Regional Seminar on Social Security Health Insurance and its Role in Health for All Strategies was held in March 1989 in Seoul. The participants from 15 countries included senior officials from Ministries of Health, Labour and Social Welfare, and National Planning Agencies, as well as social security institutions with established or very newly developed programmes in health insurance.

Foreword

Representatives and observers from the WHO, the World Bank and the Asian Development Bank participated actively in the meetings and technical visits, as did one representative each of Asian employers' organisations and trade unions.

The exchange of ideas and experience that took place at the Seminar showed that officials of the Ministries of Health and of Planning appreciated the opportunity to have access to complex and rich technical material on health insurance which had not previously been made available to them.

For this reason the ILO has decided to prepare the present publication—rather than a Seminar report—by making use of the documents circulated at the Seminar and of new material drafted for the purpose of showing a fuller picture of the evolution and characteristics of health insurance, firstly in developing countries in general, and secondly in the Asian context.

This publication is addressed to a fairly large audience of persons interested in the contribution that social security can make in the field of health care in developing countries. Policy-makers and administrators will find a comprehensive treatment of the technical issues and policy options relevant to compulsory health insurance.

Dr. Aviva Ron, consultant to the ILO, took major responsibility for writing Part I, compiling the country profiles and editing the country sections in Part II. Chapter 4 of Part I, on paying the providers, was, however, entirely contributed by Professor Brian Abel-Smith of the London School of Economics, who also gave useful advice on the drafts of other chapters. I, myself, planned and designed the publication and contributed to Chapters 1 and 2 in Part I.

G. Tamburi
Director,
Social Security Department,
International Labour Office, Geneva

CONTENTS

Foreword v

Part 1. Introduction to compulsory health insurance 1

1. Health insurance as a social security undertaking 3
Social security: A fundamental concept 3
The pressures for establishing health insurance 5
The historical evolution of health insurance: A brief review 7
      Highlights in industrialised countries 7
      The evolution in developing countries 13

2. Compulsory health insurance as a social programme and a health sub-system 21
Government and health insurance 21
Sources of revenue 25
Social security as a health sub-system 29
Role of the participants 33

3. Health insurance benefits 35
Classification of benefits 35
Benefit characteristics 38
Indirect method of providing health care benefits 39
The direct method 41
      Development of hospital care 42
      Development of primary health care 43
Combined systems 49
Cost-sharing 50

4. Paying doctors and hospitals under health insurance 53
General considerations 53
      Lower charges 54
      Standardised payments 56

Paying the doctor	58
Fee-for-service	58
Salary	61
Capitation	63
Conclusion on doctor payment	66
Paying the hospital	67
Payment per itemised bill	67
Payment per inclusive day	68
Payment by diagnosis	69
Payment by budget	69
5. Organisation and administration of health insurance	**71**
The health insurance system as an organisation	71
Social and economic factors in administration	72
Centralisation and decentralisation	74
Administration	75
Control tasks	81
Control of membership coverage	81
Financial control	82
Quality assurance	83
Part II: Experiences in the developing countries of Asia	**87**
Introduction to the country profiles	89
Bangladesh	91
China	93
Fiji	109
India	111
Indonesia	133
Jordan	139
Republic of Korea	141
Kuwait	153
Malaysia	155
Myanmar	163
Nepal	167
Pakistan	169
Papua New Guinea	179
Philippines	181
Sri Lanka	187
Thailand	189

Annexes

Annex I: Glossary: Health insurance and health care terms 201
Annex II: Medical care: Extract from provisions of ILO Conventions
and Recommendations 207
Annex III: Suggestions for further reading 229

PART I

INTRODUCTION TO COMPULSORY HEALTH INSURANCE

HEALTH INSURANCE AS A SOCIAL SECURITY UNDERTAKING

SOCIAL SOLIDARITY: A FUNDAMENTAL CONCEPT

Conditions requiring medical care of a preventive or curative nature occurring during every individual's life lead to financial commitments that many persons cannot meet from their own resources or those of their family.

When, however, risks and resources are pooled among a larger group of persons with different probabilities of requiring care, the security of each individual is enhanced. The larger the group, the higher are the chances that the funds pooled together will be sufficient to pay for the care that each member is likely to require.

Obviously solidarity implies cross-subsidisation from individuals with higher resources to those who can contribute less and from those with a lower incidence of illness to those who require care more frequently. It may also imply cross-subsidisation from those currently without family responsibilities to those supporting spouses and children.

Groups practising solidarity can be formed spontaneously. Otherwise society can choose to make mandatory the constitution of "population" groups which will mutually support one another.

The former approach (i.e. voluntary affiliation) has the disadvantage that people with higher risks and/or fewer resources will join, while others will abstain. Voluntary affiliation leads to "adverse selection", i.e. an undue attraction of the "bad" risks and, consequently, a much higher collective cost.

In contrast, when legislation makes affiliation compulsory for a prescribed and large section of the population (i.e. all employees or certain categories of employees), good and bad risks are shared and resources are pooled. The financial viability of the joint undertaking becomes much higher than when affiliation is voluntary.

When this process of solidarity is compulsorily applied to health-related risks, each individual can expect to receive *as of right* appropriate medical care whenever it is needed.

The individual's right stems from membership of the group of persons protected, irrespective of the amount of the contribution made to the joint fund. Such contribution will normally be related to ability to pay, rather than to the individual's health risk which will vary according to age, sex and physical condition.

Compulsory health insurance thus holds a strong social purpose, unlike private or commercial health insurance where individual risk is the basis used by the insurance carrier for establishing the insurance premium. For this reason "social insurance" is the term currently used to describe compulsory health insurance or similar benefit programmes based on social solidarity. The emphasis is on the term "social" more than on the term "insurance".

The mechanism to cover health risks described above creates a *demand* for health services and health care, a demand sustained by ability and capacity to pay.

The response to this demand must be an acceptable *supply* of services and care. A choice of "providers" of medical care is generally offered. These will include public non-profit institutions, private non-profit providers and, in all cases, also self-employed professionals and often profit-making hospitals.

Subject to the detailed explanations on the crucial question of how to match demand and supply to everyone's satisfaction, it must be said at the outset that in developing countries the relative availability and performance of the various types of "providers" is markedly different from the situation prevailing in highly industrialised and fully developed nations.

In many countries adequate supply is scarce or lacking in rural areas or in less accessible and less populated parts of the country. Shortages may be found in many other areas. In developing countries the availability of doctors, of para-medical staff and of suitable health infrastructure (premises, drugs, supplies, transport, equipment, etc.) is as important and crucial to the viability of a compulsory health insurance programme as the acceptance of the concept of solidarity.

Whatever the supply, any medical care *provided* to the membership of a health insurance programme must be *paid* for. The price to be paid is the fundamental issue on which a reasonable agreement must be found between the demand created by compulsory health insurance legislation and the supply which responds to it.

One of the peculiarities of the health "market" is, however, that society may well have agreed and arranged for some or all kinds of health services to be available free of charge. The State assumes the role of provider, drawing the necessary resources from its general revenue based on direct and indirect taxation. In an extreme situation where all services are virtually free at the point of delivery and every citizen is covered and is satisfied with the free care available, there would be no point in encouraging or promoting the creation of groups practising solidarity to meet their health care needs, simply because the need has already been met.

Unfortunately such an ideal situation is rarely found, particularly in developing countries. A free public health sector often exists but coverage is limited. Supply falls short of the current and the emerging demand. General revenue financing for health has severe budgetary constraints that it would be foolish to ignore or underestimate. History shows that there is ample scope for organising the process of solidarity—normally understood and defined as compulsory health insurance, a social security undertaking. If this path is followed a number of questions then arise, such as those related to the definition of the membership, the sources and level of the funds pooled together, the definition and scope of individual rights, the institutional approach to be applied and many other sometimes complex questions that public policy must address and solve in the best interest of the country at large.

Such issues are reviewed in detail in Chapters 2 to 5. First, the very broad results made so far are combined with a short analysis of the political premises and of the attitudes of the various groups who in developing countries are called to participate in health insurance as a social security undertaking. A sketch of the historical evolution of health insurance concludes the present chapter.

THE PRESSURES FOR ESTABLISHING HEALTH INSURANCE

There are a number of important factors at play in extending social security programmes to health care. Dissatisfaction with the quality and quantity of curative services provided by public systems, along with a growing inability of a substantial proportion of the population to pay for private medical services, often stimulate debate on whether basic health care should be provided as a right of every citizen. The demand usually comes from the political representatives of the users of health care. Criticism may first be aimed at the lack of resources for medical care, at the poor efficiency of services, and at the level of out-of-pocket disbursements needed to purchase care from the private sector.

Although social security programmes cannot be transferred from one country to another, least of all to developing countries, there is now a wealth of long and varied experience to learn from, and a review of the basic principles and experience should offer possibilities for suitable and successful adaptation. Overall political acceptability may be favourable but it is necessary to take account of the attitudes of the major players which, on Third World conditions, may have special limitations.

Particularly when the outlook for major progress in health service delivery through Ministry of Health resources is bleak, organised labour may promote consideration of the social insurance option for health care protection. Economic development and industrialisation lead to regular employment for more people. In the absence of social security, sickness means the loss of wages and often the loss of a job. Urbanisation, which usually accompanies this shift from a largely peasant economy, leads to smaller families, with fewer persons to pool risks and to care for sick family members. In this situation, we are also likely to find rising expectations for social security benefits. The wage-earning population becomes discontent with the generally long distances and waiting times involved in receiving a low level of public services, and with their own inability to afford private services.

Employers' attitudes are generally favourable, as they understand that a healthy labour force is more productive. To some extent, employer support for social security benefits generates worker loyalty, and it is simpler and often cheaper than bearing the responsibility for providing or paying for medical care for the worker as it is needed.

Acceptance by the providers of care will depend first on the level of supply, and the implications of the social security health care scheme both for earnings and professional freedom, particularly of physicians. In developing countries the providers may in fact be very receptive to health insurance. Despite a low level of manpower supply, underemployed doctors look for the secure and additional incomes that health insurance can generate. Low occupancy in private hospitals can make collaboration with the health insurance scheme extremely attractive, as a third party payer increases access to medical care.

Consumers do not necessarily accept a programme just because it presents opportunities for equity in access to medical care. Sociological and cultural attitudes to possible controls imposed by "public" arrangements may clash with preferences regarding, for example, privacy or freedom of choice of doctor and other providers. At the same time, health insurance contributions may be more willingly paid than general income tax. They are also easier to collect, if a network of contributions already exists for other social security schemes, such as a provident fund.

The ultimate feasibility of introducing a social security health care scheme will depend on the availability and stability of the relevant infrastructures. These are the medical resources, both manpower and facilities, the ability to contribute on the part of all three sources (employer, employee and government), and the administrative capacity to implement and operate the scheme with increasing efficiency. Along with these factors, political determination in creating the necessary legislation is needed. Very often such major issues face long delays in debate as the country goes through periods of socio-economic instability without real gains in the health status of the nation in the interim. During this period, the argument is often put forward that health insurance raises labour costs and may be inflationary. However, regular contributions may in fact replace ad hoc costs already made by employers in providing health care for their workers.

If we consider these factors, the feasibility of introducing statutory health insurance schemes in many developing countries may seem limited at the outset. But since the right path is one of gradual implementation, possibly by industrial sector or region, as the relevant infrastructures becomes available, many constraints can be lifted and a modest beginning can be made which can be extended when conditions improve.

One must bear in mind that there are political dividends for the promoters of social programmes—like health insurance—which make a tangible impact on living standards of large groups of low-income workers and their families.

THE HISTORICAL EVOLUTION OF HEALTH INSURANCE: A BRIEF REVIEW

The history of the development of compulsory health insurance as a social policy concern confirms that there must have been substantial political commitments and advantages in applying the concept of solidarity to health care. Otherwise the initial efforts, which are now at least a century old, would not have led to the situation which prevails in the world today.

Highlights in industrialised countries

The practice of pooling resources to ensure protection against the risks of ill-health grew mainly out of labour developments. In mediaeval Europe, craftsmen formed societies ("guilds") which in turn created funds to help members in times of distress due to sickness. Each member contributed to the fund on a regular basis. Industrialisation stimulated broader and more varied arrangements for dealing with the hazards of ill-health. The threat to the individual worker's earnings because of illness was seen as a risk to be shared, and from the late eighteenth and early nineteenth centuries groups of workers and small farmers in the same industry or location formed sickness funds as mutual benefit societies to serve this purpose. The term itself is important in understanding the later development of health insurance within the framework of social security, for these earliest mutual benefit societies collected contributions to provide benefits for needy members and not to gain profits for a commercial enterprise or to acquire resources for investment. The basic principles of these mutual benefit societies were solidarity, the involvement of members in their administration and the ability to adapt the distribution of benefits to the changing needs expressed by the members.

First cash benefits were provided, then the guilds asked doctors to certify sickness. To ensure services for their members, some guilds then began to contract with providers on a regular basis, and later to develop their own medical services, particularly in countries with a low supply of doctors and hospital beds. New initiatives came from employers: the schemes often becoming compulsory as employers in specific high-risk industries, such as mining, made employment conditional upon regular contributions to a fund to cover health care. With these developments, the concept of contributions related to earnings rather than to individual risk became firmly established in some countries.

It is useful to recall the medical care environment prevailing at the turn of the last century and its implications for the growth of health insurance during the industrial development of Europe. Medicine was not among the high-paid professions and the costs of medical care had not yet increased as a result of high technology. As the trend towards health insurance grew, political leaders realised the potential popularity of these essentially private arrangements. They began to adopt a firm and positive approach regarding the involvement of employers in supporting workers' initiatives, as a means of improving worker loyalty as well as health status.

The earliest and most significant political step to exploit this potential was taken in 1883 in Germany, where the Government enacted legislation providing that (i) workers in defined industries earning less than a specified amount should be compulsorily affiliated to a sickness fund, and (ii) the fund would be financed through compulsory contributions of workers and of their employers. This enactment marked the beginning of health insurance as a compulsory social insurance mechanism, a policy which spread gradually throughout Europe in a variety of forms during the first half of the twentieth century. Often voluntary schemes covered half of the populations involved before health insurance became compulsory.

Political acceptability rose steadily in many countries because compulsory health insurance was seen as the right response to the expectations of workers and their families, while it expressed in tangible terms the State's social concern with health and health care. This was a marked improvement on the traditional charitable or public-assistance approach to the provision of health care.

Following the German legislation of 1883, Austria introduced health insurance in 1887, Norway in 1902, the United Kingdom in 1910, and France enacted health insurance in 1921, with implementation only in 1930. By the early 1930s compulsory health insurance had been developed in most of the industrialised countries of Europe, under the name of sickness and maternity insurance. Probably because of the existing patterns of health care delivery, with a good supply of both general practitioners and specialists and long-established public and private hospitals, the European statutory health insurance funds operated mainly as agencies which paid providers for health care given to their members.

Health insurance as a social security undertaking

The original German law did not stipulate that the fund should pay the doctor for each specific service given to the patient, that is, on a fee-for-service basis. The method of paying doctors was not defined in the law, and most funds initially chose the capitation method, whereby doctors were paid a monthly sum for each insured person registered on their lists. The capitation method of paying physicians, rather than the ad hoc system of billing for each item of service provided, provided the insured person with a regular source of medical care, and was therefore the first mechanism to promote continuity of care at the general practitioner or family doctor level.

A different form of payment was later introduced, first in Norway, and then in France. The patient paid the doctor directly after the consultation and treatment, according to the stipulated fees for the actual services provided, and then the major part of this expenditure (initially 80 per cent) was refunded by the social insurance administration. As statutory health insurance spread in Europe, pressure from the medical profession eventually led to a shift from capitation to the fee-for-service method. About half the countries adopted the latter, either paying the providers directly or refunding the patients for most of the fee, while others retained the capitation method, at least in part. For example, the United Kingdom, Denmark and the Netherlands still pay general practitioners a monthly sum according to the number of insured persons (including dependants) on their lists. Italy changed to a capitation system in 1980.

In Southern Europe (Greece, Portugal, Spain) a national pattern developed of compulsory health insurance managed by large and broad-based public institutions enjoying administrative and financial autonomy. Large sections of the labour force including the dependants of insured persons were covered. Medical care as prescribed by the relevant legislation was dispensed free of charge on the institution's own premises (hospitals, clinics), by full- or part-time salaried medical and paramedical staff.

This direct method of providing "free" treatment to insured persons and their dependants was not always exclusive. Some schemes allowed for limited reimbursement of expenditures incurred for care given outside the system for various reasons, including the possibility that an insured person chose not to be treated at the free social medical care services.

In several European countries (i.e. Belgium, France, Germany, the Netherlands) health insurance was administered by a multitude of funds, affiliated with occupational sectors or other specific groups of individuals, and built on the existing network of mutual benefit societies. At the same time, the benefits included cash compensation for loss of income during sickness, employment injury and invalidity.

The International Labour Organisation (ILO), founded in 1919, became a major forum where health insurance policies were debated. The adoption of international labour Conventions concerning sickness insurance, the publication of research and comparative studies and the authoritative exhortations that resulted from such international action have been instrumental in the development of new legislation and the establishment of ad hoc institutions throughout Europe and in some other parts of the world.[1]

Following but not because of these developments, the practice of medicine changed significantly. Medical care became on the one hand more scientific, with new technologies increasing in number and complexity, and on the other, broader in scope to include more social and environmental aspects. As hospitals became larger, the range of professionals providing care expanded, as did the need to regulate their activities by statutory professional licensure. These increasing numbers of health care professionals then sought the trade union protection which workers in other industries had attained, and the image of large charitable hospitals, with religious volunteers or extremely low paid nursing staffs began to disappear. All this made medical care more effective, but also far more expensive. The citizens of the nations of Europe were also changing in their expectations of medical care. Just as they viewed education, health came to be considered a basic civic right. It also became apparent that it was not always feasible to place the burden for the development of health care resources, their statutory supervision and the financing of services, on government alone.

From the late 1930s a major development took place in social policy: the emergence of the concept of "social security" and its gradual implementation through reforms and the expansion of earlier social insurance legislation. This development had a major impact on health insurance.

In short "social security" emerged as a goal of societies where "freedom from want" was proclaimed as a basic human right. It meant the protection which society should provide for its members, through a series of public measures, against the economic and social distress that otherwise would be caused by the stoppage or substantial reduction of earnings resulting from sickness, maternity, employment injury, unemployment, invalidity, old age and death. Free access to medical care and the provision of subsidies for families with children was also proclaimed as a social security commitment.[2]

At the international level the new and broad social commitment arising from the social security approach was formally established and outlined in important ILO international instruments which retain even today their full significance as guide-lines for national policy.

The *Medical Care Recommendation, 1944 (No. 69),* adopted by the ILO called upon governments to meet "the need of the individual for care by members of the medical and allied professions and for such other facilities as are provided at medical institutions: *(a)* with a view to

Health insurance as a social security undertaking

restoring the individual's health, preventing the further development of disease and alleviating suffering when he is afflicted by ill-health and *(b)* with a view to protecting and improving his health".

The ILO Recommendation gave expression to a new concept of comprehensive and universal protection in the field of health which many countries were applying at the time and others were later to develop.

Public measures included a broad variety of programmes: compulsory and/or voluntary social insurance, social assistance, and employers' liability to provide benefits and services mandated by law. Such programmes pre-existed in many countries and were retained and enhanced under the new social security policy.

A major alternative was the launching of new universal health care programmes, which became known as "National Health Services" because the benefits were provided entirely by the State as a public service (rather than as a social insurance programme) to all citizens.

An example of the new approach was the enactment of a National Health Service (NHS) in the United Kingdom (1948) where the Government undertook the full responsibility for the provision of health services to the entire population as of right. The Government also undertook the commitment to pay for the NHS mainly through general revenue financing.

The national health service approach applied to health and medical care was adopted by other European countries, notably Hungary in 1920 and the USSR in 1935. Socialist countries in Eastern Europe followed on the same path joined much more recently by Italy (1980) and Portugal (1980).

In the Nordic countries the national health service approach was applied only in part, in combination with compulsory health insurance.

General revenue financing has, however, not prevailed everywhere, since contributions by protected persons and employers were in many cases retained as well.

In New Zealand the national health service aspect was applied only to hospital care, with limited insurance to reimburse general practitioners for community care. Japan, which had an extensive health insurance system by that time, did not adopt a national approach and retained the compulsory health insurance model involving a large number of separate funds.[3]

In practice each country proceeded to develop a social security system suited to traditional values, national conditions and preferences as well as social ideology. In the field of health care many different options have been chosen for the institutional framework, the method of financing, cost-sharing provisions, the organisation of medical care in terms of delivery systems, and so on. However there is a common trend toward comprehensive coverage, access irrespective of income and broad solidarity between income or socio-occupational groups.

Health insurance in developing countries

The only large industrialised country that followed a different path has been the United States. Throughout periods of intense debate on the political acceptability of national health insurance, the United States retained a preference for private insurance, including schemes developed by both non-profit and commerical sponsors. None the less, statutory health insurance was adopted at the federal level for specific groups, namely the aged and the indigent, through the legislation of the Social Security Amendments of 1965 which introduced the Medicare and Medicaid programmes.[4] Coverage has been expanded to include the severely disabled and persons suffering from terminal kidney disease.

Health insurance for the working population is dominated by employers' plans. There are significant gaps, however, particularly among those who work for small employers for whom the only alternative is individual private insurance, the cost of which is usually prohibitive. An estimated 38 million Americans are thus without any health insurance. At the state level, legislation requiring employers to provide health insurance has already been enacted in Massachusetts, and other states are likely to follow suit in the future. National health insurance Bills are once again under discussion.

While Canada had initially followed the example of the United States in developing private insurance, that country introduced a Hospital Insurance and Diagnostic Services Act in 1957 and took an even more radical step, compared with its neighbour, when it enacted a comprehensive national health insurance system in 1966 (following initiatives taken earlier at provincial level).[5]

During the past decade social security institutions in industrialised countries have focused their attention on cost control rather than on broad policy changes. This is due to unfavourable economic trends and the rising cost of health and medical care. Compulsory health insurance and national health services have endeavoured to control and moderate costs by applying measures which influence both the demand and supply of benefits. Cost-sharing by the insured person at the point of delivery (i.e. when services are received) has been introduced and/or expanded in order to moderate demand. Measures have also been taken to influence the supply of services financed through social security budgets, particularly with regard to hospital care, pharmaceutical supplies and expensive equipment. A vast documentation is available on cost containment policies and their effect on health insurance.[6] Throughout the present difficult period of adaptation of health and social security policies to the economic environment and its major constraints in the large majority of industrialised countries, continued popular support and government assent for the existing social security option and objectives in health care have been strongly emphasised and reaffirmed.

Health insurance as a social security undertaking

The evolution in developing countries

The historical development of compulsory health insurance in developing countries is generally less known. Events which have occurred in Latin American countries over the past 50 years are relatively well documented. Less reference material is available as regards the evolution of compulsory health insurance in other regions of the Third World, particularly in Asia, North Africa and the Middle East.

The purpose and scope of the present study does not permit a detailed review, country by country or region by region, of the conditions underlying the enactment and the subsequent development of statutory health insurance legislation or of the institutional patterns which have emerged. Study of the available national and international sources such as those listed at the end of this chapter is indispensable in order to assess the success and the failures of the policies developed so far as well as the issues now facing individual Third World countries in relation to the subject of health care, health financing and the role of social security.[7]

As a broad, general and necessarily incomplete overview, the following paragraphs highlight nevertheless some fundamental observations concerning the origin and the evolution of compulsory health insurance in developing countries. They are a necessary introduction to the substantive chapters which follow.

Initially (that is a few decades ago), compulsory health insurance legislation and institutions took shape in developing countries which reflected the social policies which had gained—or were gaining—acceptance in Europe. Such policies either had an intrinsic appeal to political leaders in the Third World or were part of the broad cultural inheritance from colonial powers and of the education of the élite nurtured abroad. Health insurance was therefore an acquired or imported concept, rather than an expression of the traditional national culture, and this has remained an element for criticism.

There was nevertheless always a rationale behind the desire to introduce the health insurance approach, which stemmed from the urgent need to satisfy people's aspirations to better and more accessible medical care combined with the unlikelihood that the State could—in the foreseeable future—meet such aspirations through the traditional public health services supported by general revenue financing.

Since the social and economic context was different from the European one, developing countries had to adapt the approach to health insurance to their own situation, in particular with regard to coverage and the methods of delivering health care as benefits mandated by law.

The typical initial situation which one was likely to find in the late 1940s or early 1950s could be sketched as follows: low living standards for rural dwellers and for most of the urban population witnessed by depressed or barely subsistence incomes, poor housing, widespread undernourishment, a great deal of ill-health and contagious disease traceable among other factors to environmental conditions, poor sanitation, inadequacy of diet and insufficient education; a severe shortage of medical personnel made worse by their uneven geographical distribution, resulting from a widespread tendency for doctors to concentrate in larger cities or towns; and inadequate transport facilities further limiting access to medical and non-medical personnel to the rural areas. As a rule these conditions were accompanied by an inadequate and scarce infrastructure in all respects, including short supply of out-patient facilities, lack of hospital beds, equipment and therapeutic technology. Low standards of public administration, and weaknesses and instability in the economy, completed the picture.

Against such a background three main strategies were adopted.

The first and most important was that health insurance institutions began to build physical facilities for both hospital and ambulatory care of insured persons. Such facilities were staffed by full- or part-time medical, para-medical and administrative personnel employed by the health insurance agency or institution and remunerated by salary, that is, for the value of the time spent within the delivery system. Dental, pharmaceutical, home nursing and other health services were also organised and dispensed on a similar basis. The financial resources required to build such infrastructure (and to operate it) were drawn from compulsory health insurance contributions of employers, insured persons and, occasionally, state support. Additional resources for capital expenditure were obtained through loans (or direct investment) of pension insurance funds which were often managed by the same institution. The creation of a health care sub-system by and within the prevailing social insurance mechanism was socially acceptable and encouraged.

The countries which first followed these policies were in Latin America. During the 1950s similar situations developed elsewhere (Egypt, the Libyan Arab Jamahiriya and Turkey).

The second strategy was "gradual implementation". This meant that compulsory insurance coverage was limited according to various criteria such as geographical area, size of the undertaking and category of dependant. Employees in urban areas working in large undertakings were first covered, then gradually the type of persons protected expanded, to include more categories of employees, their dependants and eventually also groups of self-employed.[8] However, coverage could not be extended indefinitely since major political, financial and material constraints could not be overcome. Thus large population groups, particularly in the rural areas, could not be covered. This imbalance is still a crucial issue today, even in countries with a long tradition of compulsory health insurance.

The third strategy was to give consumers and contributors a say in decisions concerning the management of health insurance either through

Health insurance as a social security undertaking

designated representatives or an elected governing body. This created a political asset in consolidating the new institutions.

With the improvement of the health and social conditions which ensued, such strategies were adapted, modified or further refined with varying success according to country or time.

At present, for instance, the free and direct provision of medical care to insured persons through the health insurance's own facilities and personnel is no longer the prevailing or unique type of organisation now found in developing countries. There has been a process of diversification of delivery patterns over time as other public and private facilities and health services have become available in the country, with which the insurance institution could subcontract. This process has included the "purchase" of services from public and private hospitals, clinics, dispensaries, or individual doctors at stipulated fees and payments and it has led to the coexistence of various methods of delivering the mandated medical care benefits within the same national programme, as exemplified by Brazil, Colombia and Peru among others.

Simultaneously, other patterns of medical care organisation for statutory health insurance have been tested. Typical examples include the following:

(i) the transfer of responsibilities for building up and managing all or most of the required infrastructure and the treatment of insured patients to the Ministry of Health on the basis of yearly lump-sum payments from social insurance agencies (Tunisia, 1960);

(ii) the partial reimbursement to insured persons of medical expenses freely incurred, according to a schedule of fee-for-service formally negotiated and agreed upon between the health insurance agency and the public and/or private providers of services (Lebanon, 1963, Republic of Korea, 1963, Algeria, 1949);

(iii) the state Government arranges for the provision of medical care on behalf of the health insurance agency through a variety of public and private providers, including social insurance hospitals and dispensaries where available, using salaried doctors, capitation contracts and other methods of remuneration (India, 1948);

(iv) employers, required by labour laws to provide specified health services to their employees and dependants, jointly entrust the organisation and delivery of services to the social security institution.

Most developments in health insurance came about gradually in developing countries. Some were triggered by social revolutions. In Cuba (1979), the Libyan Arab Jamahiriya (1980) and Nicaragua (1982), compulsory health insurance systems covering selected sectors of the population were transformed into national health service type programmes, though they retained payroll-related contributions of employers and workers.

Health insurance in developing countries

The recent evolution of compulsory health insurance has undoubtedly been influenced by the historic International Conference on Primary Health Care in Alma-Ata, USSR (1978), which called for a new approach to health and health care in order to achieve a more equitable distribution of health resources and to attain the goal of "Health for All" by the year 2000. The unanimous acceptance by governments of the strategies outlined at Alma-Ata may have been responsible, at least to some extent, for the following significant trends.

The first is an increased awareness of the place that compulsory health insurance, although limited in its population coverage, occupies or should take within a national health policy.

Developing countries (mainly in Africa, Asia or the Caribbean) that had so far ignored compulsory health insurance, either deliberately or by neglect or because of special circumstances, show signs of a change in attitude. It has become evident since Alma-Ata that serious shortages in the allocation of resources from state or from local health budgets would impair progress in the implementation of national strategies to achieve the goal of health for all by the year 2000. The need to mobilise additional resources has obliged governments to look for new options in health care financing. It has thus been recognised that one of the most promising options was compulsory health insurance in the form of a social security programme. This view has been supported internationally by the competent United Nations specialised agencies (the ILO and the WHO), as well as by leading international financial institutions (the World Bank and regional development banks).[9] Countries such as the Bahamas, Fiji, Indonesia, Malaysia, Morocco, Nigeria, Thailand, Zambia and Zimbabwe are exploring the potential of social security programmes as a means of broadening the access of the population to modern health care, both preventive and curative.

In these countries the starting-point, that is, the social and economic base on which to graft and build a health insurance policy, is not the same as that which prevailed 20 or 30 years ago. The options are wider. The health infrastructure has improved. Much more experience is available, for instance, with regard to primary health care strategies. Conceptually, the health insurance policy-makers are now in a far better position than their predecessors.

New policies are thus designed on the basis of past experience which shows that the self-financing mechanism which has supported the development of health insurance combined, where applicable, with the deliberate choice of providing medical care through a delivery system financed and operated by social insurance agencies, has brought about over the years a massive input of fresh resources into the health sector. This might not otherwise have taken place in the countries concerned if general revenue financing had continued to be the only source of non-private health care funding.[10]

Health insurance as a social security undertaking

The second major trend revealed by recent developments is that the Health for All goal has inevitably led governments to search for more coherence, compatibility and complementarity between different health insurance sub-systems and the public health services organised under the responsibility of Ministries of Health at central and local level.

Delicate and sometimes intractable political obstacles as well as legitimate institutional interests tend to keep health insurance administrators apart from Ministries of Health both at the policy and operational levels.

Starting mainly in Latin America, experiments have been made to promote suitable co-ordination between social security health insurance and government-financed public curative services (Ministry of Health).

Occasionally a complete integration has been envisaged with varying degrees of success according to time and place. Institutional pluralism in programme development and implementation has emerged as a potentially positive feature of the overall health care system. This trend has also gradually involved private sector providers and has opened up new avenues for a more efficient sharing of functions within the health system in developing countries.

In the uneasy dialogue between the various parties and pressure groups involved in making institutional pluralism in health care a positive rather than a divisive feature, the following important point has been made. The beneficial effect of compulsory health insurance development in various parts of the Third World has been felt beyond the welcome expansion in national resources devoted to health. Other induced effects include a significant development of human resources (medical and paramedical staff), the creation of jobs in the health sector and the alleviation of a burden traditionally carried by the Health Ministries enabling them to shift resources to rural areas and to preventive-oriented services and programmes, a positive demonstration effect which has triggered better standards all around.

As we approach the end of the century the economic and social background against which the developing countries have to contemplate further progress in the health sector is constantly changing. For many, Health for All objectives to be met by the year 2000 will continue to be a major challenge and perhaps an impossible task.

What matters most is that gradual progress is sustained and that all options are seriously considered. Compulsory health insurance is one of the options that governments should not ignore.

Notes

[1] ILO: *The International Labour Organisation and social insurance,* Studies and Reports, Series M, No. 12 (Geneva, 1936). This publication describes in detail the development of social insurance and the work of the International Labour Office. A large section deals specifically with Sickness Insurance. The origins and the development of health insurance in several European countries have been described recently in:

Health insurance in developing countries

Peter A. Köhler and Hans F. Zacher, in collaboration with Martin Partington: *The evolution of social insurance 1881-1981: Studies of Germany, France, Great Britain, Austria and Switzerland,* Max-Planck-Institut für ausländisches und internationales sozialrecht (London, Frances Pinter, 1982); and
Peter A. Köhler and Hans F. Zacher: *Beiträge zu Geschichte und aktueller situation der Sozialversicherung,* Colloquium des Max-Planck-Institut für ausländisches und internationales sozialrecht (Berlin, Duncker and Humblot, 1983).

[2] The trends and innovations in health care policy emerging with the formulation and acceptance of the social security doctrine are reflected, for instance in:
ILO: *Approaches to social security: An international survey,* Studies and Reports, Series M, No. 18 (Montreal, 1942).
Medical Care Recommendation, 1944 (No. 69), in ILO: *International Labour Conventions and Recommendations, 1919-1981* (Geneva, 1982), pp. 567-578.
ILO: "Post-war trends in social security: Medical care I", in *International Labour Review (ILR),* Aug. 1949.
———. "Post-war trends in social security: Medical care, II", in *ILR,* Sep. 1949.
———. *Objectives and minimum standards of social security,* Report IV(1), International Labour Conference, 34th Session, Geneva, 1951; in particular Chapter III.

[3] T.E. Chester and Mitsuya Ichien: "Health care in Japan: Its development, structure and problems", in *Three Banks Review,* Mar. 1983.
National Federation of Health Insurance Societies–Kemporen: "Trends and prospects for the medical care security system in Japan", in *International Social Security Review (ISSR)* (Geneva, International Social Security Association (ISSA)), 1986, No. 1.
Social Insurance Agency: *Outline of social insurance in Japan 1986* (Tokyo, Japanese Government, 1987).

[4] The peculiar features of the public, private and non-profit health care programmes in the United States are reflected in an abundant literature which is well known. The following publications provide an insight into the major programmes:
Robert J. Myers: *Social security* (Homewood, Illinois, Richard D. Irwin, 3rd ed., 1985), Part IV.
Beth Stevens: *Complementing the welfare state: The development of private pension, health insurance and other employee benefits in the United States,* Labor-Management Relations Series No. 65 (Geneva, ILO, 1986).

[5] Carl A. Meilicke and Janet L. Storch (eds.): *Perspectives on Canadian health and social services policy: History and emerging trends* (Ann Arbor, Michigan, Health Administration Press, 1980).
Dian Cohen: "Canada's health insurance program", in *Journal of the Institute for Socioeconomic Studies,* Summer 1986.

[6] Brian Abel-Smith: *Value for money in health services: A comparative study* (London, Heinemann Educational Books, 1976).
———. "Who is the odd man out?: The experience of Western Europe in containing the costs of health care", in *Health and Society* (New York, Milbank Memorial Fund), 1985, No. 1.
ISSA: *Cost-sharing by persons receiving health care under sickness insurance,* by L. Leeber, Report III, 21st General Assembly, Geneva, 1983.
ILO: *Report of the meeting of experts on the rising cost of medical care under social security* (Geneva, doc. RCMC/1977/D.12 (Rev); mimeographed).

[7] The main sources available in English include:
Brian Abel-Smith: "Funding health for all: Is insurance the answer?", in *World Health Forum* (Geneva, World Health Organization (WHO)), No. 1, 1986.
Asian Development Bank, Economic Development Institute of the World Bank, and the East-West Center: *Health care financing,* Regional seminar on health care financing, 27 July-3 August 1987, Manila (Manila, 1987).
Inter-American Center for Social Security Studies: *Primary health care under Mexican social security: The experience of the IMSS-COPLAMAR Programme* (Geneva, ILO, 1987).
ILO: *Problems of social security,* Report I, Preparatory Asiatic Regional Conference of the International Labour Organisation (New Delhi, 1947).
———. *The role of social security and improved living and working standards in social and economic development,* Report III, Part 1, Eighth Conference of American States Members of the International Labour Organisation, Ottawa, 1966.
———. *Social security in Asia: Trends and problems,* Report II, Sixth Asian Regional Conference, Tokyo, 1968.
ISSA: *Medical care under social security in developing countries,* Studies and Research No. 18 (Geneva, 1982).
Pierre Mouton: *Social security in Africa* (Geneva, ILO, 1974).

Milton I. Roemer: *Medical care in Latin America*, Studies and Monographs, III (Washington, DC, Pan American Union, General Secretariat, Organisation of American States, 1963).

———. *The organisation of medical care under social security* (Geneva, ILO, 1972).

Giovanni Tamburi: "Social security in Latin America: Trends and outlook", in Carmelo Mesa-Lago (ed.): *The crisis of social security and health care: Latin American experiences and lessons*, Latin American Monograph and Document Series, No. 9 (Pittsburg, Center for Latin American Studies, University of Pittsburg, 1985).

WHO: *Financing of health services*, Technical Report Series No. 625 (Geneva, 1978).

———. *Economic support for national health for all strategies,* Background document, 40th World Health Assembly, Geneva, 1987.

[8] See, for instance:

ILO: "Gradual extension of social insurance schemes in Latin American countries", in *ILR,* Sep. 1958.

L. Leal de Araujo: "Extension of social security to rural workers in Mexico", in *ILR*, Oct. 1973.

S. K. Wadhawan: "Health insurance in India: The case for reform", in *ILR*, July-Aug. 1987.

[9] ILO in collaboration with the Pan-American Health Organization (PAHO), the Permanent Inter-American Committee on Social Security and the World Bank: *Primary health care and health strategies in Latin American social security* (Geneva, ILO, 1986).

World Bank: *Financing health services in developing countries: An agenda for reform* (Washington, DC, 1987).

[10] Milton I. Roemer and N. Maeda: "Does social security support for medical care weaken public health programmes?", in *International Journal of Health Services*, 1976, No. 1.

2 COMPULSORY HEALTH INSURANCE AS A SOCIAL PROGRAMME AND A HEALTH SUB-SYSTEM

GOVERNMENT AND HEALTH INSURANCE

It may seem odd to begin a review of the main issues relevant to health insurance policy and planning in developing countries with an analysis of the institutional framework and its political implications.

However, experience has abundantly shown that the institutional issue, and more specifically the relationship between the Ministries of Health and the managers of social security institutions, represents the most sensitive and crucial factor in obtaining political acceptance of a sound health policy for the country as a whole. Without such political acceptance little or no progress can be expected.

During the period in which health insurance spread across continents, health care became far more institutionalised. Ministries of Health and social security systems developed to become complex institutions, dealing with personal health care of individuals and necessitating consideration of the relationships and interaction between the two in each country. Each type should be reviewed in terms of the scope of its current responsibilities.

The Ministry of Health generally is responsible for the planning and supervision of the overall health services of a country. This covers responsibility for the development of the health care infrastructure, including manpower, facilities and equipment, as well as the continued licensing and monitoring of performance of the resources developed. The Ministry of Health has traditionally been responsible for the promotion of public health. This includes both the safeguarding of the health of the public by controlling the environment and the setting of standards regarding public services, as well as the provision of personal preventive care for the entire population. The scope of modern preventive services goes beyond immunisation against infectious diseases. It includes a safe water supply, sanitation, nutrition, family planning and the prevention and early detection of chronic disease as well as the promotion of behaviour to improve health in the population at large.

The Ministry of Health is by no means confined to the above role. It also undertakes responsibility for personal *curative* care for the indigent, for vulnerable groups and, in some countries, for much larger sections of the population.

There is no law which defines in specific and legally formulated terms who is entitled to curative care by the public health authorities such as the Ministries of Health, although the common understanding is that every citizen has a potential entitlement. Care may be free or against payment but—in principle or in theory—is available to all. In developing countries this proposition loses its practical meaning to the extent that the resources available to public health curative care generally fall short of needs. There may be a few exceptions (i.e. small oil-rich States such as Kuwait or the Gulf States) and, understandably, shortages can be more or less serious depending on the wealth of the country.

Over and above these tasks, government ministries are responsible for the development of national health plans, which should also cover the financing of health care and the regulation of the supply of facilities in the public and private sectors.

Social security organisations with health care programmes are responsible for the protection of the populations they insure from the hazards of ill-health, by guaranteeing funds for the individual to acquire medical care as needed. They have traditionally been responsible for *curative* care, but are increasingly taking on *preventive* care. This reflects the current view that to protect the population from ill-health in the future, preventive as well as curative services must be included as social insurance benefits. Primary health care strategies are increasingly applied by social security institutions dealing with health care.

In other words, while the Ministry of Health is generally charged with promoting and enhancing the health of the population, health insurance protects all or part of the nation's citizens from the inability to acquire health care because of financial barriers.

Both are large, complex institutions, operating on the foundations of political ideologies and not as profit-making concerns. The need for public accountability exists in both organisations. While each should have a defined sphere of responsibility there is likely to be overlap between them and with other agencies.

Historically, when compulsory health insurance was first introduced in developing countries the Ministries of Health did not show much concern or interest in the legislative process which took place and the institution building which followed.

Later they realised that the political and financial weight which social security programmes were acquiring in the broad field of health and medical care deserved attention. Their attitude was frequently hostile, motivated by concern about or fear of duplication and institutional competition. At the same time, they began to realise that the greater the reliance placed on the employer/employee payroll contribution, the stronger was the trend towards autonomy in the use of resources for the benefit of contributors, rather than for that of the population at large. In some countries it also became clear that the insured population was receiving medical care of a much higher level than the general population. This realisation did little to promote a more positive relationship.

In carrying out possibly overlapping functions, the Ministry of Health is generally more restricted, as its operations are funded as part of the state budget. Social security institutions are likely to have more flexibility. Changing contributions to meet changing demands for health care may involve a long legislative process, but health insurance schemes will generally find it easier to finance or to introduce new programmes than government ministries. This situation can well breed competitiveness rather than co-operation between the two major systems involved in health care in a country.

It is obvious that the continued successful growth of health insurance will require a concerted rather than competitive approach among all the forces involved—government in general, its Ministries of Health, Labour and Finance, as well as industry and the workers themselves. National policies may determine the scope and type of legislation, but implementation will primarily be the responsibility of the health care bodies and the result of co-operation between them.

It has been widely recognised that a well-designed and efficiently administered compulsory health insurance scheme lessens the Ministry of Health's burden of assuring access to personal health care, thereby allowing for more efforts and financial resources to be spent on badly needed public preventive health services.

It is accepted that a common dilemma in developing countries today is the funding of health care, as well as of other social and welfare services, particularly when countries are burdened by debts to international agencies which exert strong pressure on government to reduce the subsidisation of goods and services. Statutory health insurance allows for the diversion of part of government responsibility for the delivery of health care to social security, which is self-financing.

While health insurance may serve as a response to financing the access of individuals to health care, the Ministries of Health and Finance will still be concerned with costs. As government bodies, they may be wary of mechanisms that provide financing but can lead to an escalation of the overall expenditure on essential services. The Ministries will seek representation in the management body of any separate social security institution to exert an influence on the level and utilisation of revenues from the two major sources of funds—contributions from employers and workers. There is also concern, again on the part of the government ministries, with the stability of these sources in a developing economy, and the extent to which government participation will be needed.

The development of social security programmes in general may be slow, not only in increasing coverage of larger parts of the population but also in broadening the range of benefits. Despite this slow growth, social security organisations may demonstrate relative "wealth" and autonomy as compared with government agencies, and thereby create some imbalance between the real scope of their activities in the country and their political influence. This may well lead to some negative feelings among the officials of ministries dealing with the day-to-day burdens of providing health and welfare services to the nation.

A somewhat different issue in determining the relationship between the Ministry of Health and the insurance scheme is responsibility for the development of the infrastructure. A health insurance system that undertakes to provide care in its own facilities should do so only within the scope of policies and plans agreed by the Ministry of Health. The initial impetus for the health insurance system to develop its own resources may indeed stem from the past difficulties of the Ministry of Health in finding the money to build an adequate infrastructure. In many countries planning policy is poorly developed and the health insurance scheme may want to proceed according to its own perceptions of need and demand for specific services. This may lead to conflict, duplication and competition, and imbalances in the provision of services between different population groups.

The main areas of co-ordination remain the volume and character of this infrastructure and standards for the delivery of care, including provider payment levels.

Given all these factors, the relationship between the Ministry of Health and the health insurance scheme will ultimately depend on the nature of the social insurance partner, its degree of autonomy, the scope of persons protected and the organisation and management of the scheme.

The international organisations concerned (the WHO and the ILO) sought early in this process to foster the necessary co-ordination and institutional co-operation.[1] A series of recommendations to this end was made in 1970 by a joint ILO/WHO Committee of Experts. More was to follow in the American region or at national level whenever international co-operation from the United Nations family of agencies was sought: the prevailing slogan being that "social security programmes for personal health care should be planned within the framework of an overall national health plan".

It would be naive to state that such recommendations have found unanimous acceptance. Over time, local political considerations in some countries have played a divisive role rather than creating a climate of co-operation and understanding. The general trend, however, is towards the search for more coherence and sharing of functions between the various agencies within a given health system. In other words, it has been recognised that in some countries the introduction of health insurance did in fact initially evoke opposition from government ministries dealing with health, and that this was often due to the lack of clarity on relationships between ministries and the new schemes. It was also realised that co-ordination must be encouraged from the beginning, just as conflict between the organisations involved should be avoided.

As health insurance develops, it should be seen by the government, particularly in a developing country, as more than a stable mechanism for financing personal health care, and not as the cause of increasing costs. If health insurance schemes are involved in the direct provision of health care, they should be viewed as partners rather than competitors in the recruitment of resources, negotiations with providers and in gaining professional esteem. The relationship which develops over time with the ministries responsible for health, labour, welfare and finance should be based on the *mutual respect for the institutional mandate of each partner*. In addition, there has to be professional and social integrity on all sides.

Professionalism and co-operation at the planning and operational levels should provide at least some immunity to the demands of current political issues, as they arise. It may well be that effective co-operation can only be achieved by having an inter-agency body, charged with overall planning and co-ordination, and responsible directly to government. However, the maintenance of a constructive relationship will also require mutual recognition of the need for changes in health care over time, with consent on changing roles. This should give continued credence to the approach, stated earlier, that the Ministry of Health, or government, protects the health of the nation, while the health insurance system enables continued access to health care for its members.

SOURCES OF REVENUE

The self-financing mechanism established and set in motion by legislation is the key characteristic of compulsory health insurance and perhaps its main appeal in developing countries.

It is therefore important to examine the nature and significance of the most common financial provisions found in existing legislation in developing countries.

By virtue of the principle of solidarity (sometimes called risk-sharing) the sources of revenue of compulsory health insurance are:
— contributions by employers;
— contributions by insured persons;
— state subsidies; and
— miscellaneous income (cost-sharing, etc.).

Contributions by employers and employees are, as a rule, wage or earnings-related, although flat-rate contributions have sometimes been applied. The earnings subject to contribution are very often limited to that portion of earnings that does not exceed a prescribed "ceiling". The rate of contribution due from employers is almost unvariably higher than the rate of the employee contribution.

In the case of a self-employed person ad hoc rates are established because it may be impossible to obtain acceptance of the principle that the self-employed should pay both the employer and the employee contribution, calculated or determined on the basis of declared earnings. It should be borne in mind that among the self-employed there are high-income groups (self-employed professionals and businessmen) as well as small artisans, small shopkeepers, street vendors, etc., who have very limited capacity to pay substantial and regular contributions.

Whatever the method of calculating contributions, the principle of equity in the social security context means that all members are entitled to the same benefits. That is, although there may be some limitations on the volume of specific benefits, there is basically no link between revenues accruing from contributions and expenditure at the individual level. To the extent that the social security programme is spread among different population groups, by geographic region or industrial sector, its economic viability as a whole will benefit from inter-community subsidisation.

The "public" and statutory nature of social insurance does not necessarily imply government funding, as social security is normally financed by regular contributions from wage earners, their employers and the self-employed. However, legislation does often provide for government subsidies, or contributions, depending on the extent and desirability of a national commitment and the ability of employers and employees to sustain the scheme financially, given the prevailing economic conditions.[2]

There are several examples of government contributions to compulsory health insurance.

One is that the government takes responsibility for financing the health infrastructure required while income from employer/employee contributions is expected to cover current benefit costs and administrative overheads.

Another possibility is for the government to pay the administrative costs only or to assume permanent responsibility for any shortfall of income that may result at the end of a fiscal year. There are examples of government subsidies earmarked for specific insured groups who are unable to cover all or part of the contribution that they should normally pay.

The most common view is, however, that when coverage in terms of persons protected is small, government subsidies are less justified than in the case of broad country-wide programmes. It seems correct and understandable to question the wisdom of using general revenues only for the benefit of a limited section of the population. In practice the harsh reality of public finance in the majority of developing countries (excluding obviously oil-rich and similar States) makes it unrealistic to rely on government subsidies. On the other hand, Ministries of Finance see in the flow of statutory social insurance contributions an opportunity to obtain funds to strengthen, for instance, the budgets of Ministries of Health.

Assuming however that coverage in terms of persons protected is comprehensive, as it is in some newly industrialised countries, government participation in health insurance financing would be justified on the following grounds.

First of all, the insurance schemes must accept all those within the defined population group to be covered; there is no basis of rejecting an applicant with a history of previous illness, a chronic disease requiring constant care, a high risk of illness or large number of dependants. Second, the benefits will inevitably include medical care in fields that were once considered the public's responsibility, such as certain infectious diseases and mental health. Third, cost control by the regulation of supply and of provider fees requires the active partnership of the relevant government bodies and failings in this area deserve some government support in order to preserve the level of benefits covered.

Among miscellaneous income of a compulsory health insurance scheme one sometimes finds the amounts that the patients may be required to pay at "the point of delivery", such as a flat-rate sum for each prescription, for each pair of spectacles or for each call at the hospital. This type of income traditionally defined with the term "cost-sharing" is also referred to as "user charges" and there is an abundant literature about its application or suitability in *private* health insurance (particularly in the United States).

However, in compulsory health insurance as applied in developing countries cost-sharing is a less relevant issue and it accounts only for a minor part of annual revenue of a compulsory contributory scheme. The main considerations are the following. First, unlike public health services, medical care under social security is a right granted against payment of a specific individual contribution. It is argued therefore that the patient has already paid—by a deduction from his salary—for the right to the medical care benefit. Consequently cost-sharing at the point of delivery is not so much imposed to raise additional revenue but to prevent abuse or misuse of available benefits (such as pharmaceutical products) when the benefit is provided free of charge *directly* by the insurance institution to the insured person. This disincentive has however to be handled with great care among population groups which are at subsistence level or who chronically lack cash, because cost-sharing may have the opposite result: to prevent people who should be treated for illness or injury from claiming the service and aggravating their health condition, the treatment of which will later be more costly.

The subject of cost-sharing is dealt with in detail in later chapters, since it may take different forms according to the type of organisation of medical care delivery under social security, which may include, for instance, the partial refund of expenses incurred rather than the direct provision of services.

Returning to the main source of revenue, that is compulsory contributions, it is important to note some additional features which emerge from current practice.

Compulsory contributions from the insured person and his employer are—as explained earlier—earnings-related or, sometimes, flat-rate, but as a rule the individual rate disregards the number of dependants who may also become entitled to medical care by virtue of the insurance status and the contribution of the insured person (the employee, the self-employed).

Equal contribution rates regardless of marital status and family size are often questioned when a health insurance scheme is first developed. With greater understanding of the principles of pooling of risks across populations and over time, this concept has become an accepted principle of health insurance within the framework of social security. There are similar questions regarding cross-subsidisation between different income groups, such as higher urban regular wage earners and lower often seasonal rural workers. This is a common argument in developing countries, and may be solved quietly or require considerable political effort in attaining maximal risk-sharing across a nation. In a national programme the aim is generally to achieve cross-subsidisation in all planes: from high to low incomes, from the healthy to the sick, across socio-economic and occupational groups and from single persons to families.

The total level of contributions required depends on a set of variables such as:

— the scope and nature of benefits provided (Chapter 3);
— the organisation of medical care benefits (Chapter 4);
— the level of earnings on which contributions are calculated;
— the participation of the State in financing the scheme (subsidies, etc.); and
— economic and market conditions relevant to health care in general.

Contribution rates are calculated on the basis of statistical and financial information relevant to the "population" to be covered. Short-term assumptions are generally applied to the main variables since compulsory health insurance is financed on a pay-as-you-go basis. Rates of contribution are revised from time to time in the light of experience (i.e. every three or five years). Provision for small contingency reserves is normally made in order to protect the finances of the scheme from unforeseen deviations in income or expenditure trends.

When the insurance scheme has among its tasks the construction, maintenance and expansion of its own health infrastructure (such as hospitals and dispensaries), the total rate of contribution may include a portion earmarked for financing an infrastructure development fund.

Finally it should be recalled that some developing countries may contemplate an alternative option in order to mobilise additional resources for health. Rather than establishing compulsory health insurance they may wish to levy a tax on wages. Such "health levy" is merely an earmarked tax on one sector of the economy and the revenue that it produces is channelled into general revenue or into the revenue of the government ministries or departments administering health services. This approach has advantages and disadvantages depending on the circumstances. The shortcomings seem to far exceed the advantages because the health levy option has rarely been applied so far in developing countries.

SOCIAL SECURITY AS A HEALTH SUB-SYSTEM

The main difference between health services provided by public health authorities (Ministries of Health, etc.) and medical care "benefits" through social security is that as a counterpart of imposing compulsory health insurance contributions, those covered are given a *right* to specified individual items of care (curative and preventive). In public health services in developing countries a local dispensary will often supply only such "care" as its resources permit, irrespective of the potential demand. No such discretion operates in a health insurance scheme.

In other words, if contributions are to be collected for health care on a compulsory basis through legislation, then a benefit programme should simultaneously be established to provide for those entitled to it.

Social security in the field of health is therefore a *social programme* with a *public commitment* to "take and give" under prescribed conditions stipulated by laws and regulations.

Compulsory health insurance is therefore much more than a financing mechanism, as some planners and academic writers are inclined to believe.

If both contribution and benefit specifications are sound and programme administration is efficient, compulsory health insurance becomes a useful means to rationalise, redirect and optimise household expenditure on health. Studies have shown that in developing countries household expenditure on health is significant—particularly for low-income households—but that it is inefficient or ineffective in terms of results obtained.

The specific nature of the financing mechanism and the legal requirement that medical care benefits should be provided "as of right" to prescribed categories of persons, confers on compulsory health insurance the status of a "health sub-system" within public provision for health.

In developing countries the establishment and the operation of such a sub-system has to come to terms with two fundamental issues. One is the institutional strategy and the other is the concept of gradual implementation.

The first has been analysed in earlier sections, showing the need for coherence and co-ordination among all the health agencies within the public sector. In addition, it should be remembered that when compulsory health insurance is established, political pressure inevitably develops to claim administrative and financial autonomy for the sub-system. The claim is put forward by representatives of the groups which are financing the scheme: i.e. employers, employees, and self-employed, as the case may be.

Though such a claim may seem legitimate, it is equally understandable that the government in power can hardly be expected to divest itself completely of any responsibility for the "management" of compulsory health insurance. This is partly because the scheme is founded on legislation and partly because the State often has a financial stake in the sub-system, even if it is only to underwrite its viability. But in addition the government needs to ensure that its own services continue to be viable: it cannot stand idly by while, for example, the health insurance scheme attracts health professionals out of the government services by offering much higher remuneration. Nor can it allow a scheme which starts with higher-paid industries to become so expensive that further industries with lower pay cannot be brought within it.

The presence of state representatives in the governing bodies of compulsory health insurance may guarantee—assuming that the role is played competently—that the sub-system achieves a "responsible status of autonomy", whereby the sub-system does not develop into an unfair competitor of other public sector agencies (e.g. the Ministry of Health).

The concept of "responsible autonomy" also implies the realisation by the State that compulsory health insurance is not merely a fund-raising device for the benefit of the Ministry of Health, but a partner with less rigid budgets and probably more capacity for innovation and adaptation.

The second issue deals with "gradualism" in the implementation of health care programmes and the benefits that the law entrusts to the sub-system. Ideally, coverage in terms of persons protected should be as wide as possible but most developing countries do not have the resources (infrastructure, human resources, ability to pay, etc.) to honour from the start all the mandated benefits in respect of large and often geographically scattered population groups. Experience shows that a step-by-step approach has definite advantages, provided that it does not become, at a later stage, an "excuse" for avoiding larger responsibilities and wider coverage.

Gradualism can be applied with regard to various criteria, such as:
— the size of the enterprise;
— geographical area;
— category of insured persons or of dependants automatically covered; and
— type of benefit.

Starting with coverage of large enterprises (for instance those employing ten or more workers) allows the administrators of compulsory health insurance to gain experience in both collecting contributions and paying benefits without having to cope with the identification and control of small and often unstable employers. Once the administrative procedures are established and the staff has become familiar with them, coverage is "extended" to employees of smaller enterprises. There have been many examples of this approach, particularly in Asia.

The gradual implementation of compulsory health insurance according to geographical areas is perhaps the most frequent feature in developing countries. It is the obvious response to the uneven distribution of medical infrastructure and personnel throughout the national territory and to the obstacles facing administrators in the identification, registration and control of paid employment or self-employment in rural areas or in regions where records and communication systems are not sufficiently reliable. There may also be shortages of trained personnel which cannot be surmounted in the initial stages. One often finds that the capacity of employers and employees to contribute is much lower outside the modern urban sectors of the economy. Naturally the size of the country plays a decisive role. Small islands or States have rapidly reached full geographical coverage while large countries (e.g. Colombia, India, Indonesia, Mexico), have followed the pattern of extending compulsory health insurance by geographical areas over a number of years.

It is also common for compulsory health insurance coverage to be applied first to selected categories of persons in the labour force. A clear preference is to start with categories of employees, leaving compulsory insurance for the self-employed for a later stage. Ability to pay is one of the main reasons underlying this option, as well as the problems connected with the identification of self-employed persons and with the determination of their earnings or income to which compulsory contributions are normally related. Financial considerations are often advanced when coverage is restricted initially to the employee with the exclusion of his family dependants. Although the per capita cost of providing health insurance benefits is not *directly proportional* to the size of family, each eligible dependant increases the potential liability and the cost of the programme, which, in turn, must be reflected in higher employer/employee contributions. As explained earlier, most schemes in developing countries do not vary the health insurance contribution by family size: the total contribution paid by or on behalf of the insured person entitles to benefit both the insured person and the dependants as defined in the legislation (normally the spouse and the children under a prescribed age). Very broadly, assuming that coverage of the worker alone requires, for example, a contribution equivalent to 4 per cent of earnings, when the workers' dependants are also insured the rate of contribution rises to 6 or 7 per cent of earnings.

Finally, the principle of gradualism in implementation may affect the "package" of the benefits provided.

For instance, the types of medical care benefits provided in the first stages of implementation can be limited, excluding the less essential ones or those whose cost may be deemed high. Such limitations may apply to dental services, psychiatric care, cosmetic surgery, domiciliary visits, and so on. Alternatively, the initial limitation can be applied to selected types of diseases or to certain expensive treatments.

Adoption of the principle of gradual extension can affect the legal framework in two different ways. In certain countries the legislation describes in detail the conditions and requirements for entitlement to benefit as well as the contribution rates. In others the health insurance law lays down only the general principles of the benefit and contribution systems, leaving to regulations and further enactments the details of the operative provisions. The second framework is more amenable to a process of gradual extension than the first.

To conclude, there is general agreement that the initial limitation of the scope of compulsory health insurance and the principle of extending it gradually, which have been adopted by a number of developing countries, are wise and realistic policies.

Any attempt to embrace the whole of the country or the entire active population within the health insurance sub-system from the very beginning is likely to lead to inefficiencies and shortages which can only undermine the credibility and the authority of the insurance institution.

On the other hand, implementation by stages creates in effect privileged groups and possible discrimination between enterprises. Consequently, any initial restriction of coverage can be ultimately justified only as a transitory measure which must be constantly kept under review and superseded as soon as circumstances permit.

The danger is that progress in implementing desirable extensions of coverage may be too slow. This may be due not only to economic and financial constraints, but also to the lack of dynamic initiatives from the social security management and their political leaders. Instability in the management has been identified in developing countries as a cause of their unwillingness to explore ways and means to extend coverage, particularly towards rural areas.

The "sub-system" has therefore its boundaries in terms of coverage: they are flexible and they should extend gradually. The final profile of coverage depends on the country, its ideology and its peculiar social and economic conditions.

ROLE OF THE PARTICIPANTS

The mutual benefit societies founded a century ago were characterised by democratic administration by the elected representatives of members, as indeed all the decisions on contributions and benefits were made by the members themselves. Funds were not diverted to other welfare programmes and there was a strong identification with the "sickness fund". In the large statutory health insurance schemes of today, it is far more difficult to maintain administrative participation of the members. What is important now is to broaden the concept of participant to include the three contributing bodies—members, employers and government—as well as the sponsoring bodies. In some countries the providers are also represented. If health insurance is to remain a stable option for the delivery of health care, each of these partners must have a vested interest in providing good medical care within a reasonable time, and within the constraints of a controlled and balanced budget.

The major issues requiring the input of these "participants" are the updating of contribution rates and of benefits, acceptability of reimbursement rates or payment to providers, the definition of quality controls and basic standards of care, and the promotion of special developments, particularly at the community level. The effects of failure to reach a minimal spirit of participation among all these "agents" may not be felt at the beginning of the operation of a health insurance scheme. The concepts of solidarity and community pooling of risks are not always understood at the beginning of a social insurance programme. However, dissatisfaction with the programme may lead members to seek private care outside the system. This then promotes the growth of private medical care which ultimately drains resources from the "public" system, leaving the latter with long waiting times for essential services and poor administration to serve the patients with the highest health risks, particularly the aged and indigent. The achievement of this "participation" is not simple, but depends to a large extent on the type of system developed and administrative sensitivity. The major measure of dealing with this sensitivity is reflected in the extent of decentralisation at the regional and local levels.

Notes

[1] WHO: *Personal health care and social security*, Report of a Joint ILO/WHO Committee, Technical Report Series No. 480 (Geneva, 1971).

Health insurance in developing countries

PAHO: " Coordination of Social Security and Public Health Institutions", Resolution adopted at the XXXII Meeting of the Directing Council (Washington, DC, Sep. 1987, CD32/17 Eng.)
———. *Coordination of Social Security and Public Health Institutions*, Background document prepared for the 99th Meeting of the Executive Committee of the Directing Council (Washington, DC, June 1987, CE99/19 Eng.)

[2] The only international source of comparative income and expenditure data from social security health insurance schemes is ILO: *The Cost of Social Security: Twelfth International Inquiry, Comparative Tables, 1981-1983* (Geneva, 1988) and *Basic Tables* (Geneva, 1988; mimeographed).

HEALTH INSURANCE BENEFITS 3

CLASSIFICATION OF BENEFITS

In a statutory health insurance programme, medical care benefits are given as of right. Each member, regardless of his contribution, has a legally enforceable individual right to defined and mandated benefits, appropriate to his medical needs at the time of use. The range of benefits may change as the health needs and patterns of care of the population change, requiring a legal adjustment of the statutes defining benefits.

Health insurance benefits are classified in two groups: cash payments and health care services. The cash benefits do not include cash refunds for outlays to health care providers made directly by the insured, but rather allowances or compensation for the loss of income or expenses of a patient, and typically include the following:

1. Sickness allowance—payment of a fixed percentage of the insured's daily wage for a limited period (and after a defined waiting period) as compensation for loss of income due to illness.
2. Maternity allowance—payment of a fixed percentage of the insured's daily wage for a set period around the time of confinement to cover the loss of income during maternity leave.
3. Funeral grant—payment of a lump sum to cover funeral expenses to the legal survivor of the deceased member.

In some systems the cash allowances are not part of the health insurance scheme, but are administered by the agency dealing with other social security benefits, such as old-age, invalidity or survivor's pensions. Since the cash benefits are usually restricted to the workers and not their dependants, this arrangement does not imply a limitation in the scheme. Placing the responsibility for cash benefits in the general social security organisation may in fact relieve the health sub-system of the burden of dealing with large cash transfers.

The health care benefits are traditionally divided as follows.

1. Medical care benefits, further classified as:

- hospital in-patient care;
- general practitioner services in the community;
- physician specialist services, which may be in individual practices, polyclinics or hospital out-patient departments;
- medicaments;
- ancillary services, such as X-ray and laboratory tests;
- vision tests and spectacles; and
- prostheses and appliances.

2. Dental care
   - basic dental maintenance; and
   - reconstructive dental care, such as prostheses.

The classification within the medical care benefits has become increasingly problematic. In the past, the insurance system was expected to provide for the curative services needed following the onset of illness. Any kind of preventive care was considered the responsibility of the agency responsible for public health, i.e. the Ministry of Health. According to the same logic, mental health services were considered "public health" issues and their inclusion in health insurance benefits, particularly in systems with direct provision of services, was generally neglected. Expenses for infectious diseases that were seen as a "public danger", such as tuberculosis, were also left to the public authority in a few countries. At the other end of the spectrum of medical care, rehabilitation was often neglected as a necessary and integral part of convalesence and the return to productive life, if not productive work. Particularly for the working-age population requiring rehabilitative services, part of the burden was often transferred out of the medical field, as it was considered more of a social and occupational problem. All such distinctions have been gradually eliminated in most advanced health insurance programmes.

Another problem area is the length of hospital in-patient care. When the benefits cover acute hospital care, there is generally no limit for those patients requiring more than the average length of stay. Difficulties arise when it is clear that long-term care is required, and that the nature of the long-term care is more nursing than medical. In developing countries the practice adopted so far has been to extend the regular, that is, acute care benefits to cover longer hospital stays. Other systems simply do not include long-term hospitalisation among their benefits. As the population grows older and is composed of an increasing percentage of individuals who paid regular contributions into the health insurance fund for decades of their working life, this exclusion is viewed as a serious denial of rights. It has led to the enactment of supplementary insurance programmes for long-term care, or a proliferation of private services to provide nursing care.

The current approach to health care is that the comprehensive spectrum of care includes promotion, prevention, curative and rehabilitation services, for the organic and psycho-social needs of individuals. This encompasses the classification of medical care not into hospital and community services, but into primary, secondary and tertiary care, with the emphasis placed on the need for a sound primary care base to ensure good and efficient use of health care at all levels. The recent debate on whether insurance schemes should cover and even take the initiative for health promotion and the prevention of disease is finally reaching a positive conclusion, although this does not mean that all early detection screening will be covered. In any insurance scheme, the very concept of reducing risk is considered as a means of spending less on benefits.

The trend now evolving is one integrating preventive care at the level of the insured individual with efforts towards health promotion at the high risk or vulnerable group level. This approach means that health insurance benefits should include a broad range of personal preventive care, including not only immunisation for the relevant diseases, but also health education for health promotion and screening for the early detection of chronic diseases. This does not necessarily mean that health insurance schemes should undertake mass screening programmes in select population groups, but that they should not reject reimbursement or programmes for those services which allow for the earliest possible treatment of disease.

Another recently debated concept is the "basic health care package" or core benefits to be covered by health insurance. It is understandable that a newly developing social security health insurance system may want to limit the medical care benefits in an initial stage. The problems with this approach come from the dynamics of change in medical science, where a new if more costly diagnostic or therapeutic measure may be more cost effective. Rigidity in defining a core package may ultimately lead to patients using the conventional measure in the health insurance system, but seeking the "new, scientific and more sophisticated" measure in the private medical care system. The real issue here is not a rigid definition but, first, creation of a strong primary care base, with an intelligent and efficient referral system for those patients needing the more sophisticated measures. Second, the effective use of these new measures will require a level of trained and experienced health care professionals to provide the services within the health insurance framework, and the constant monitoring of the appropriate use of both new and old technologies. Compulsory or statutory health care benefits should in no way be exempt from quality assurance and technology assessment, which are now gaining favour as the correct terms for the evaluation of health care.

Medicaments are another benefit category in which there are

variations in the range of services covered. In some schemes only drugs prescribed by a physician are covered, thereby excluding non-prescription or "over-the-counter" medicaments which the insured can purchase at his own discretion for minor symptoms. Other schemes cover a list of basic or essential drugs as defined by the WHO, while at the other extreme many of the European funds cover any drug included in the Ministry of Health's list of pharmaceuticals approved to be sold in the country. The current trend is to limit the list of drugs to a regularly updated list, usually comprising around 2,000 pharmaceuticals, with insurance coverage (reimbursement or direct provision) of only those drugs included in the physician's prescription, regardless of whether a particular drug may also be purchased without a prescription. In some developing countries with health insurance schemes operating their own services, the policy has been to select a limited list of essential drugs for the free dispensing of drug benefits. The list, as adopted by Mexico for example, includes fewer than 100 drugs that may be dispensed without charge in community health care facilities, and about 300 drugs for hospital use.

BENEFIT CHARACTERISTICS

To meet the needs of appropriate health care within the health insurance system, the benefits must have certain essential characteristics. Equity is a basic principle and the factors that serve to provide this condition are primarily equitable accessibility and availability of services to all parts of the population covered. There are obvious problems in fulfilling these conditions, as apart from a general inadequacy of health care resources, we usually find very significant geographic inequalities, including urban-rural and central and peripheral regional differences. Within the health care resource supply, we may find imbalances in the categories of professionals, with a disproportionate number of specialists, and high technology diagnostic services concentrated in cities that are at the same time sorely lacking in primary care providers needed to deal with the social welfare problems of rapid urbanisation and industrialisation.

The health insurance system also has to deal with public expectations and preferences. There tends to be greater reliance on hospital care, although in many areas, hospitals are still linked to high fatality rates. There may also be unnecessary drug dependency, with the insured believing that any encounter with the health system at a time of illness must include a drug prescription. For many, the transfer from a "free" public system to a regular contributory system creates a tendency to seek maximal use of the benefits covered. This "milking" of the system further complicates the attempt to reach rational and balanced utilisation of health care.

The solutions to dealing with these problems are often passed on to the patient (that is, the insured seeking care at the time of illness) rather than the providers, for instance in the form of cost-sharing, as will be discussed later. Many aspects of what may be considered abuse of the system can be dealt with by rigid administrative procedures, but these tend mainly to overburden the insured with unnecessary bureaucracy, which often results in delays in seeking care or the use of "simpler" if expensive private sources motivated by the attitude that nothing is more important than health. The ability of the health insurance system to regulate use towards a rational pattern depends to a large extent on the type of system involved, that is, the direct reimbursement or direct provision of care, as will be discussed in the following sections.

INDIRECT METHOD OF PROVIDING HEALTH CARE BENEFITS

The mutual benefit societies of nineteenth century Europe were designed to collect contributions to pay providers directly for health care expenditure, based on the volume and type of services given, mainly by physicians. Later, France introduced the method of reimbursement to patients for all or part of payments already made to providers. Hospital costs were usually reimbursed on a fixed daily rate for all the care given during the days of hospital stay. Physician services given in hospital were included in the daily charge, or billed separately. Less frequently, hospital costs were reimbursed according to an itemised bill for all the procedures given to a patient during his stay. Reimbursement to providers was generally limited to physicians and hospitals on a "list", that is, with some contractual agreement with the health insurance fund to adhere to charges negotiated between the fund and the provider organisations.

This is termed the "indirect" form in health insurance programmes, as opposed to the "direct" provision of services by facilities operated by the scheme itself. The indirect form has two methods: direct payment to the providers, and reimbursement to the patients for expenses already paid to the providers for medical care.

While these two indirect methods may seem to be convenient in terms of a fund's unwillingness to get involved in the delivery of medical care, it has become increasingly complex beyond the problems relating to provider payment, which will be dealt with in the next chapter. The list of health care professionals has grown, and payment must now be made to doctors at general and specialist level, as well as to a range of other health professionals. The services of some of these professionals were previously confined to hospitals, but in keeping with the current trend to keep patients out of hospital, more and varied community health care brings new demands for tariffs and conditions regarding the method of payment. For example, is payment to be based on a single fee for a visit to the doctor, nurse or physiotherapist, or separate fee for each item of service? Which of the two indirect methods—payment to the provider or reimbursement to the patient—is more suitable in each health insurance scheme? If payment is made to the provider, should it allow an additional and non-reimbursable sum to be paid by the patient to the provider? And if the method chosen is reimbursement to the patient, should it be partial or full reimbursement?

Partial reimbursement to the patient, regardless of whether the patient had to first make the total payment out-of-pocket to the provider, is the most common form of cost-sharing. (This is different from a user-charge, which is a specific non-reimbursable amount paid by the patient for a specific service at the time of use.) The part not refunded is therefore considered a "deductible" in insurance terms. One of the common problems is that while the percentage of the fee not refunded may be stipulated, the total amount charged by the provider may exceed that fee, creating what is termed "over-billing". As the national health insurance system of Canada developed following legislation in 1966 on a fee-for-service basis for physician care, over-billing became a common practice, particularly for specialists in the cities. Legislation was finally passed in 1986 to ban over-billing, leaving physicians who wished to charge more than the negotiated fee with the choice of "opting-out" of the insurance system.

In recent years the control of fees has been seen as an important measure in the health care cost-containment battle.

A fundamental task in the setting of fees is the calculation of what constitutes a reasonable charge as opposed to the cost of a service provided in a public non-profit environment. There is often little appreciation of real cost in public services, and equally little information to derive itemised costs. In the transition from cost to charge in an entrepreneurial setting, the process has to take into account a long list of additional factors, such as capital investment in the physician's practice, equipment depreciation, support staff, post-graduate training and vacation allowances, and the total volume of services expected in the contract.

The issues involved in negotiating fees are sometimes considered minor in comparison to the problems involved in the actual payment. The indirect system using fee-for-service payment involves a tremendous amount of processing and paying itemised claims. On the positive side, the system does allow for detailed utilisation review, at both individual provider and individual insured member levels. This would be even more beneficial if we could develop better criteria to determine rational use, so that the providers with profiles indicating abuse of the system could immediately be identified. This again leads us into the field of quality assurance. Unfortunately, methods of evaluation of provider profiles and methods of sanctioning the "abusers" have not been adequately developed to give the direct fee-for-service method a significant advantage from the health insurance side. In developing countries the sophistication of such procedures would exceed the administrative capacity of most institutions.

The indirect method of providing health insurance benefits can, of course, be based on the capitation system of paying for a significant part of medical care.

Another issue in dealing with the indirect method, as well as combined systems, relates to the ownership of health care facilities. Under the indirect method, a basic question is to what extent the health insurance scheme directs referral and use of defined services, such as public versus private for-profit hospitals. Government (central or local) may have lower charges, negotiated through special agreement with the health insurance scheme, but longer waiting times and more crowded conditions than private hospitals and clinics. On the other hand, the volume and quality of care may be more difficult to monitor and control in private institutions. As the public and private mix of health care facilities changes, health insurance schemes become concerned with far more than the costs of care. A moral issue arises regarding the restriction of patient preferences versus the real possibility of damaging equity in access to health care among all members of a scheme. This happens when members with the financial means can avail themselves of faster and more comfortable services (though not necessarily of a higher quality) if they can add the supplementary charges, that is, after the health insurance scheme has paid the regular allowances in a private facility.

THE DIRECT METHOD

The direct provision of health services by a health insurance scheme requires a completely different kind of undertaking and organisation. In the past, this type of system evolved out of the sheer necessity to develop resources in order to provide the benefits, as we saw in the Latin American experience, and in the initial development of health insurance schemes in other developing countries. If this type of system is undertaken today, it may well be for similar reasons and, more importantly, because direct provision enables health insurance to apply more effectively the primary health care strategy, a vital approach to the achievement of efficient and less costly treatment of the insured population.

Moreover direct provision is suitable for ensuring cost and quality control as well as the ability to shift resources within the system to meet changing needs over time. To achieve these gains, we now appreciate that the process must begin with a careful assessment of the availability and economics of health care resources, and an assessment of the needs of the population covered.

One of the initial questions is whether the health insurance scheme needs to develop the entire range of services, or whether it can use already existing public, voluntary or private institutions. Since no system can develop all the necessary services at once, priorities have to be determined as to what category, or mix of categories, should be built first. Very often, this may differ greatly from one area of the country to another. Each aspect requires analysis of the resources available and the prevailing economic and organisational factors, including the logistics of moving staff, supplies and patients through the system. A case in point is whether or not to organise the direct provision of drugs within the community services of the health insurance scheme. Where this has been done, the expenditure on pharmaceuticals remains comparatively low. This first aspect involves decisions on a list of drugs, then central purchasing, storing and distribution to regional depots and community clinics around the country, and finally dispensing by salaried pharmacists.

However the list of priorities in developing health services is finally decided, the important issues will always be equity and continuity. Just as we are sensitive to certain categories of patients "falling between the chairs", we try to avoid repeat services for the same patient in different frameworks. This happens not only when a patient is shifted between institutions under different ownership for different services or levels of care, but sometimes within the same system, when co-ordination between community and hospital care is poor.

Development of hospital care

The building and operation of hospitals have been considered the major achievements and showpieces of health insurance schemes, for instance in Latin America. This approach, with the hospital being the focus of medical care, may be changing, but modern comprehensive clinical medicine still relies on the hospital. Neglect of this facility is usually not acceptable to the public. A health insurance scheme which undertakes developing hospital care cannot be content with operating only small rural or district hospitals with a limited range of services. The quality of care of the providers in a direct health insurance system is influenced by the extent of post-graduate training, exposure to modern methods and an overall academic atmosphere.

If the scheme becomes involved in hospital care, it should also include the large urban hospitals, and strive for university accreditation as teaching hospitals in medical, nursing and para-medical fields. It may seem that this sort of academic involvement is outside the field of interest and practicality for a social security health programme. In the long run, however, the insured will not be content with "second best", particularly regarding specialists and more sophisticated hospital care, which their providers will ultimately become without continuing medical education and research. At the same time, university teaching hospitals may be persuaded to send out senior staff and trainees to the smaller rural or district hospitals as well as to community facilities, all of which will contribute to co-ordination between the community and hospital services provided to the insured population.

The direct operation of hospitals will also assist the health insurance scheme in controlling visits to specialists, as most of their services can be concentrated in hospital out-patient departments or polyclinics staffed by the hospital departments. In systems which rely on the total provision of outside secondary care, patients often have unnecessary visits to specialists practising solely outside the hospital, only to be referred to out-patient departments where they can be seen by the specialist who will treat them if in-patient care is needed.

With health insurance systems generally spending over 50 per cent of their budgets on hospital care, this remains the largest single area for cost control. Direct provision of all or part of the needs of the insured population has significant advantages in this respect.

Development of primary health care

The primary health care concept deserves special focus in this chapter, and is vital to understanding the development of health insurance within the social security framework. The Alma-Ata Conference of the World Health Organization held in the USSR in 1978 adopted the following definition of primary health care:

> Primary Health Care is essential health care, based on practical, scientifically sound and socially acceptable methods and technology made universally accessible to individuals and families in the community through their full participation and at a cost that the community and country can afford to maintain at every stage of their development in the spirit of self-reliance and self-determination. It forms an integral part both of the country's health system, of which it is the central function and the main function, and of the overall social and economic development of the community.

As pointed out repeatedly in the literature on this subject, primary care should in no way be considered second-class care intended only for rural communities or poor people, to be dispensed by auxiliary or untrained personnel. Its potential for good-quality care, as its very definition implies, should be recognised and understood, as it is provided by professionals in a number of disciplines using the appropriate medical, ancillary and social technologies.

Primary health care is not a term meant to reflect all the medical services that can be performed in the community as opposed to hospital setting. It is first-level care, aimed at serving as a front line for the bulk of medical conditions, before and as they arise, and excluding as such only trauma requiring the immediate services of a hospital casualty or emergency unit.

The front line cannot handle all the services that may be needed by an individual patient following the initial contact. The task of the primary care provider will first be to gather as much information as possible to reach a diagnosis, a process which may involve the use of services outside the basic primary care unit, such as a laboratory or radiology service. If the diagnosis is clear and the treatment of choice can be given by the same primary care unit, the patient will remain under such care for therapy and follow-up. If, however, this cannot be done, the primary care or front line doctor, nurse or auxiliary may refer the patient, with the relevant information gathered, to the hospital.

It is not only the individual patient's condition that determines whether referral is appropriate. Very often, the primary care doctor is faced with a situation where he cannot carry out simple procedures for which his medical training prepared him because he lacks the basic facilities. This applies mainly to simple specimen tests and minor surgical procedures. The generalist may also be faced with patient expectations for more specialist and hospital care, as his own lack of equipment may promote the tendency to see such services as higher-quality care. These factors play a part too in his own motivation towards acquiring these basic aids, while he may at the same time feel underpaid and overburdened with minor complaints compared with his specialist colleagues.

Before going into how primary health care can be organised to meet the challenges of modern health care, it may be useful to recall why it is so important. As it requires less sophisticated personnel and equipment, it can be better distributed among population groups, thereby putting real value into the concept of equity of access. It is very significant in controlling costs within its own framework as well-organised primary health care will be based on the optimal use of the personnel making up the primary health care team and the range of drugs and equipment used. It is equally important in controlling the overall costs of hospital care. The insured public cannot be expected to accept reductions in access or limitations in their patterns of using hospital care unless they are guaranteed strong medical support in the community. There is little point in, for example, reducing the length of hospital stay by early discharge programmes for specific categories of patients if the necessary care cannot be provided in the patient's home.

If we now accept that the promotion of health and the prevention of disease are integral parts of medical care, all the elements fall into a spectrum which must have continuity, just as life itself is a continuum. The curative parts may well relate to episodes of ill-health, but we now also understand that prevention occurs in stages, particularly as the population ages and we are faced with more individuals with chronic diseases.

In the first stage, that is, in primary prevention, we try to reduce the risk factors that may lead to a particular disease. While the main effort may be on groups of high risk individuals, there is tremendous value in having the message reinforced by the primary health care provider, particularly as such messages usually deal with personal habits, such as personal hygiene, clean water and sanitation in the home, as well as smoking and correct nutrition. Secondary prevention deals with the early detection of disease, and here again it is the primary care provider who receives relevant information on the possibility of a chronic disease in early stages when the patient comes for attention with relevant signs and symptoms. Unless there is a system of rigorous and regular screening of high-risk groups, it is not likely that a better substitute for the primary care doctor's role in this capacity will be found. In tertiary prevention, that is, the prevention of progression of a chronic disease, it is the time factor that first determines who will look after the patient. Whether we are referring to a diabetic in middle age or an 80-year-old with a malignancy, the patient should be in his community for most of the duration of his illness. Here the primary care physician and team will play a crucial part in keeping the patient out of hospital, and maintaining his health to the extent possible in the workplace, home and social environment.

For the medical profession in general, these "new tasks" are easier to accept and implement in systems which are organised, and which offer regular post-graduate training as part of their work conditions. If advances in clinical techniques and therapies take time to be adopted by the majority of physicians, advances in "medical care" ideologies take even longer if left to individual initiative. From the social security health insurance standpoint, however, these ideologies make good and immediate sense.

The question then arises as to how primary health care should be organised in the community to attain these goals. There are countries with a tradition of excellent primary care given by general practitioners, many of them with specialised training in family medicine, practising alone in their own independent clinics or "surgeries". They are paid by the health insurance schemes on a capitation basis for each insured person on their own list, regardless of the volume of services used or the frequency of visits. This form of primary care also ensures continuity. However, our focus here is on the direct provision of care in facilities developed and operated by the health insurance scheme itself. We are also more concerned with countries in which health manpower is not plentiful and population dispersal, travel time and distance are different from that in long industrialised nations.

Taking the current approach to medical care, the basic primary health members accept responsibility for home visits and the health centre serves as the base for preventive care given in schools and other institutions as prevention activities are merged with curative functions. Larger health centres may have a more varied range of services, including pharmacists, social workers, health educators and laboratory and radiology technicians if very large populations are served. Such centres may also have examination and consultation facilities for the regular use of some specialists. These will primarily be gynaecologists and pediatricians, but a large centre may have physicians in surgical and internal medicine specialities to assist the family doctors in the diagnosis of more complex conditions or even routinely carry out minor surgical procedures.

Whether or not there is a health centre, owned and operated by the health insurance scheme, every community depends first on the definition of community. The location of centres will obviously be determined first by population size, along with consideration of transport, travel time and distance between the population centres of a region. The centre may well serve a total insured population of up to 20,000 or even more individuals residing within a radius of several miles, depending again on the mode of travel in the area. On the other hand, rural health centres serving the populations of several villages with small populations (under 1,000 individuals) often fail in the basic purposes of primary care when patients with acute problems find it simpler to travel to the hospital in the city than to reach the health centre. Sometimes cultural and ethnic factors discourage building a single health centre to serve a geographic region, or the socio-economic conditions of a single or group of communities may warrant having a smaller centre in its midst, particularly to stimulate the better health and living conditions. Smaller health centres serviced by one doctor splitting his time between them but backed by a full-time nurse or health aide are sometimes more effective in poorer areas than a large but poorly attended health centre.

The community health centre may include a limited drug supply (that is, drugs that can be administered by a nurse), a dispensary staffed by a licensed pharmacist or the scheme may rely entirely on existing private pharmacies. However, the availability of licensed pharmacists is usually limited, and the health insurance scheme cannot offer salaries which are competitive with incomes in the private sector. Drug dispensaries operated by the scheme may therefore have to rely on pharmacist assistants and an efficient pre-packaged pharmaceutical supply system to reduce the workload of the fully qualified pharmacists.

This implies a far more serious drug supply undertaking by the health insurance scheme. Indeed, the major savings on drugs and medicinal supplies in a direct delivery scheme come from having a central purchasing and supply system, rather than from the actual dispensing function. When the health insurance scheme covers a large population and operates its own hospitals, it acquires considerable bargaining power in purchasing drugs directly from the pharmaceutical producers, sometimes with the help of international agencies such as the WHO and UNICEF. It can also reduce waste by ordering bulk and unit quantities according to appropriate dosage and projected needs. However, even if the basic list of drugs stored and dispensed in the scheme's hospitals and health centres is limited, the regular communications and transport infrastructure needed for efficient dispensing are not always feasible in developing countries. The inclusion of drugs will therefore depend on local resources, public attitudes and the ability to control costs within the primary care system. The advantages of including this function have been dealt with above, but the important determinants of this issue may be different between countries, and even within countries, such as between urban and rural districts.

Whatever the ultimate size and form of the health centre, team-work in its staffing must be stressed. The actual establishment of a primary care health centre by the health insurance scheme generally brings new health care professionals into the area. Their first task is to co-operate with the existing health care providers in the community, such as the local midwife or traditional birth attendant, and to the extent possible, co-opt the help of indigenous health practitioners. The task of the staff in providing health care as well as in community social and environmental projects will be made much easier by team-work, with clear definitions and division of duties between them. In the larger urban centres with two or more doctors, general practice becomes far more manageable and rewarding when each doctor knows he is working within a group of peers, ready to share problems, knowledge and duties when one of the group is attending hospital duties, on post-graduate study or vacation.

A primary care centre developed by the health insurance scheme has an additional advantage for young medical graduates. In many countries their education has been attained at great expense and effort. A clinic post means no additional investment in setting up a practice in terms of equipment and patients, and at the same time may provide the newly graduated doctor with the valuable assistance of at least a nurse if not more experienced doctors. All this is of considerable advantage to the young doctor. The trend towards specialisation in family medicine has taken root in most countries, and this too should be considered. The residency programme that has been evolving in Western countries includes several years of supervised primary care clinical practice. If the health insurance scheme has chosen the system of direct delivery of care, it will have to encourage this additional training and provide positions in its health centres. The short- and long-term results of this "investment" is a primary care provider better qualified to serve the needs of the entire family outside the hospital.

If all these tasks have to be carried out, and in a spirit of team co-operation and commitment to the health of a community, the design of the centre warrants attention here. The rural unit, which is usually the smallest health centre, basically consists of an examination and consultation room, a treatment room that may serve for immunisations, family planning or observation for several hours, a maternity room, a small drug and equipment storage room and a waiting area. Larger centres such as rural health centres serving a number of communities or urban neighbourhoods, may have, in addition to more doctors' and nurses' rooms, facilities for specialists and regular visits by para-medical health care workers (social worker, nutritionist, health educators), a dental clinic, drug dispensary with adequate storage space, small area for basic laboratory tests, an office, and a staff meeting room. All the relevant areas must be large enough to take into account that in some societies, several family members may accompany adults as well as children on a visit to the doctor.

As the traditional preventive and curative functions are integrated into the primary care centre's functions, care has to be taken to do this without negative effects on either of the two areas. If the disease pattern of the population is marked by a high frequency of acute infectious and parasitic diseases, it may be necessary to have a separate area for the maternal and child care preventive services, or at least separate waiting areas and in any event, separate practice hours. The design and size of rooms must allow for privacy and patient dignity, while the overall centre layout should encourage team-work and health education activities in an environment that promotes pride in the centre as a community asset. If the health insurance scheme is the sole provider of health care in the community, an obvious problem will be whether to permit access to individuals who are not covered. Local conditions, co-ordination with the health and welfare agencies and the extent of insurance coverage will probably determine the response to this question.

An issue which has not been addressed is the extent of choice the insured member has in seeking medical care. Primary health care is the service which will be used most frequently, yet it may be the very area where it is difficult to provide choice because of small population and health centre size. If the health centre is indeed the only source of care available, the lack of choice can be compensated by sensitivity to the desires of the community regarding location and centre hours. In larger areas, it may be possible to allow some choice among several doctors. Choice of specialist is also difficult if all the specialists coming to the centre are part of hospital teams staffing both in-patient and out-patient facilities. However the system is ultimately developed, it is extremely important in the long run that the insured feel they have some control over choice and that their personal identity is preserved and not abused by, for example, long waiting lines, centre sessions in which senior staff do not show up, and unnecessary administrative demands. The insured also need to feel professional commitment on the part of the health centre staff. The major result of solving these problems is a strong primary care base which goes a long way in achieving a balanced health insurance system.

COMBINED SYSTEMS

Regardless of all the advantages of a health insurance scheme's direct involvement in health care, it is extremely difficult for the system to be self-sufficient. In most of the countries in which social security benefits are currently being extended to medical care, we will not find a complete vacuum, particularly in hospital facilities. These may have been developed by the Ministry of Health, charitable and private institutions or by universities as teaching hospitals for their medical schools. If the health insurance is aimed at the majority if not all of the population, the continued utilisation of these hospitals will be expected, as long as all the facilities providing care to the scheme's members are not operating at substandard levels. In the spirit of healthy pluralism, with constructive competition among providers stimulating efficiency, the health insurance scheme is more likely to develop with a combined system, with due consideration of which elements to provide directly and which to "purchase" from outside providers. Combined systems may in fact be very important in Asian countries, where much attention may be given to maintaining privacy and allowing for ethnic and religious considerations.

Taking the primary health care model described in the previous section, the health insurance priority will probably be the development of community clinics to provide this level of care on a self-sufficient basis. How specialist care is provided will depend on the scheme's involvement with hospitals. If the scheme owns and operates a major part of the hospitals, it may want to restrict consultations in some of the specialities, that is, those with low hospitalisation requirements, to the out-patient departments of its own hospitals. Or, it may develop regional polyclinics visited regularly by the specialists from its hospitals, who may also do some minor surgery on an ambulatory basis. If, on the other hand, this proves inconvenient for most of the insured, it may "purchase" specialist care from the same non-health insurance-owned hospitals providing in-patient care.

The mix of direct and indirect systems will give the health insurance scheme the opportunity to compare utilisation patterns and to try to regulate the tendency of outside providers to generate unnecessary services. In several countries, including Canada and Israel, the health insurance schemes have reached contractual arrangements with the main hospital providers whereby an annual global payment is calculated for hospital care to defined populations, based on the expected utilisation of in-patient care.

Such arrangements and the delivery of care in general in a combined system require a considerable amount of good will and co-operation between all the parties, at central and local level, and preferably under the leadership of the Ministry of Health. The situation to be avoided is one in which the health insurance scheme competes with the Ministry of

Health in the provision of services, and the private providers compete with the insurance scheme. Inclusion of all the accredited providers in an atmosphere of co-operation is likely to increase both public and professional acceptability and generate a sufficient level of competitiveness to maintain efficiency throughout the system.

COST-SHARING

This section is included here as it is an area of divided opinion and repeated debate in both direct and indirect systems. Although not an integral part of the method of paying providers, and not a significant factor in dealing with sources of financing health insurance, it comes up in discussing these areas. More important, in developing countries it is usually debated in the context of the moral question regarding the wisdom of giving care "free of charge" at the time of service. The following review is aimed at providing a better understanding of the cost-sharing and user-charges arguments.

The two basic reasons for cost-sharing are to control demand and/or to increase revenue into the health insurance scheme. Hence the use of different terms in addition to cost-sharing, such as user-charges, co-payment, deductibles and co-insurance *(ticket modérateur)*. The demand and revenue considerations are often supplanted by the attitude that health care should not be "free" and that therefore some charge should be made to the patient at the time of use. However, this ignores the underlying principle of health insurance in which a regular contribution or payment is made into a fund just for the purpose of avoiding the hazard of payment at the time of use. Therefore social security medical care schemes have taken the position that cost sharing should be kept to a minimum, in recognition of this principle.

The Social Security (Minimum Standards) Convention, 1952 (No. 102), adopted by the ILO stipulates that "the beneficiary or his breadwinner may be required to share in the cost of medical care the beneficiary receives in respect of a morbid condition: the rules concerning such cost-sharing shall be so designed as to avoid hardship". This is extremely difficult to do in developing countries where a large portion of the population may exist below the poverty line, and the term "poor" cannot be clearly defined for the purposes of providing health care benefits.

It is now fairly well accepted that unless the user-charge is substantial it has no lasting effect on controlling the demand for care. Also recognised is the fact that even nominal charges may have a detrimental effect on seeking certain kinds of services, particularly those which may assist in the early detection and treatment of disease. A new consideration on the demand side has been to impose user-charges as a means of controlling referrals to control higher cost services. For example, charges are applied if the patient goes directly to a specialist rather than through the primary care channel. On the revenue side, a more recent concept is that imposing user-charges can serve as an additional source for underfunded or new areas, which the insurance schemes find difficult to finance without increasing contribution rates.

Efforts to balance health insurance budgets have therefore led to some increase in cost-sharing in recent years but so far such revenues—direct payments by patients at the time of service—have not accounted for significant proportions of health insurance income. The dangers of creating barriers to access and of increasing administrative complexity has kept cost-sharing at limited levels. Complex yet flexible measures are needed to exempt various categories of the insured from payment.

The most controversial application of cost-sharing from this point of view is for doctor visits. Cost-sharing for hospital care has generally been based on the concept that the patient is paying towards the "hotel service" as opposed to medical service received as an in-patient. Another approach has been to levy or increase cost-sharing after a specific length of stay. The cost-sharing may be applied above a specific level of expenditure, or as a flat-rate charge for each day in hospital. To date, most social security health insurance schemes have not imposed cost-sharing for general hospital care.

The only benefit for which most systems have imposed patient participation is for pharmaceuticals. This is perhaps the only service where a major reason for introducing cost-sharing was the reduction of demand, despite the fact that the actual demand for prescribed drugs is generated by the doctor and not the patient. Partial or total exemptions are usually given for young children and pensioners, patients requiring continuous drug therapy for chronic conditions, or for life-saving drugs. Even with all these exemptions, the user-charges for drugs in health insurance schemes which dispense drugs through their own system can bring in a considerable amount of additional revenue, simply because of the large volume of this service. One result is conflict between the budgeting side of the scheme, concerned with increasing revenue, and the medical side, concerned with decreasing the high dependency on drugs that has developed in many countries. With the changes in approach towards more health promotion and patient responsibility, this is a conflict that should be resolved, and in which essentially minor budgetary considerations should not be counter-productive to improving health care.

It is extremely difficult to make a case for no cost-sharing at all, mainly because of the very different economic, cultural and health factors in each system. In developing countries the insured population includes very large groups of low-income and fairly poor beneficiaries, many of whom could hardly be expected to share the cost of care at the point of delivery in addition to the compulsory regular deduction made from their incomes in order to pay the social insurance contribution. In the final analysis, the most attention should be given to the objective of cost-sharing, so that the appropriate measures are taken while maintaining the principles of insurance and patient and provider responsibility.

PAYING DOCTORS AND HOSPITALS UNDER HEALTH INSURANCE

4

GENERAL CONSIDERATIONS

All systems of payment create incentives for suppliers of goods and services. Indeed this is their economic function. They reward those who produce, supply and sell them and thus induce them to do so. Competition prevents these rewards becoming excessive. The consumer decides how much to buy at the prices on offer.

Health insurance interferes with the market mechanism by reducing or removing price as a system of controlling how much the consumer wants to buy. Indeed this is its purpose: people contribute regularly when they are well, so that price will not be a barrier to obtaining care when they are sick. Insurance may also remove competition if the insurer pays all providers at the same prices. In this situation providers inevitably want to sell as much as possible to maximise their rewards. In the health market this is dangerous for two reasons. First, the consumer is poorly equipped with knowledge to budget what he needs or how much he needs. Second, the advice on what he needs comes from suppliers of services: health professionals who can, depending on the payment system, have a financial interest in supplying more services than are strictly necessary.

Health insurance can be based on one of two models. In the first the insurer gives a subsidy towards the costs of health care incurred by the insured person but does not attempt to control the prices which the insured person has to pay. The subsidy may be claimed by the provider or the patient may claim reimbursement up to the limits that the terms of the insurance policy allow. The model operates, for example, in the Medicare scheme for hospital insurance in the Philippines. Here the insurer needs to be satisfied that the service provided is of acceptable quality and that the claim was justified. The costs falling on the patient are not the insurer's concern. One disadvantage is that the provider finds himself able to charge higher prices than he would have been able to charge before insurance was introduced. Second, the costs falling on the patient can still be substantial and unpredictable. When the scheme began in the Philippines in 1972 it was reimbursing 70 to 100 per cent of hospital costs. Owing to higher prices, possibly largely due to drug prices and the inclusion of dependants, by 1982 the proportion of costs covered had fallen to 48 per cent for primary care hospitals, 30 per cent for secondary hospitals and 15 to 18 per cent for tertiary hospitals. Moreover, the admission rate rose from 3 per cent per year to around 6 per cent per year, partly because care outside hospitals was not covered.

The second model tries to regulate charges made for health care even though part of the cost may have to be paid by the patient either by the insurer's reimbursing only part of the cost or by allowing providers to make certain specific charges for health care. The insurer may own the health facilities and pay all the providers' salaries—the *direct* system. Alternatively the insurer may make contracts with providers (e.g. with doctors and with hospitals which are owned by other agencies)—the *indirect* system. In either case the insurer will want to be satisfied that the services provided give value for money. The services must be acceptable in terms of convenience, comfort and courtesy. They must be of good technical quality but at the lowest cost this can be bought. This is of critical importance in developing countries in schemes which are intended eventually to achieve wide coverage. They must be sufficient but not excessive in the sense either that the same health outcome could be achieved with fewer services or that interventions are not made which unnecessarily place the patient's health at risk by, for example, using potent drugs or surgery when there are insufficient indications for using them. Finally, the health insurer wants the cost of providing the services to be as predictable as possible per person covered as is consistent with sufficient services of good technical quality. These aims can lead to conflict with the interests of providers in two ways.

Lower charges

First, the concerns of the insurer for low and predictable costs are inevitably at variance with the interests of both hospitals and doctors. As the insurer sees it, he is widening both markets by enabling patients to use doctors and hospitals without having to worry about the cost or only such charges or co-payments as are built into the insurance policy. This widening of the market will enable doctors and hospitals to treat more patients with the same overhead costs. The insurer expects to capture these savings or a large part of them. In other words, charges for insured persons should be below those previously charged in the private market because the insurer is a bulk purchaser. Thus, for example, when health insurance was introduced in the Republic of Korea payments to both hospitals and doctors were set out at about 50 per cent of prevailing charges. This remained the level for doctors' fees but hospital charges were later allowed to rise to about 60 per cent of what was charged to the non-insured.

The level of charges is a critical consideration for a developing country introducing a health insurance scheme which can only hope to cover a minority of the population for a long time to come. The rewards to health professionals for insurance practice cannot be allowed to become much greater than salaries in the government service or recruitment to the latter will be damaged and doctors may leave it to join the insurance scheme. Or health trained manpower may be less willing to work in rural areas because of the high incomes which can be earned in urban areas where employed persons who can be most readily covered by insurance mainly work. Despite the lower fees and charges under health insurance in the Republic of Korea, the number of doctors working in rural areas fell by 9 per cent and nurses by 47 per cent in the nine years after health insurance was introduced.[1] Thus what a doctor is paid for treating an insured person may have to be several times lower than fees in private practice. Under the Employees' State Insurance Scheme in India salaries for the doctors are the same as for government servants except for the addition of some special allowances.

Doctors and hospitals which have not previously had to bargain about price are naturally reluctant to lower their charges. Moreover, neither take kindly to being asked to justify what they provide for patients. But the insurer is wise to do this in the interests of ensuring that costs are predictable and value for money is obtained. This underlying tension about the level of charges influences attitudes about the system of payment. The provider obviously wants a system which will enable him to recapture some of the losses due to lower charges by giving each insured person extra services while the insurer wants a system which will contain costs and not lead to excessive services.

So far it is assumed that doctors and hospitals operate like any other business concern. A private profit-making hospital is clearly oriented to sell extra services and there is considerable scope in offering extra amenities such as air-conditioning and special meals. Even a hospital owned by a non-government organisation may have to cover costs and any surplus enables it to update its equipment and expand its facilities. Doctors, however, are bound by ethical standards. They are expected to act in precisely the same way however they are paid or indeed whether they will be paid or not. But in practice doctors, like other human beings, respond to financial incentives. There is a considerable area (e.g. more pathology tests) where further services *might* possibly help in the care of the patient and for a number of operations there is a considerable "grey area" where there is room for disagreement among doctors on whether surgery would be appropriate. Beyond these areas the extent to which a particular doctor responds to incentives will depend on how far he places his ethical responsibilities above his financial interest. Standards of medical ethics differ between countries as well as between individual doctors and in some developing countries they are not well developed.

Health insurance in developing countries

Standardised payments

Second, different levels of fee present a problem when health insurance is introduced and the insurer wants to standardise the payments for services to make the cost of the policy as predictable as possible. Standard charges pose problems for tertiary hospitals and particularly teaching hospitals where teaching requirements impose higher costs. Thus a higher scale of payment may need to be applied to such hospitals—particularly if the payment system is per day of care.

In a private market doctors charge fees for their services, though in some countries the fee may be disguised by including it in the price of the medicine provided. A doctor with a high reputation can charge a higher fee than a doctor who is not so highly regarded. High fees can be used to limit the size of a practice to what can be comfortably managed. In some countries a specialist has always charged more than a general practitioner for the same service. Obviously doctors with high incomes do not want to see these reduced when their patients become covered by compulsory health insurance. Thus high-earning doctors, who are often the leaders of the profession, may well oppose the introduction of compulsory health insurance for this reason, whatever other reason they may give in public: they may even try to persuade all doctors to boycott health insurance.

A number of different answers have been found to this problem. One is to exclude higher earners from the compulsory scheme (i.e. in the Philippines). Another answer is to pay higher fees to specialists than general practitioners when they perform the same services. A third answer is to have a choice of payment systems for patient and doctor. Those patients who want their health care to be free at time of use can consult doctors who accept not to be paid on a fee-for-service basis or have agreed to accept a negotiated schedule of fees. But those doctors who wish to do so can charge their usual fees and those patients who wish to consult them can do so but the patient has to pay part of the fee. A variant is to restrict freedom to charge their own fees to particular categories of particularly distinguished doctors. A fourth answer is to have a completely different payment system for general practitioners and specialists, with a system of merit additions for the most distinguished specialists.

A system of payment by salary neatly deals with this problem by providing different rewards to different doctors. This is one of the advantages of the *direct* system of providing insurance in which the insurer employs the doctor. But it is also possible for the insurance to pay for part of a doctor's time each day by a sessional payment. The doctor may spend the rest of his time working in private practice. Alternatively he may be working in the government health service and provide early evening clinics for insured persons as in the scheme for civil servants in Indonesia. While fees are undoubtedly the oldest way in which doctors were paid, salaries have a long history in some countries. For example, over a hundred years ago the majority of doctors in Sweden were paid salaries: to be selected for a salaried position was an honour. In countries with a long tradition of salaries and where the level of salaries had been generally regarded as fair, salaried payment may lead to a quality service which is acceptable to insured persons and does not lead to some of the worst problems listed below from the experience of some other countries.

The third way of paying doctors involves the greatest degree of standardisation of medical incomes. This is capitation payment. Partly for this reason the system is normally only applied to general practitioners. The patient chooses a doctor and once that doctor has accepted and registered the patient, the doctor receives a monthly income from the insurer for each registered patient whether that patient uses the doctor's services during the month or not. There are arrangements for patients to change doctors. Doctors are therefore in competition for patients as their incomes depend on how many they attract to register with them. The system originated in voluntary health insurance in Europe in the eighteenth century (or earlier) and was widely used in the nineteenth century in Denmark, the Netherlands, Germany and the United Kingdom. Three of these countries have retained the system with modifications when insurance became compulsory. It was adopted because it was simple to administer and made costs predictable. Originally, the doctor was expected to pay for the drugs out of the capitation fee. Later drugs became separately paid for by the insurer.

It is by no means unknown for more than one payment system to be used in one country. Different health insurance funds may use different payments systems as in, for example, Israel where the largest fund uses salaried payment. It is also quite common for the same insurer to use more than one system. It may, as often in the Employees' State Insurance Scheme in India, use salaries under a direct system of provision in areas where there is a heavy concentration of covered persons and capitation for outlying areas where there are too few covered persons to justify a whole-time salaried doctor.

The advantages and disadvantages of each of these three systems—fee-for-service, salary and capitation—are discussed in the rest of this chapter from the point of view of the patient, the provider and the insurer. Pointing to the problems which have been found in some countries or among some doctors can easily leave the impression that ALL doctors are unscrupulous and motivated only by the desire to make money. This is by no means our view. But it is useful to point out what can happen under a particular payment system even if only in the case of a small minority of doctors or in the context of a particular country, so that those choosing a payment system for a new scheme of health insurance can consider whether or how far it might occur in their country. Exceptionally, the experience of industrialised countries will be quoted in this part of the chapter together with information from developing countries. The examples are drawn from America and Europe as well as from Asia. This is where the long-established schemes are to be found. Some problems with health insurance may take a considerable time to emerge or to be identified. Moreover research on comparative experience has a long history in Europe.

PAYING THE DOCTOR

Fee-for-service

This system of payment is used, for example, in the United States, Canada, Australia, New Zealand, the Republic of Korea, Belgium, France, the Federal Republic of Germany, Norway and as an option in Sweden. The advantage to the doctor of fee-for-service payment is that it gives him the flexibility to increase income by providing further services by, for example, encouraging the patient to make repeat visits, ordering more diagnostic tests or undertaking more procedures. The payment system reflects the work actually done. The disadvantage is that the doctor has to give a record of all the medical acts performed for each patient in making claims from the insurer or providing bills on which the patient can claim reimbursement. This is a time-consuming operation. Further time and irritation may be caused when the insurer starts questioning the claims and this process can lead to delayed payment.

The advantages for the patient are that the doctor has incentives to make the services he provides acceptable by attractive premises, prompt service and courtesy. The doctor is unlikely to complain even when consulted on matters which he may regard as trivial. Further advantages are that the patient can be given complete free choice of doctor for each illness or even during the course of any illness. If the doctor has access to a hospital, the patient can be treated by the same doctor in and out of hospital. One possible disadvantage may be that doctors appear to be in a hurry as time is money. Moreover patients living in areas where doctors find it unattractive to work may find that there are not enough doctors and those who are there are extremely busy. It may not be possible to get an appointment with a particular doctor on the day it is requested. Moreover the insurance contribution is likely to be high.

The advantage from the insurer's point of view is the high level of satisfaction of covered persons. Doctors have no incentives to underprovide and some incentive to keep up to date—particularly in the use of new procedures for which charges can be made. There are also incentives to obtain specialist qualifications in so far as patients prefer to take particular problems direct to specialists.

The disadvantages for the insurer are high administrative costs in processing claims, high, rising and unpredictable costs and in some cases concerns about quality. In China, since the decline of the co-operatives with barefooted doctors paid by salary, fee-for-service payment has led to a decline in preventive services, excessive prescription of drugs and overuse of sophisticated services.

A wise insurer will not simply price the medical acts claimed and pay the bill. Claims will be queried if the acts claimed are inconsistent with the diagnosis (if this is disclosed) or inconsistent with the diagnosis suggested by other treatment or generally appears to be excessive (e.g. too many repeated X-rays). The insurer has to be on the look out for false claims—medical acts charged for and not actually done quite apart from acts actually done but attributed to the wrong patient. Even when a doctor sends to the insurer a bill that has been paid to a laboratory for tests, this is not total protection against fraud as there can be an agreement between the laboratory and the doctor only to do some of the tests requested so that they can share between them the profit from tests charged for but not actually done.

Even a very simple fee schedule with payments only for visits and consultations can lead to a high use of services and consequently high costs as the doctor can encourage a patient to make repeat visits during the course of an illness. In Ireland, where such a fee schedule applies for the poorer half of the population, the visit rate is 11 per cent per year compared with 4.5 per cent in the United Kingdom.

Where the fee schedule is complex as in the Federal Republic of Germany and the Republic of Korea and claims can be made for over 600 medical acts in the former or 2,000 in the latter, it is inevitable that some procedures are high earning for the doctor for the time involved in undertaking them as fee schedules generally reflect skill and complexity not just time. Thus there are financial incentives to over-use these procedures. The high use of diagnostic tests has been identified as a particular problem in Belgium.[2] Moreover, where the doctor has purchased a particular piece of equipment, there are strong financial incentives to use it frequently so as to pay off the capital cost as fast as possible with claims for the particular medical act for which it is used. This has been a special problem in the Federal Republic of Germany.

High costs are not confined to the claims made by doctors for their own fees. Repeat visits may lead to further prescriptions. In the Federal Republic of Germany about two-thirds of visits are "doctor-induced" compared with one-third in the United Kingdom. It may not just be chance that a study of Member States of the European Community showed that the number of prescription items per person covered was about twice the rate where the doctor was paid on a fee-for-service basis than on a capitation basis. And where a doctor has rights to admit to hospital there are financial incentives to do so as there are hospital staff to help undertake medical acts and the doctor not the patient decides how often the patient should be visited.

Concerns about quality can arise in a number of contexts even if they apply to only a few doctors. Where doctors are responsible for in-patients, one concern is unnecessary surgery. A much quoted study from the United States showed that varying geographical rates of surgery seemed to be best explained by the number of surgeons in each geographical area.[3] And complete freedom of choice of doctor has risks beyond those of high costs. The patient can consult several doctors in the course of one illness and each of these may prescribe: the drugs actually taken by the patient may be dangerous in combination. While the doctor has some incentives to keep up to date, competition leads doctors to tend to work in isolation rather than in teams: the restraint of colleagues knowing about the way a doctor practises medicine and the possibility of informal consultation between doctors within the premises are then absent. Moreover, doctors may be tempted to undertake some procedures, including surgery, in which they have no recent experience, rather than refer a patient to a specialist surgeon, lest that patient will go direct to that specialist in a further illness. Finally, the doctor has no real incentive for preventive work as only limited preventive acts can be incorporated in a fee schedule.

To try to limit all these problems, the insurer needs to monitor claims closely and maintain statistics or "doctor profiles" to indicate which doctors have high-claim rates in particular respects. The insurer may try to persuade high-claiming doctors to modify their behaviour by circulating their profiles to them with the averages for all doctors, arranging for doctors to be visited by control doctors, reporting doctors to the Medical Association or licensing authority, threatening to remove offending doctors from insurance practice or actually doing so. Second, the insurer may try to negotiate changes in the fee schedule to make certain acts less financially attractive. Third, the insurer may introduce systems of independent prior approval for hospital admissions and/or surgery. Moreover these types of activity by the insurer involve extra administrative costs and cause strained relations with the doctors concerned. This is particularly the case when payment is delayed while the necessity for a particular medical act is disputed as has happened frequently in the Republic of Korea. While fee-for-service payment appears at first sight to interfere least with the practice of medicine or professional freedom it may end up by interfering far more than under any other payment system.

A fourth solution is to require the patient to pay part of all the costs or only for those medical acts which cause particular concern. In the Republic of Korea, when the health insurance scheme began in 1979 for government employees and private school teachers, insured persons had to pay up to 30 per cent of out-patient expenses and 20 per cent of in-patient costs. In 1980 the co-insurance rate for out-patient visits was raised to 50 per cent in the case of hospitals but out-patient visits continued to rise from 4.8 per person per year in 1980 to 7.4 in 1985. In 1986 a flat rate sum was added for out-patient care at clinics and in the case of hospitals the insured was required to pay the whole cost of the doctor consultation fee plus 50 to 55 per cent of the other expenses. Thus the patient had to pay 65 per cent of the cost for a hospital visit. This at last caused out-patient visits to fall.[4] But this, of course, considerably reduced the scope of the insurance which it was originally intended to provide.

Salary

This is the most common way of paying doctors who care for in-patients. Senior doctors may be allowed to supplement their salaries by charging on a fee-for-service basis those patients who choose to pay extra for single rooms or higher classes of care. This can cause worries that some doctors are devoting too much time to such patients at the expense of insured persons in standard wards. For this reason, some schemes forbid full-time salaried doctors from having any private practice. This is the normal rule, for example, in the Employees' State Insurance Scheme in India.

Salaried payment is also used for primary health care in health centres, clinics or dispensaries in, for example, Finland, Sweden, the USSR, Spain, Portugal, Greece, Turkey, India, Indonesia and the largest fund in Israel. It is also the most common method used in Latin America. The doctor may be employed whole time or more often on a part-time basis, for example, four hours per working day.

The advantage for the patient of health centres with salaried doctors is that having arrived at the centre he is likely to be able to see a doctor on that day, subject to any problems of recruitment. Moreover all primary health care may be provided in the same building. In some health centres a patient can be referred for pathology tests, X-ray and a specialist's opinion all within the buildings. The staff of the centre may all be trained to promote preventive medicine, for a full range of facilities are also available. Where a health centre serves a defined geographical area it is possible to remind patients about attendance for immunisation, screening, ante-natal and post-natal care, child health monitoring, family planning, health education and other preventive work. In practice, however, in most Latin American countries and also in Spain, Portugal and Greece, health insurance originally developed as primarily a curative service with preventive services provided in separate premises under the control of the Ministry of Health. In the three European countries and in some Latin American countries, these services are being brought together into the same buildings. Under a salaried system of payment, posts for doctors can be established in ratios to the number of insured persons in each area. It does not, however, follow that all these posts will be filled.

Health insurance in developing countries

But the existence of health insurance can improve the geographical availability of doctors.

The disadvantages for the patient are that a large health centre or clinic may seem impersonal. Moreover even in Sweden and Finland where efforts are made to do so, a patient cannot be reasonably sure of seeing the same doctor who was originally consulted on a repeat visit during the same illness or in a later illness. If the centre provides a 24-hour service seven days a week, there has to be a rota so that doctors are given days off after night or weekend duty. In many other countries little attempt is made to accommodate the patient's preference so that a different doctor is seen on virtually every visit. While this doctor may well have in front of him the patient's record, both patient and doctor have to make a new relationship. At its worst such a service can degenerate into short consultations with poor courtesy after long waiting times because doctors arrive late and leave early. In China it is reported that the faults of rural co-operative health insurance with salaried paid doctors were that "health workers were lazy, showed up late, left early; there was a lot of absenteeism; workers were rude to the patients and the quality of care provided was bad". After the consultation there may be another long wait at the pharmacy because suddenly, after no work for the first hour or two of the working day, there is a flood of prescriptions to be dispensed. It is because of major patient dissatisfaction with the salaried system of payment revealed by a survey that Costa Rica is currently moving over to a capitation system of payment to create continuity of care and competition between doctors.

Patients may respond to poor service by tipping the doctor in the hope of getting better attention. Or patients may be given the impression that only by seeing the doctor privately in the evening can they hope to be given the time for careful diagnosis and conscientious treatment. Indeed the doctor may consciously use insurance work to recruit patients for private practice.

The advantages for the doctor are a secure income, clear hours on duty and off duty and the possibility of promotion to higher grades in the organisation. In a well-run health centre many doctors enjoy the team work and the collective effort to improve the health of the local community. Moreover the work may not be arduous. Some medical unions in some countries in Latin America have negotiated what work the doctor is expected to do. Thus a doctor may only be asked to see five, four or even three patients an hour—even for repeat visits. Where the doctor is paid for a four-hour daily session, this means that the workload is only 12 or 16 patients a day.

The disadvantage for a doctor working in a large health centre or clinic is lack of continuity of care. He does not have his own patients. He does not normally know the result of his treatment. His job is to process patients on to a next step with the help of the medical record. There is little incentive to get to know a patient and understand the patient's work and family history because that patient may never be seen again. This can lead to low morale and poor job satisfaction.

The advantage for the insurer is control of costs. Personnel costs are within his control and budget ceilings can be imposed on other expenditures—even on the pharmacy. The insurer can more readily select and control the list of drugs made available and economise by using generic drugs bought by tender. Access to specialists and hospitals is only on the basis of referral by the general practitioner. Where extensive preventive services are provided the insurer may hope that these will keep down long-term curative costs as well as improve the health of the insured. Moreover, doctors can be required to attend continuing education and team work can be encouraged. The disadvantage is the need to employ staff in a supervisory capacity—particularly to try to enforce time keeping which may lower the morale of the doctors still further. Doctors with a four-hour session and a "quota" of 12 or 16 patients to be seen may be strongly tempted to arrive late and leave early. Moreover, in some countries it is not uncommon for a doctor to have two or even three or four contracts normally for four hours plus a private practice done in the early morning and in the evening. As a result of this exhausting workload, insured patients may receive a very poor service indeed.

While the system is economical in some respects it may not turn out to be so in others. Where time keeping is enforced, doctors may work at a leisurely pace compared with what happens under other payment systems. Moreover, doctors who do not know their patients well may make a high use of prescriptions, diagnostic tests and referral to specialists to make quite sure that they have missed nothing and because all these facilities are in the building and can be used without great inconvenience to the patient. Thus it is not unknown in Latin America for about one visit in three to lead to referral to a specialist, who will frequently order expensive diagnostic tests.

Capitation

This system of payment has long been used in a pure or modified form for paying general practitioners in Denmark, the Netherlands and the United Kingdom. Before 1980 it was used for a minority of the insured persons in Italy but after the 1980 reform it became the sole method of payment. One reason for the change was that doctors paid on a fee-for-service basis prescribed about one-third more drugs than doctors paid on a capitation basis. It is currently being introduced in Costa Rica and Indonesia and operates under some Health Maintenance Organisations in the United States. In Indonesia, as in Costa Rica, it had been found that salaried service did not lead to what patients regarded as a satisfactory service.

The main advantages for the patient are free choice of doctor (up to the limits imposed on doctors' list sizes) and continuity of care. A patient may only be listed with one doctor at any one time and that doctor will refer the patient for specialist care (including in-patient care) and the specialist later refers the patient back to the general practitioner with a letter explaining the diagnosis and treatment. The doctor under most systems has responsibility for his patient 24 hours a day, seven days a week and 365 days a year. The doctor may fulfil this responsibility by working in a partnership so that partners can deputise for each other during nights and weekends on a rota basis. Or there may be a special deputising service available locally for the doctor to employ. The doctor is not allowed to see a patient on his capitation-paid list in private practice and is unlikely to suggest that the patient visits another doctor on a private basis lest the patient leaves his list. Patients may also welcome home visits when seriously ill which may be required of the doctor as part of the contract (as in the United Kingdom).

The disadvantages for the patient are that the system may give rise to some waiting time and the doctors' premises may be poorly equipped and poorly furnished, as in a pure capitation system the doctor has to pay for the upkeep of his premises out of the capitation payments unless he has also a considerable income from private practice.

Premises may be particularly cramped and run down in the high rent areas of large cities and in poor city areas there may not be many doctors. While the doctor has an incentive to be courteous to keep his patients and give them adequate consultation time, he may show impatience with patients who visit frequently with problems he regards as trivial. The patient may also dislike being handed over to the care of other doctors on admission to hospital.

The doctor likes being his own boss and running his own practice in his own way with the only paper work for the insurer being the reporting of patients added to his list apart from maintaining his own medical records. There is very little interference with his clinical freedom, though his prescribing may be monitored by the insurer. If he is a member of a partnership, this has been by choice and he has chosen with which partners to work and has agreed what will and will not be shared, what supporting staff there will be and how they will be paid.

The disadvantage for the doctor is that his maximum income is fixed by the maximum list size. Depending on the area, he may achieve this by his early thirties and then, unlike other professionals, his income cannot increase except through the negotiation process which will affect all doctors of all ages. If in late middle age he decides that a maximum list is generating too much work and he lets it fall, he loses income. As supporting staff have to be paid for out of the capitation payment he may choose to do his own clerical work but nevertheless resent it. A doctor who wants to combine general practice with hospital practice, particularly surgical practice, will find it hard to do so as capitation leads to a strong line between hospital work and general practice. They are not easily combined.

The insurer has the advantage of the costs for general practitioners' services varying only with membership and thus contribution income, though prescribing costs can be unpredictable and an area of concern. However it is possible to introduce positive or negative lists of products which can be prescribed to keep costs down and to watch and warn high prescribers. Capitation payment does, moreover, generate some incentive for new doctors to settle in under-doctored areas where it will be easier to build up a full list. There is some incentive for doctors to encourage prevention where they think it will lighten their work load in the long run. Doctors and patients are likely to be reasonably content and there is a simple answer to a dissatisfied patient which is to try another doctor in the scheme—though in remote rural areas this may not be practicable. As the main clerical work is to maintain a record of which doctor should be paid for which patient, administrative costs are low and there need be little supervision, possibly only a procedure for adjudicating serious complaints such as doctors' breaking the rule about seeing their listed patients on a private paying basis or refusing to make a home visit where the case is serious.

The insurer may, however, be concerned about the quality of service provided by some doctors, even though the patients appear to be satisfied. There are the questions of poor-quality premises, doctors who use too few diagnostic tests, overuse deputising services and make themselves hard to contact by, for example, using telephones with tape recorders which are not helpful to patients trying to make an appointment from a coin-operated public telephone box. Moreover, doctors have little incentive to keep themselves up to date or attend continuing education; and some doctors may lighten their workload by referring any time-consuming case to a specialist—though in the United Kingdom at least the average referral rate is low.

The insurer can modify the pure capitation system to counter some of these problems and this has been carried furthest in the United Kingdom. The doctor is reimbursed his rent and this opens the door to the inspection of premises and refusal to reimburse the rents of unsatisfactory premises. The salaries of two supporting staff are subsidised at the rate of 70 per cent. Restrictions are placed on the use of deputising services though these are hard to enforce. Attendance at continuing education is subsidised and extra allowances are paid to doctors as they get older. Controls are enforced on the entry of new practitioners to areas with too many doctors and there are financial incentives to work in remote rural areas.

Up to this point the capitation system has been considered in the context of the capitation payment covering only the doctor's services. As mentioned earlier, there was a stage in the development of health insurance where the doctor was expected to provide drugs out of the capitation payment. This might well be a possible model in developing countries. In some types of "Health Maintenance Organisations" in the United States the insured person pays a group of doctors for all health care and the group meets all costs. A recent Committee set up by the Government in Nigeria has proposed this model with some modification for compulsory health insurance. Already some doctors are offering employees such inclusive contracts and employ other doctors to help them provide the services. The main risk is that there are strong incentives to provide fewer services than are needed—particularly care in hospital.

Conclusion on doctor payment

As can be seen from the above, there is no perfect way of paying doctors. All methods have advantages and disadvantages. It is possible to point to examples where each of the three systems works well, though not always from the same point of view. Salaried practitioners give a good service in, for example, Sweden and Israel though in both the use of the wholly private sector has been growing in the past ten years. Capitation works well in the Netherlands and the United Kingdom: in the latter there is very little private general practice though there is substantial private specialist practice. The fee-for-service system works well in, for example, Canada, the Federal Republic of Germany and France but in all three it is expensive for the insurer. Where virtually the whole population is covered under this system, the role of wholly private practice is negligible.

Doctors get used to the way they are paid and seldom want it changed. Many salaried doctors in Israel welcome the fixed hours which enable them to add to their incomes by private practice in the evenings.

British general practitioners have long fought and won battles against becoming salaried and have considered and rejected the paperwork and greater competition which would be involved in fee-for-service payment. Doctors in France, the Federal Republic of Germany, Australia and New Zealand fought early battles to prevent or abolish capitation payment and strongly prefer fee-for-service payment.

In a developing country where the level of contribution is an overriding consideration if a scheme is to attain wide coverage, there is a strong case for avoiding fee-for-service payment, particularly if the social controls on ethical standards are weak. It may only be possible to run it at tolerable cost by introducing substantial cost-sharing which limits the whole purpose of the insurance scheme. In the choice between capitation and salary, the key question is whether doctors paid on salary can be expected to give a conscientious and courteous service without the spur of any financial competition, bearing in mind that salaries for insurance practice cannot be much higher than salaries in the government service because of the risk of damaging recruitment for the latter. Systems of payment can be combined. For example, there can be a basic salary or capitation payment plus a payment per visit. Or part of the remuneration can be a salary to cover defined preventive work with a capitation payment for curative work as is being tried out in Costa Rica. Countries are wise to experiment with systems of payment on a small scale and monitor the effects before introducing them on a large scale. But it must be recognised that reforming governments are often in a hurry.

PAYING THE HOSPITAL

A hospital will normally want not only to cover its running costs but make a surplus. The surplus will be needed to buy new medical and other equipment to modernise and extend the buildings and, if it is a profit-making hospital, give a profit to its owner(s). A profit-making hospital is likely to be more aggressive in the search for profit. An insurer on the other hand wants to get quality and necessary care for insured persons at low cost. A hospital can be paid by an itemised bill, by an inclusive charge per day, by diagnosis or by a negotiated budget.

Payment per itemised bill

In the extreme application of the system everything used by the patient is listed and charged for separately as in a hotel—each meal, each drink, drug, test, procedure right down to rubber gloves and telephone calls. This type of system is often used under private health insurance but the patient generally has to pay a proportion of the cost so that he has an incentive to keep costs down. The patient will find such a hospital charging on this basis keen to meet any of his requirements from special food to hire of television and will welcome visitors at almost any time and they in turn will be offered services which will be added to the bill. Such an open-ended system of billing is clearly inconsistent with the objective of keeping costs down. While the level of charges for each service can be negotiated, the hospital, or the doctor in charge, is in a position to decide whether the patient should have special nursing and how many and what diagnostic tests and procedures should be provided. The insurer is in a weak position to question afterwards how much of this was strictly necessary.

Under the government scheme for public employees in Thailand, the employee and dependants can either use government health services without charge or use private services (including hospital services) if they are prepared to pay half the cost. Private hospitals charge by itemised bills. It was hoped that making the patient pay half the cost for private hospitals would keep costs reasonable. But the problem which has been found is false claims. Payments by the insurer for services never actually provided were being shared between the provider and the insured person. Itemised bills are also used in Thailand to pay the medical costs of persons injured at work under the insurance scheme for industrial injury. The bills are reviewed by the insurer and "unnecessary items" struck off and left for payment by the employer or employee. Hospitals have been found charging more for medical services than they pass on to the doctor. There are proposals to extend this scheme into a general health insurance covering conditions not due to work injuries or occupational disease. The problem is that in industrial injury the diagnosis is normally clearly established and thus unnecessary treatment can be assessed against a clear diagnosis. In a general health insurance scheme the insurer is much less able to check the correctness of the diagnosis and thus whether treatment is necessary or unnecessary. An itemised bill creates clear incentives for a private hospital to provide excessive treatment and use a higher level of technology than is necessarily required.

A variant of the itemised bill is used in the Republic of Korea. There is a standard daily charge for room and board but the hospital can charge from a scale of some 2,000 items for medical acts. This creates incentives to increase the number of acts per day beyond what is strictly necessary. Inevitably certain acts are seen as more profitable for the hospital.

Payment per inclusive day

Here an inclusive rate per day is negotiated in advance between the insurer and the participating hospital. Rates may be renegotiated each year. This is a system which has been commonly used in continental Western Europe. The hospital has an incentive to make the patient comfortable lest the patient should seek to be discharged as soon as possible. From the insurer's point of view the fixed rate per day gives the hospital a clear incentive to be economical in the services it provides. The hospital has, however, an incentive to encourage long hospital stays because the costly days for the hospital are the early days of the stay when the patient is being diagnosed and treated and may need substantial nursing time. The costs falling on the hospital during the recovery stage become much lower as the patient becomes able to do more for himself. Thus the longer the stay, the greater the profit. To counter this possibility, the insurer may employ a doctor or nurse to visit patients in hospital and review the possibility of early discharge, as is currently under consideration in Indonesia.

It should be appreciated that an unscrupulous hospital management may be tempted to compromise on the quality of what is provided by, for example, not employing a sufficient complement of trained nurses or other personnel, doing an insufficient number of diagnostic tests or even using drugs of inferior quality.

Payment by diagnosis

A complex system has been developed in the United States for classifying diagnoses into some 470 groups, for each of which a lump-sum payment is made to the hospital for the whole period of care. Several European countries have been experimenting with such systems. The groupings developed in the United States are unlikely to be appropriate elsewhere because of the different ways in which medicine is practised and the different facilities which are available. The system has the advantages of predictability and cost control and removes the incentive for long stays. But the hospital has incentives to manipulate the system to its advantage in two ways. First, when the diagnosis is not clear-cut the more high paying of the possible diagnoses may be claimed ("diagnostic escalation"). Second, patients may be discharged and readmitted soon afterwards so that two stays can be claimed for the same diagnosis. Insurers have developed procedures to detect the latter. The risk from the patient's point of view is that discharge may be too early particularly when there have been complications or the patient is elderly and needs longer than a younger patient to recover.

Such systems may be unsuitable for most developing countries because they are complex to develop and difficult to police. But the general idea can and has been adapted in certain specific fields. For example, rates may be agreed in advance per delivery or for certain specific operations leaving other cases to be paid for on an inclusive day basis as above. Or the inclusive day payment may be supplemented by negotiated lump-sum payments for operations classified as major, minor and intermediate. Both of these systems of payment are used in Indonesia.

Payment by budget

This is usually associated with direct systems of organising health insurance where the insurer owns the hospitals it uses, as is often the case in India and several countries in Latin America. It can however be used without ownership, as is the case in Canada where general hospitals are owned by separate non-profit-making organisations. Budget ceilings have more recently been applied to hospitals in Belgium, France and the Netherlands, even though a variety of different insurers are paying for the care of patients. If the hospital "earns" more revenue than it is allowed in the year, it must pay it back to the different insurers in the proportion of patient days each have financed. These are, however, countries where insurance has a very wide coverage. But it would be possible for an insurer to contract to buy the use of X number of patient days and associated facilities at a negotiated price from a particular hospital.

The main advantage of the budget "envelope" is that the cost is fixed for both the insurer and the hospital and the latter can plan in advance the most efficient use of the limited resources. The disadvantage is that the hospital has no incentive to increase its productivity by shorter lengths of stay, because the more patients are admitted to a fixed number of beds, the larger the number of expensive early days of care which have to be financed out of the fixed budget, with the associated treatment and diagnostic costs. There are two ways of countering this. One is to negotiate a formula which gives extra payment for "productivity improvements" or, alternatively, any improvement in productivity can be rewarded in the negotiations for the budget for the following year.

A developing country will want to choose a system of payment which is simple to operate. If it is decided not to own hospitals, possibly inclusive daily payments, supplemented by payments for operations with lump sums per confinement, can work effectively. But the insurer may still need to monitor lengths of stay at the different hospitals which are contracted and threaten not to renew the contract with those hospitals where the length of stay is high and cannot be explained by the type of cases admitted.

Notes

[1] Ok-Ryan Moon: "The National Health Insurance Policy in Korea", School of Public Health, Seoul National University, 1987.

[2] Brian Abel-Smith: *Cost containment in health care* (London, Bedford Square Press, 1984).

[3] K. McPherson et al: "Regional variations in the use of common surgical procedures", in *Social Science and Medicine*, 1981, pp. 273-288.

[4] Young, Joo Kim: "Health care financing in Korea", Paper presented at a Seminar on Health Care Financing, Asian Development Bank, Manila, 1987.

ORGANISATION AND ADMINISTRATION OF HEALTH INSURANCE 5

THE HEALTH INSURANCE SYSTEM AS AN ORGANISATION

The administration of a social insurance programme providing medical care benefits requires a degree of technical management and of financial flexibility justifying the establishment of a separate administration. The health insurance organisation may take one of a number of forms:

(i) a separate administration under an existing government ministry;
(ii) part of a national social security administration;
(iii) a separate autonomous government or quasi-government body;
(iv) a non-government organisation (as, for example, when the health insurance scheme is sponsored by a trade union); or
(v) a number of non-government organisations, affiliated with different voluntary bodies, and with or without an umbrella organisation to manage all or part of their functions.

In countries which have separate schemes for government employees and for the private sector, each scheme may take a different form among these options. Naturally, when health insurance becomes universal, that is when it applies to all the resident population and is organised like a public service (i.e. in the United Kingdom), an administration within a government department becomes fully justified.

Each scheme, or group of schemes, may have an external board of directors or public council, with representatives from the relevant government departments, the contributing employers and the workers. This board might serve as an overall policy-making body, and may also constitute a form of public control as well as co-ordinate between the health insurance schemes themselves and between the schemes and government agencies.

In developing countries one finds (almost without exception) that compulsory health insurance is first established as a semi-autonomous public agency or institution under the supervision of a government department, often the Ministry of Health or the Ministry of Labour or their equivalent. There may be more than one health insurance institution where different categories of the population establish such a programme separately. Semi-autonomous institutions enjoy financial and administrative autonomy and independent legal status. They are accountable to their management bodies and, through them, to the government. Their regional and local boundaries may not follow those of government, the staff may be considered public sector employees but not civil servants, and the scheme's facilities may not be classified as state property.

Before dealing with the administrative functions of a health insurance system, it is important to review some of the basic problems involved in its operation, mainly towards understanding why the organisation must be characterised by stability, professionalism, flexibility and a high level of integrity. This is quite apart from the organisation's need for a strong leadership that will command the respect and co-operation of the major health, economic and social institutions in the country. This relationship should not be unduly influenced by prevailing political considerations.

Social and economic factors in administration

The first set of problems stems from the social, economic and material context in which compulsory health insurance has to be implemented in the different regions of the country with different population groups. In developing countries the context is crucial for the potential administrator. Procedures and techniques which have been successful in countries where the background is different may fail altogether. To take an extreme example: computer processing of data becomes inefficient in areas where power cuts or power failures are frequent. Or, when mass unemployment is a national concern, managers may well be advised to moderate the thrust towards expensive automation of administrative procedures. The irregularity or the instability of employment and incomes are most relevant to the design of suitable administrative and recording techniques, particularly for the collection of contributions and the registration of protected persons. Inflation, precarious economic conditions and poor transport and communications infrastructure, illiteracy and related factors (lack of unique identifying family names) turn various administrative tasks into major difficulties. Experience shows that initial registration of employers and employees is a slow process. The settlement of claims (when reimbursement methods are used) often encounters unexpected complications due to all these factors.

Another basic problem which the organisation of a new health insurance system may face is the level of management prevailing in the country. A display of committed leadership should not be confused with managerial capabilities in all aspects of management. A common

Organisation and administration of health insurance

problem in many such organisations is not simply the difficulty in generating valid and reliable data on the relevant aspects of activities, but also the ability of management and the top executive level in particular to use information in the decision-making process.

In addition, such organisations have a tendency to be large, by nature of their basic undertaking. This necessitates consideration of three separate but equally important issues. First is the concept of individual accountability in a large non-profit public institution. An integral part of the tasks of a new health insurance scheme will be to instil a moral obligation for individual accountability in all sectors and at all levels of the organisation, and regardless of whether political or professional functionaries are involved.

Most people using health services will be in some sort of distress, even if temporary, resulting from the ill-health which has led them to seek medical care. In such a setting, empathy is a crucial factor in the operation of the system. Just as with accountability, there is a moral obligation to instil and maintain a feeling of empathy throughout the organisation, and not only in those sectors dealing directly with patients. Another related feature of large organisations is that they tend to become impersonal from within and somewhat out of touch with their members as well as the providers of health care. Alienation is a term that has been increasingly used in the analysis of large health service systems, including health insurance schemes.

The third factor is the cost of administration in a health insurance system. It is difficult to provide guide-lines for the overall costs of administrating the system as a percentage of the total budget, but this proportion does not generally exceed 8 to 10 per cent. A problem often encountered is how to define "administrative expenditure" within the system of accounts, particularly when the institution operates its own hospital and medical facilities, buys drugs and equipment, or invests capital. The amount spent on administration should not only be kept low for cost containment reasons, but also as a reflection of the basic purpose of the organisation. It is important to show the insured members that funds from their compulsory contributions are not wasted on unnecessary bureaucracy or excessively highly paid executives with ostentatious working conditions.

In both compulsory and voluntary insurance systems it is common to find some degree of politicisation of the executive management level. The real issue and indeed challenge is for the executive to understand the multi-disciplinary professional character of the tasks involved in both health insurance and the delivery of health care. This is especially important in new health insurance systems, where there may be a danger of the authorities seeing their new and high-priority project as a location for high-level placements as favours to individuals within their political sphere.

The managers of both compulsory and voluntary health insurance will have to develop a strong professional cadre within the system. The very nature of the system requires professionals in the health care field, which must cover public health and epidemiology as well as various general and specific medical areas, for example, paediatrics, geriatrics and mental health. The financial, personnel management, logistics, health care and facilities planning, information systems, as well as computerised data processing and public relations, are all functions that require high professional and technical expertise, and cannot be directed solely by appointed or elected laymen.

To some extent, this professionalisation may be easier to develop when the organisation is a separate entity, again in all types of health insurance schemes. As a separate body, the health insurance scheme may have more flexible abilities, as well as better opportunities for paying professionals, than in a rigid governmental setting. The caution here is not to develop conditions so favourable that they drain the appropriate professional health manpower from the Ministry of Health. Whatever the organisation of the health insurance scheme, this government Ministry must remain a strong statutory body to oversee the operation of health insurance, health care and the health of the nation.

Centralisation and decentralisation

It has repeatedly been mentioned in earlier chapters that compulsory health insurance allows for the maximal spreading of risk among large populations. This "maximum population" element may be crucial in gaining a balance between revenues from health insurance contributions and expenditure for health services, but it does mean that the organisation of the system must be decentralised. Unless we are dealing with very small area population and size, one central bureau cannot take care of the administrative needs of the system for the entire country. Some form of regionalisation is necessary both to enable sound direction of units of a manageable size and to operate the system with the required degree of sensitivity to local needs.

This brings us to the currently popular trend from centralisation towards decentralisation in modern organisations. The challenge in this area is to develop sound central policy regarding those issues which follow national guide-lines, and then to ensure the appropriate scope of decentralisation. The concept of decentralisation itself is often misunderstood. In some systems and environments it is interpreted as complete freedom in the use of the budget by the regional or local administration, regardless of the fact that the revenue side of that budget may be determined by central factors, which generally stipulate both contribution rates and the range of benefits. In times of economic constraints decentralisation may become less desirable. A limited budget

Organisation and administration of health insurance

decreases the ability of local management to allocate resources according to its own desired response to special interest groups. Decentralisation in large organisations therefore has two prerequisites: first an understanding of the concept and implications of changes in resource allocation, and second, an analysis of the functions in the administration of the health insurance scheme that are amenable to decentralisation.

It may well be that priority functions in the move to decentralisation are the control and audit of provider performance. These are usually less popular and more complex tasks, as they should involve professional judgement of the necessity of medical services. The feasibility of performing the various functions, including medical audit, at the regional and local levels needs clear appraisal before the change towards decentralisation is made. It may seem obvious that the registration of members and the collection of contributions are far easier to do as local functions. However, the efficient performance of the tasks involved may require resources and skills that first have to be acquired at the local level. The resources may begin with such basic equipment as a safe to store cash. The regional level may have the appropriate equipment but will need to develop the tools to supervise and check the new functions.

If decentralisation works well, it should permit greater efficiency and satisfaction at the regional and local levels. This may be achieved by allowing regional administrators more authority and flexibility in negotiating with providers and introducing new health care programmes, within the accepted benefit package.

Whatever the decision regarding decentralisation in the organisation, there must then be clear understanding regarding the locus of the authority and responsibility for the numerous tasks involved in the system at central, regional and local levels.

All the above issues are not insurmountable problems but have to be constantly looked for, so that they are prevented from becoming barriers and stumbling blocks to the effective operation and growth of the health insurance system.

Administration

Essentially, the health insurance system has two major groups of administrative functions:

(a) tasks related to membership registration and identification;
(b) tasks dealing with members' claims.

If the scheme is also a health services delivery system, these functions will be expanded to include:

(c) the development and operation of health care facilities.

In both cases, that is, in systems with and without the direct provision of care, the overall administrative functions will cover basic management requirements, as described above. Particular emphasis should be placed on the necessary planning functions to meet the needs of the insured, given the changing demographic and disease patterns in the population and the dynamics of technology in health care. For economic as well as other reasons, such as the natural tendency for a large and complex organisation to develop resistance to change over time, the introduction of new technologies is often deferred. The new medical care methods may indeed be more costly at the outset. However, they should not be rejected without a careful cost-benefit analysis that takes into account the possible savings afforded by the replacement of conventional methods with more efficient alternatives. The point to be stressed in this context is that stagnation in the area of medical technology or in the extension of health insurance benefits to new methods and services can ultimately promote stagnation in the performance of the health care providers. This is obviously a basis for dissatisfaction among consumers and providers and may well undermine the development of the health insurance system over time.

The three major groups of administrative functions should be expanded on, although the discussion here is limited to a very basic description of the functions involved.

Membership registry functions

Once the definition of eligibility has been made, the real tasks begin with the registration of employers and employees, as well as individuals who may not be contributing directly to the health insurance fund. The major problems, however, are with the working population. Particularly in developing economies where not all members of the labour force understand the direct benefits of social security in general, or the more indirect benefits of income taxation, there may be a latent consensus on the part of both the employer and the employee to avoid registration. This is obviously a process which cannot be accomplished overnight and requires an appropriate public relations campaign.

The collection of contributions can take several forms, either as the responsibility of the overall social security mechanism, or as a separate administrative function of the health insurance system. If the health insurance is administered by a number of funds, the collection may be done separately by each of these agencies. Central collection is usually preferred as it avoids considerable duplication in effort, but is possible only when the existing social security programmes cover the same population as the medical care programme, and also enable collection from a minority of individuals who may be outside the general social security framework.

In most systems the contributions are deducted from wages and transferred to the social security mechanism directly by the employer, with arrangements for both parts (employer and employee) in the case of the self-employed.

The task of identification of the insured really means being able to provide authorisation that the individual seeking care is indeed eligible, at the time of service. The traditional way of doing so was to provide each member or unit, such as the family, with a stamp book, in which stamps representing a receipt of the payment of contributions for a specific period would be pasted. In many countries the stamp book has been replaced by a magnetic card, from which information can be read by electronic communications and linked with the members' contributions file in the central computer. This may potentially be the most elegant way to guarantee that services are indeed provided to those who are not behind in paying their dues. However, it requires a sophisticated network of computerised equipment, including magnetic card readers at each of the points of delivery of service, and electronic communications and central data banks to serve fully the purposes of authorisation or eligibility control. The danger of implementing such a sophisticated system too early, that is, before all the required elements are in place and operational, is that the actual process of checking eligibility is overlooked when the tools are not in working order, or installation is only partial. An intermediate device is a card issued or revalidated once a year after payment by the employer of the last three months of contributions. The question with such cards is whether the names of dependants are added, whether separate cards are issued for each family member and whether photographs are included.

An additional problem arises in schemes which limit membership to wage-earners below a specified level. For reasons ranging from promotion within the same place of employment to the failure to update the wage ceilings during a period of rapid inflation, members can lose their eligibility "overnight".

A third membership registry function is the updating of a complete list of insured persons. In some health insurance systems this effort is limited to contribution paying members, and neglects the listing of dependants. While this may meet the requirements of limited programmes, it will hinder the analysis of utilisation by specific population groups. At this point we need to consider the importance of central versus regional or local data banks. If a basic membership registry is maintained at the central level, it should eventually enable the kinds of analysis of patterns of utilisation and changes in the insured population that will assist in policy-making and planning. The registry would therefore have to contain basic demographic information to allow for such levels of analysis.

Basic information on the individual for whom employers have made and deducted contributions may come from the dues collection agency. However, the task we are referring to here is the updating of the registry of all the insured persons, and not just those who pay into the fund. If the coverage is universal or limited to entire sectors of the population, such as the residents of specific areas, and if the scheme is a statutory health insurance system or part of the national social security mechanism, the updating may be done through linkage with the general population registry. The advantage is that this source is responsible for the ongoing recording of births, deaths and population movement in the country. The updating becomes more complex in voluntary insurance, where members reporting to local branches of the health insurance administration may be the only source of information. In this case it may be difficult to motivate the insured to inform the local health insurance branch of changes in marital status or place of residence. Even events which involve the use of health services, such as births and deaths, may be reported only after considerable delays.

Another issue which favours a central data bank is duplication. It is not uncommon to find the same member registered more than once, particularly if the system relies on reporting from local branches and has no mechanism to erase previous entries after a change of residence. The degree to which inaccurate registries will create problems again depends on the type of system. If the percentage of duplication is high in a system which pays primary care physicians on a capitation basis, we will have the same degree of duplication of payment for individuals. In all systems a high percentage of inaccuracy in the membership registry creates an undefinable bias, particularly in planning and budgeting tasks.

Tasks dealing with members' claims

These administrative tasks are of major importance in schemes based on the payment to providers directly, or to the insured for expenditures already made in using services. At the same time, they should not be neglected in systems providing health care directly, as the routine collection of data is necessary for the kinds of analyses described above. These tasks basically involve the administrative and technical processing of providers' and patients' claims for payment for professional services rendered. While a completely computerised reporting, review and payments system is usually beyond the capabilities of most health insurance systems, in developing countries a minimal level of electronic data processing is essential today. The actual processing of claims in order to reimburse the providers—or the patients—within a reasonable time is the objective of the task, but it is incomplete if it does not include a professional review stage. In most such systems the reimbursement is made on a fee-for-service basis, and the provider has an increasing number of service options as medical technology advances. The quality assurance aspects of this task will be dealt with later in the discussion on control functions. At this point, it is important to emphasise that in a large and impersonal organisation, this ultilisation review process can hardly be accomplished without elementary data processing.

Close supervision of medical practice is neither feasible nor desirable in a normal doctor-patient environment, and generally not acceptable to the health care professionals working as "outside contractors" with the health insurance system. The purpose of the review is therefore not to directly oversee practice, but rather to monitor patterns of use to detect trends as well as those irregularities which may constitute misuse or abuse of the system. These activities need professional backing as well as professional criteria to determine first which claims need to be screened, and then which need to be queried in greater detail, possibly with added information from the patient's medical record. When irregularities are found, the process is still in the sphere of professional standard review, and the ultimate goal is twofold: to avoid remuneration for misuse or abuse of the system on the one hand, but also to intervene constructively and promote improvement in the providers' practice. It is for this reason that the professional reviewers must have high clinical standards. The challenge is for this review to involve education as well as utilisation and performance review in a peer environment, but with the necessary authority to reject unjust claims.

Tasks dealing with the development and
operation of health care facilities

The complexity of the functions involved in the undertaking of the direct delivery of services has been dealt with to some extent above, in Chapter 3. From the administrative point of view, direct provision of health care means more than the double challenge of handling both an insurance third party system and a delivery system at the same time. The initial question is whether the health insurance system should have both tasks under one single administrative body, with the relevant division of functions reflected in its regional offices.

On the one hand, there is an obvious advantage in a unified ideology regarding the health care benefits to be provided at a given time and in the future. There is also a better chance to provide feedback on the trends in both sectors, such as changes in the demographic pattern of the insured members, changes in their patterns of use and in the performance of the facilities to deal with these changes. Whether or not these opportunities will be realised may depend to some extent on the information system, but this in turn should be developed according to the needs of the scheme for such integration of administrative functions. A unified organisation may avoid some duplication of administrative facilities and staff to carry out both of the health insurance system's tasks, and this is crucial for cost control over time. On the financial side, a unified fiscal and accounting function may enable better short- and long-term use of the health insurance funds. The delivery system will probably benefit from revenues regularly accruing from membership contributions in its development and current budget, rather than having to seek credit from outside agencies. The advantage of central purchasing and supply functions to secure lower prices for all the equipment and drugs in all the scheme's facilities may be very significant.

On the other hand, the disadvantages of a single administrative channel should be considered. In an insurance system with direct care benefits, sharing a single administration, the health services are paid for by an internal transfer of funds from one sector to another. Specific pricing and itemised billing is therefore not required, at least not for purposes of remuneration between provider and third party payer. This can lead to a situation in which the real cost of providing services within the overall institution is not given adequate attention. The whole area of calculating costs of services produced by the scheme may be neglected. This in turn may contribute to the tendency to disregard and downplay financial accountability at the individual and organisation level. It must be remembered here that we are dealing with non-profit organisations, in which the product is not always easy to define. For example, this kind of internal accounting does not necessitate defining what is involved in the hospitalisation of a specific case, and whether the costs involved were justified or not.

Such a unified internal arrangement may proceed fairly well from the financial point of view, but can be strained in times of general economic distress. This happens, for example, when private or even other public non-profit providers of care can offer the health insurance part of the system their services at a cost lower than that of the system itself. When the regional branches of the unified health insurance system are asked to cut costs, their managers may try to do so by buying lower-cost services from outside providers, which means that they then bypass possibilities within their own services.

This may involve the regional branches in external payment obligations that they are not prepared for. These can become complex issues, depending on several factors, such as whether the membership contributions are put into a central fund to gain the maximal spread of risk, how regional budgets are allocated, and whether regional administrations have other local sources of income. For these and other reasons, it is essential that a health insurance system directly involved in providing care maintains a budgeting management and a cost analysis function that is able to assess the price of the basic health care services provided, and to compare these with the alternatives offered by outside providers.

Whether or not it is cost beneficial to develop more services internally, or to reduce these in favour of external providers, are questions which the administration of the organisation should constantly be prepared to answer. Very often, management becomes tied down with efforts to make revenues and expenditures balance, or with looking for ways to cover a deficit. As a result, cost containment, cost benefit and cost effectiveness analyses in the overall organisation are often neglected.

Another consideration in having a single administration for both the insurance and delivery of care components concerns the balance between the various administrative tasks in the organisation. The insurance part is mainly concerned with membership enrolment, revenue from contributions into the fund, and expenditures for services provided within and outside the scheme. The delivery of the health care part of the system, on the other hand, deals primarily with the provision of services of a highly technical nature. While the basic management theory in the two parts of the system may be the same, both the process and outcome of the management functions involved have important differences.

In the health insurance part, procedures are easier to define and productivity can be measured on a more objective basis of measurable tasks accomplished. In the health care delivery part of the system, the outcomes of care cannot always be measured objectively. In personnel administration, the health insurance part covers mainly those occupations involved in the various phases of management. In the health care delivery part, personnel administration will be more concerned with the professional background of those recruited, and with placement to meet very specific needs in hospitals and clinics. The challenge in having a single administration to deal with the two parts is therefore to achieve a balance in representation of insurance and health care management needs at the top executive level and throughout the organisation, without suppressing the special requirements of any one part.

CONTROL TASKS

While control and programme evaluation may be accepted as integral parts of sound management, they deserve special mention here. The major control functions in a health insurance system, with or without the direct provision of health services, can be put under three major headings, each with its special implications and sensitivities.

Control of membership coverage

As mentioned in the previous chapters, it is essential for the health insurance system to have updated information on (i) whether all the persons covered by legislation have actually been identified and registered; and (ii) who meets the eligibility conditions to benefit when a claim is made or a service is requested. Incomplete registration means less revenue and inaccuracies in the membership registry lead to duplication in expenditure, as well as misuse and abuse of the benefits. The control function in this area begins first with compliance regarding the payment of contributions. For many reasons, this may be lax. For some populations the regular payment of any kind of tax is not part of daily life, just as the expectation that individuals will need medical care for an illness is not a daily concern. If the way in which contributions are collected is relatively simple, that is, if they are deducted by employers from the monthly salaries, the task may be easier. New health insurance systems at the least would have to obtain lists of active employers or businesses from tax authorities, trade associations, etc. When the legislation covers categories of self-employed persons special contribution regulations must be designed and contributions cannot be collected by a routine arrangement without any initiative on the part of the insured themselves.

An educational process is needed before any control mechanism can be expected to achieve the desired results. This education process will have to motivate the public towards enrolment, and provide counselling on the members' rights to the scheme's benefits. A latent objective of this task is to create understanding of the appropriate use of benefits and to reduce misuse and abuse of the system.

The actual forms of controls in contribution collection and maintenance of an updated and accurate membership registry will not be detailed here. They depend to a large extent on the nature of the organisation, including affiliation to the general social security framework or other sponsors, the degree of decentralisation, and the sophistication of the data processing facilities of the scheme and country as a whole.

Financial control

The major issue in the financial control of a statutory health insurance system concerns the concept of accountability. This is both a management function and a basic characteristic that we aim to instil in such organisations. Both are often regrettably neglected, as in systems with strong political affiliations the term "financial control" is too often seen as the issue of who controls the investment of revenues, sometimes at the possible expense of the extension of health care benefits. Or it may be seen as control of the decision-making process regarding the level of contributions on the one hand, and expenditures on benefits on the other. It is extremely important for new health insurance schemes to understand what is really meant by financial control, and to build such measures into the system from the start.

From a technical point of view, this control encompasses the monitoring of financial performance—that is, of revenues and expenditures—throughout the various sectors and levels of the health insurance system. This function has to be carried out despite the non-profit nature of the system, which may wrongly contribute to an attitude that achieving a balance between revenues and expenditures is less important. This tendency may also be prompted by the lack of strong professional economic input in the administration of the system, and by the lack of objectives, measures and of sanctions regarding "overspenders" or "overusers" of the system.

The conceptual side of accountability in terms of financial control should try to compensate for these deficiencies. If the administration of the scheme understands the benefits of a balanced budget, regardless of who bears the responsibility for covering the deficit, it is likely to put more effort into its planning process. Sound planning, beginning with the formulation of policies regarding the major fields of operation of the scheme, contributes to a health insurance system's ability to reach its goals, one of which should be financial viability. At the same time, instability in the financing of the health insurance scheme undermines the planning function. The constant requirements for cuts in expenditure in a deficit budget often prevent well-designed plans from being implemented. The hope here is that awareness of the need for accountability, both within the system and in relation to external bodies, may promote more attempts to solve budgetary problems by changing the internal allocation of resources and constantly examining alternatives to prevailing health care patterns.

It is this kind of attitude—or manifestation of the accountability concept—that may lead a health insurance system to look more seriously at cost containment methods. One result may be a more positive approach to including health promotion and disease prevention services in its regular benefits. Another may be renewed interest and investment in primary care. These points could be summed up as saying that financial control is not merely an exercise in monitoring the flow of funds in and out of a health insurance scheme, but could become the stimulus to ensuring resources for the volume and level of health care required for the members. At the very least, this approach could go a long way in promoting co-operation in the decision-making process of the lay and medical management components. This itself is extremely important if cost containment plans need to be implemented with the full backing of all sectors of the organisation.

Quality assurance

The third control function to be reviewed here, though briefly, is quality assurance of the health care benefits. This is an investigatory process to assure quality in the practice of medicine, and it is important that it be viewed as a positive and educative function rather than a regulatory medical control task. Whether we are dealing with a health insurance scheme that only reimburses or a scheme with its own delivery system, this function will be concerned with the quality assurance of the structure, process and outcomes of the medical care benefits.

Structure may involve evaluation of a single type of health care resource used to provide the care, or the availability of certain types of resources versus others. Quality assurance of process in health insurance will deal mainly with utilisation review, and cover both general services, such as hospital care, or specific items, such as laboratory examinations or drugs, in and outside the hospital. The assurance of the outcomes or results of health care is more difficult to carry out, mainly because we cannot always make clear statements on direct relationships between the medical care benefit and measurable indicators of health status. The concern in the evaluation of outcomes in this framework can be more limited, and deal with the basic question of whether the diagnostic procedure used provided the relevant information or whether the treatment selected led to the expected therapeutic result. These may not be simple questions, but the point to be made here is that the evaluation of the outcomes of health care in a health insurance system does not have to be neglected because of the difficulties in measuring health status.

Matters of this kind raise the question of appropriateness and not simply quality, avoiding the issues of having to rate services as good or otherwise. The concept of appropriateness covers the necessity of the medical service, its timeliness, and the method used, in addition to the outcome. In recent years emphasis has been placed on studying variations in the relevant parameters, again within the framework of variations in the provision, utilisation and outcome of medical care. Interest was first raised by cross-national comparisons of the utilisation of specific services, from hospital in-patient admission rates, visits to doctors and variations in rates for the same surgical procedure in different countries. The current emphasis is on regional and small area variations, in which the aim is to compare population-based rates for specific medical procedures across defined medical catchment areas, or across individual hospital, clinic or physician practices. The study of variations at such small practice levels raises important questions beyond possible clinical and epidemiological explanations. As far as the health insurance system is concerned, the variations provide the challenges in both quality assurance and cost containment.

When significant variations are found, and no negative outcome factors can be related to rates which are around the norm for the entire group, it is legitimate to ask to what extent savings could be made by more normative behaviour, meaning a reduction in the rates of those practices with the highest rates. It is also important to look for ways of changing variations through effective intervention in medical practice. This should involve direct educational efforts rather than sanctions directed at providers with grossly different practice patterns, unless the latter action is clearly called for. If the health insurance system itself cannot undertake these educational efforts, they can be provided with the co-operation of other agencies, such as medical schools. Participation in such programmes can then become requirements for the extension of contractural agreements with the health insurance system or for continued practice within its own system.

As with financial control, quality assurance is not an automatic administrative function that can easily be taken on by the health insurance organisation. It requires a strong professional input, with the co-operation of clinicians, epidemiologists, statisticians and data processing staff to begin defining the parameters to be studied and the details of the information system to support this level of analysis. However, all these efforts will have limited effect if two conditions are not fulfilled: first, the professions involved must understand and accept the potential for positive steps that can result from quality assurance, and second, the administration itself, including its financial as well as medical components, must be committed to using the information and the results of the analysis in the decision-making process. Even when the information system enables the collection and analysis of data considered complete, reliable and valid by all the parties, failure to use the data over time will ultimately weaken the effort. Use of the results should again not be viewed in negative terms of sanctions, but rather in very positive terms of opportunities to bring about changes in resource allocation, and to create incentives for improved practice patterns.

The control functions of a health insurance system, covering the three areas described here—membership, finances and health care benefits—are obviously functions for which the relevant branches of the administration will assume direct responsibility. At the same time, these are perhaps the most sensitive administrative tasks in the view of the public, or insured population. Depending on the nature of the health insurance system, reports on the scope of activity and progress of these functions will be made known to the sponsors and membership, and their publication should be able to promote support for extension of the health insurance system rather than criticism or ambivalence.

PART II

EXPERIENCES IN THE DEVELOPING COUNTRIES OF ASIA

INTRODUCTION TO THE COUNTRY PROFILES

The brief profiles of the present state of development of health services and of health insurance in developing countries of Asia which are gathered in Part II have been compiled from the following sources:

— Country papers submitted by national experts to the ILO Asian Regional Seminar on Social Security Health Insurance and its role in Health for All Strategies (Seoul, March 1989).
— The Report of the Seminar on Health Care held in Manila in 1987, and sponsored by the Asian Development Bank, the World Bank and the East-West Center.
— *The state of the world's children 1989*, issued by UNICEF, and the latest statistical yearbooks of the United Nations.
— Information made directly available to the ILO by individual countries.

The contribution of the following experts in particular is acknowledged with thanks:

Mrs. Kusum Prasad (India), Professors Chong-Kee Park and Heung Bong Cha (Republic of Korea), Dr. James Jeffers (ADB Consultant on Malaysia) and Dr. Damrong Boonyoen (Thailand).

BANGLADESH

DEMOGRAPHY AND HEALTH DATA

Bangladesh had a population of over 110 million in 1987, with an annual growth rate of 2.6 per cent for the period 1980-86. In 1987, 13 per cent of the population were in urban areas. The per capita GNP was US$160 in 1987, and the average annual GNP growth rate was 0.9 per cent for the period 1980-86.

In 1987 the infant mortality rate was 120, and the child mortality rate (under 5 years) was 191 deaths per 1,000 live births. The average annual rate of reduction in child mortality was 1.41 per cent between 1980 and 1987. Life expectancy was 52 years in 1987. The literacy rate for males was 42 per cent and 22 per cent for females in 1985.

HEALTH SERVICES

The Ministry of Health has assumed responsibility for the delivery of health services in Bangladesh. The Ministry has constructed and operates hospitals, and aims to have a hospital in each subdistrict by 1995. The patient pays a nominal charge for services in these hospitals. The Ministry of Health operates 3,000 dispensaries, to serve populations of 25,000, and is planning to have another 2,500 dispensaries by 1995. Services given in these community health centres are provided free of charge, regardless of the individual ability to pay. Drugs are manufactured by government-owned companies, and dispensed free of charge by government hospitals. The central Government allocated 5.6 per cent of its total expenditure to health care in 1987. The private sector and non-government organisations have been encouraged to develop more clinics and nursing homes to supplement public health care resources.

HEALTH INSURANCE

Health insurance has not yet developed in Bangladesh. Workers in some corporations and private companies have health care expenditures reimbursed in full. Government workers have a standard lump sum added to their salaries, but the amount is not considered adequate for health care. The Government is currently debating compulsory health insurance, following recognition that it cannot cover costs of all the health care needed. A major problem in promoting health insurance is the high proportion of the population existing below the subsistence level which would not be able to afford the contributions. In 1987 it was estimated that 86 per cent of the urban and rural population were below the absolute poverty level.

CHINA

DEMOGRAPHY AND HEALTH DATA

The population of China reached over 1,100 million in 1988, with 21 per cent in urban areas. The growth rate has decreased significantly over the past years, and the annual average for 1980-86 was 1.2 per cent. In 1987 the GNP was US$300 per capita, and the average annual GNP growth rate for the preceding six years was 9.2 per cent.

In 1987 the infant mortality rate was 33 and the child mortality rate was 45 deaths per 1,000 live births, with an average annual reduction of 3.08 per cent for the preceding seven years. Life expectancy was 70 years in 1987. The literacy rate in 1985 was 82 per cent for males and 56 per cent for the female population.

HEALTH SERVICES

Health care facilities are owned by different government organisations in China, with wide variations throughout the country, in both the organisation of medical care and the types of resources available. The total expenditure on health in 1987 came to 1.5 per cent of the GNP. About 40 per cent of the amount was government expenditure, and about 23 per cent was borne by private households.

HEALTH INSURANCE

Various forms of social security health care schemes have developed over the past 30 years, with wide variations by province and between urban and rural areas. The major forms are described in the two papers presented at the Seminar: *Health insurance for workers in China*, prepared by the Ministry of Labour, and *An introduction to Chinese rural health insurance experiments,* from the Ministry of Public Health.

Health insurance in developing countries

Health insurance for workers in China

In China workers can enjoy the necessary medical services for illness, injury and childbirth in accordance with the state provisions. This is the basic right of workers stipulated by the Constitution and laws. Article 45 in the Constitution provides: "Citizens of the People's Republic of China have the right to material assistance from the State and society when they are old, ill or disabled. The State develops the social insurance, social relief and medical and health services that are required to enable citizens to enjoy this right." There are specific provisions on items and standards of health insurance for enterprise and government workers respectively in "Regulations on labour insurance of the People's Republic of China" (abbreviated as "Regulations") and "Principles of the State Council on Free Medical Service for Government Workers in government agencies, political parties and groups, and their affiliated non-profit institutions at all levels in China" (abbreviated as "Principles"). There are more items with higher standards in the medical coverage for injury on the job without expense borne by the injured and fewer items with lower standards for illness and non-occupational injury with a small part of the expense paid by individuals.

The medical coverage usually implemented for state-owned enterprise workers (including Chinese workers employed in Sino-foreign joint ventures) and retired persons is called labour insurance medical coverage. Another system carried out for workers and retired persons of government agencies, political parties and groups, non-profit institutions as well as for university students and disabled soldiers with second degree or above disability who are demobilised to be back home (the above-mentioned persons are called government workers) is referred to as a free medical service. According to the "Regulations" and "Principles" as well as the following supplementary provisions set up by competent authorities concerned, most of the items and standards under labour insurance medical coverage and free medical service are the same with few exceptions.

When enterprise and government workers go to the appointed medical institutions for their illness, non-occupational injury and childbirth, they have to pay a registration fee, nutritious medications and board expenses during hospitalisation, while enterprise and government will bear their therapy, medications, operation, examination, delivery and hospitalisation fees. Travel cost for those who are allowed to go to other areas for medical care are borne by the workers themselves, based on regulations of labour insurance medical coverage and in conformity with the provisions of free medical service.

All therapy fees, travel costs and costs for artificial limbs, steel waist-coat, steel waist pad, artificial teeth, ocular prosthesis, wheelchair, walking stick, audiophone, etc., will be supplied by the enterprise or the

State for workers suffering occupational injury and disease; and one-third of board expenses during hospitalisation will be paid by the workers themselves; the rest will be financed from enterprise earnings or the state budget. Model workers and combat heroes, who have made greater contributions to the revolution and socialist construction and now are demobilised to work in enterprises or government agencies, can enjoy the above-mentioned rights for their non-occupational illness and injury.

Labour insurance medical coverage stipulates that direct dependants of enterprise workers can enjoy medical allowances for their illness, that is: half of the cost of operations and medications will be financed from enterprise earnings and other costs will be contributed by patients if they go to appointed hospitals.

Fees for registration, examination, operation, medication and hospitalisation of enterprise and government workers for sterilisation, putting in and taking out IUDs or induced abortion will be totally borne by enterprises or the State.

Enterprise and government workers can enjoy these medical services until their recovery, their resumption of labour ability or being determined as disabled, with the exception of contract workers and casual workers who can enjoy a certain period of medical treatment for illness and non-occupational disease according to their length of service.

Resources of funds and administration systems are different between labour insurance medical coverage and the free medical service. Funds for medical coverage for enterprise workers and their direct dependants are taken from costs according to a certain ratio of total wage and paid from a "welfare fund of enterprise workers". As for retired workers, their medical cost is financed from a "beyond-business" budget and managed by the enterprise itself, whereas the cost of free medical service for government workers is financed from the state budget on the basis of per capita quota and is used as a "free medical service fund" managed by health departments. Officers of the free medical service subordinate to health departments are specifically responsible for the comprehensive management and use of medical costs.

By the end of 1987 about 180 million persons were covered by these systems. Among them 94.11 million were in service enterprises or government workers, about 50 million were direct dependants of workers, 14.24 million retired workers and 20 million workers from large collective enterprises.

For more than 30 years the implementation of the medical coverage scheme has played an important role in preventing and curing disease, improving the quality of the labour force, and promoting production. However, some problems still need to be solved. The main problems are:

1. The medical cost borne mainly by the State without payment from individual workers leads to inefficient control. Because workers know

little about medical costs, rational medical consumption cannot be stimulated to any great extent. In addition, the examination and reimbursement functions are not strictly carried out, so some persons who are not fully entitled take rest for light illness, stay in hospital without illness, or receive a lot of medicine without cause.

2. The mechanism is not adequate for increasing medical funding according to need. In 1987 the total medical cost of enterprise workers was 10.7 billion yuan (among which 8.4 billion yuan was for in service workers, and 2.3 billion yuan for retired workers) with an increase of 207 per cent compared with that of 1978, and the annual increase at an average rate of 13.3 per cent; the annual per capita expenditure was 137 per cent with an annual increase of 10.1 per cent. The increase was caused by the change in objective needs. For example, the number of worker recipients increased from 72.81 million in 1978 to 94.11 million in 1987; other examples are the introduction of new medical technology, the application of new equipment and restructuring of medicine taken, price rise of sanitary materials and hospital management, readjustment of parts of medical cost, increases in the price of medicine, the ageing problem of workers and the increase of incidence of some diseases such as heart attack, cerebro-vascular disease and cancer. The annual increase of these costs is reasonable, but the existing ratio of the fund for medical coverage and the standards of free medical service was not raised with the change in the needs. Some of the welfare fund and other funds have to be used to make up for the increasing medical cost in some areas and units.

3. Management institutions are not perfect, and there is little pooling of risk. At present, labour insurance medical coverage is managed by labour departments and trade union organisations, while the free medical service is run by health and financial departments without an integration between the two systems. Under the free medical service, special management institutions have been established in only eight provinces, autonomous regions and municipalities, with 143 full-time staff members. In terms of labour insurance medical coverage, it is managed on the basis of individual enterprise, so that the solidarity attribute of medical insurance is not reflected. Therefore small and medium-sized enterprises can only manage payments for general diseases, and they usually cannot bear medical costs in the case of large payments for serious diseases. Moreover, some pharmaceutical factories sell medicine with articles in daily use, as a package, and some hospitals write out expensive prescriptions or make unnecessary examinations for patients to get more money. The medical cost is also increased in this way.

How the health insurance reform is carried out is of much concern to everybody. Intensive discussions have begun in recent years between theoreticians, teachers, and those engaged in social insurance and health services. Some experiments have been conducted in some areas and agencies. A tentative reform plan was proposed recently by the departments concerned based on the discussions and experience as follows:

1. There should be a change in resources for medical care through the establishment of medical insurance funds for workers. The funds will be put aside from total wages at a ratio decided by local medical insurance organisations according to the principles of "real needs, collection decided by payment and small surplus", and will be shared by the State, enterprise and workers. As wages are rather low in China now, most of the medical insurance funds will still be financed from the government budget and enterprise earnings and only a small part will be borne by individual workers based on wage increases. The preliminary idea is that wages of workers will be raised by 3 per cent, 2 per cent of which will be paid by individuals to medical insurance funds and 1 per cent of which will be used as medical cost for illness.

2. Workers should bear a small part of the medical cost. Apart from the registration fee and out-of-pocket expenditure for medications, individuals have to pay 10 to 20 per cent of out-patient and hospitalisation fees, and 2 to 5 per cent of bed cost. If the amount paid by individuals exceeds their annual wage income by 5 per cent, it could be reimbursed from medical insurance funds.

Individuals should also pay partially for some expensive examinations and therapy using high technology (specific items will be decided additionally). Those who have financial difficulties could get subsidies from enterprises.

The method of medical allowances will be continuously implemented for direct dependants supported by workers.

3. Special medical insurance institutions should be set up at different government levels (or affiliated to social insurance). They will be responsible for studying policy-making and regulations, as well as for integrating, co-ordinating and managing matters related to medical insurance.

The above ideas on reform are an ideal approach and envisage speedy implementation; therefore it is difficult to implement them throughout the country. A few areas could be selected for experiments, then the coverage could be extended step by step. Nowadays, many non-experimental areas and units are taking some measures of reform according to their respective conditions in order to deal with problems existing in the present medical coverage scheme. These measures are:

— cost criteria will be readjusted with an increase of medical cost based on real needs before the existing resources of funds are reformed;
— some of the medical costs will be passed on to workers, depending on their length of service or age. In this way individuals will supply a small part of the medical fees. Savings will partly or totally go to

their pocket while overspending could be partly or totally reimbursed;
— comprehensive medical funds for serious diseases will be established within a trade or sector and will be managed by competent departments; and
— the reimbursement system will be reformed with charged bills cancelled, cash paid for illness with medical certificates, and reimbursement made with prescription and receipt.

The concept of cost will be primarily introduced in the existing free medical service system with the adoption of these measures, which will improve the cost control mechanism to a certain extent. At the request of the State Council, the departments concerned will actively conduct experiments in health insurance reform and at the same time they will sum up their experience and create the necessary conditions for overall reform of the health insurance system.

The reform of health insurance is not only the concern of the State, enterprise and individuals, but is also related to the reforms carried out in health services and management units. The departments concerned and medical insurance institutions will divide labour among themselves and work out the necessary reform measures in close collaboration, with a view to ensuring the successful development of the health insurance reform. This will include such activities as:

— making regulations on the standards of medication covered by health insurance and on the limitations of reimbursement. Methods of reimbursement are to be complete. For example, nutritious medications can never be reimbursed, and prescriptions must be written with carbon paper, with one copy being used as a reimbursement receipt;
— educating medical staff to improve their morals and style of work so as to carry out the principles of medical care in accordance with the patient's illness and right use of medications;
— setting standards of charges based on the technical levels and equipment of different medical institutions. Collecting more money than that defined by the standards will not be allowed. Standards of charges must be open to the public for supervision;
— strengthening management and supervision of some related links in medical coverage. Necessary punishment should be conducted when medical staff go against the medical principles or break management provisions. If cases are very serious, prescription rights or entitlement to health insurance can be taken away for some period;
— making a strict distinction between a medicine package for domestic use and that for export. It is absolutely not permitted to use specially shaped packages and articles in daily use as packages or to prescribe

other articles as medications. Random price hiking or the sale of medications with other things is also not allowed; and
— carrying out the policy of putting prevention first, developing prevention and health work and greatly encouraging various types of physical exercises to build up workers' health and reduce diseases.

In order to reach the objective of "Health for All" put forward by the World Health Organization, China is now studying a health insurance system covering workers of non state-owned enterprises, self-employed workers, peasants and citizens, while it is continuously developing programmes on health insurance for enterprise and government workers. China will first work out principles on the above ideas and then proceed step by step. It is believed that around the year 2000, with efforts contributed by all the people and with the development of production, China will initially set up a social security health insurance system suitable for its own conditions to enable every citizen to have access to the necessary health care.

An introduction to Chinese rural health insurance experiments

Government policy on social security health insurance in rural areas

The main governing principles and policy guide-lines of the Chinese Government and Ministry of Public Health on social security and health insurance in rural areas are given below:

(a) Article 45 of the People's Republic of China's Constitution stipulates that Chinese citizens in the event of old-age, disease or disability have the right to get material support from the State and society; the State develops social security, social relief and health services needed by the citizens to enjoy this right.

(b) Chapter 51 of the Seventh Five-Year Plan (1986-90) of national economic and social development points out: "In the Seventh Five-Year Plan period, an embryonic form of socialist security system with Chinese characteristics will be set up step by step."

(c) Article 6 of the health reformation programme during the Seventh Five-Year Plan (1986-90) formulated by the Ministry of Public Health indicates that medical and health care systems in rural areas should be reformed according to the local situation, economic conditions and public opinion. Co-operative medical services may be practised, and other forms of the service may also be tried. Health insurance systems which suit the rural area should be explored and developed. The residents' committees, village enterprises and collective economic organisations are encouraged and advocated to draw a certain amount of public welfare and insurance funds to support and develop rural health services.

(d) According to the actual conditions in different places, the system will adopt various forms, items and standards to carry out health insurance co-operative medical services, and establish contracts on preventive health care, insurance for programmes of child immunisation, perinatal care, maternal and infantal safety during parturition, or simple prevention insurance systems. Co-operative medical service and health insurance is a mass health care service. It should be run by the people themselves on the principles of voluntary participation and democratic management. Under the leadership of local government, support for the health insurance system should be obtained through various channels. For example, the work of relevant departments should be actively co-ordinated and funds raised through various channels, such as the public welfare fund of residents' committee, should be used for the profit of village and town enterprises.

Different health insurance systems and their characteristics

In the 1970s the co-operative medical service system was generally implemented in the country's rural areas. But the rural economic system has changed from a collective economy system to a family union contract responsibility system since 1979. Because the co-operative medical service system was dependent upon the foundation of a collective economy system, most of them were disintegrated. Some of them have undergone reformation and have continued. Following the development of the rural economy, many places are experimenting with various forms of health insurance system according to the local economic conditions and public opinion, and assimilating the experiences and lessons of the co-operative medical service.

(a) *Health insurance:* The raising of insurance funds and the scale and range of reimbursements are through a scientific method which strives to be reasonable and feasible. The signing of contracts and other activities are carried out according to insurance rules and principles, giving the insurance a legal basis. These measures ensure that people joining the health insurance scheme get the basic medical care and a fixed part of compensation for their ailments and diseases.

(b) *Co-operative medical care:* This system is based on both individual and collective financial support in which each participant pays 4 or 5 yuan for a year and can have a part of his or her medical charges reimbursed for minor diseases, but severe diseases are excluded from coverage. Some co-operative medical care systems have reformed health insurance management methods and have increased funds with more ability to bear risks.

(c) *Clinics financed by peasants:* In this system peasants collect a small amount of money to pay the salary of the village doctors, and the cost of such services as registration and injection are free, but patients have to purchase drugs at their own expense. This system is usually used in relatively poor villages. The patients can save 20 per cent of the charges.

(d) *High-risk medical insurance:* This system is based on compensation for part of hospitalisation costs. In-patients and heavily charged out-patients are in part reimbursed. The family can get benefit when their members suffer from serious illnesses, but most of them cannot because of the high deduction. Consequently, this system is not very attractive to the peasants.
There are 41,940 administrative villages implementing the above-mentioned systems, accounting for about 5.7 per cent of the villages in the country as a whole.

(e) *Contract on preventive health care:* Each peasant pays 50 cents annually and the village doctors bear the responsibility for free preventive health care.

(f) *Single insurance for preventive health care:* One example is insurance for planned immunisation of children, perinatal care, and maternal and infant safety during parturition.

(g) *Dental care insurance for primary and middle school students:* The contracts are signed by dentists and schools, and every student pays 1 or 2 yuan as "premium" for dental care. Dentists give lectures on dental health every month and conduct a dental health screening every six months. Treatment will be given in cases where dental disease is recognised during the check-up.

(h) *Subsidies for medical care:* The village committees set up a fund for social security from which patients in economic difficulty may get a subsidy ranging from 20 to 60 per cent of the drug costs.

Health insurance of Jin Tan County, Jiangsu Province

Jin Tan County is located in eastern China with an area of 951 square kilometres. There are 630,000 people living in the 28 towns and 423 villages in this county. Ninety-one per cent of the population (590,000) is in the agricultural sector. The total output value of industry and agriculture is 842 million yuan, of which 75 per cent is the total output value of industry. The total output value of village and town enterprises is as much as 60 per cent of the total output value of industry. The peasants' average annual income is 640 yuan.

Jin Tan has 11 medical and health units at county level, five township clinics, 26 township clinics, 44 industrial and other departments medical units, and 416 village clinics. There are 1,150 technical health workers in this county. The averages per thousand persons are 2.23 medical workers including 1.17 doctors and 0.61 nurses. There are 1,025 beds in the clinics, and 1.99 beds per 1,000 people on an average. Village health care workers number 676 persons. Three-tier health care networks have been built up within the county, towns and villages. The peasants can get health services when they need them. Last August the county government announced its Strategy Programme for 1988-95 to realise Health for All by the year 2000 and this has been launched with a great effort.

The health service fund was 1,685,000 yuan in 1986, with 4.03 per cent for the county expenditure of 3.27 yuan per person on the average. The county also collects 1,400,000 yuan for the co-operative medical service each year.

The mortality rate of the county's population is 6.8 per thousand, the rate of birth 15.08 per thousand, and the natural increase rate of population 8.28 per thousand in 1986. The people's average expectation of life is 69.41 years (67.03 years for males and 72.21 years for females). The main causes of death for persons more than 1 year old are: cancer (206.37/100,000), heart diseases (174.50/100,000), cerebro-vascular diseases (104.35/100,000), and unexpected death (65.39/100,000). The infant death rate is 19.95 per thousand.

Jin Tan County has practised the co-operative medical service for 20 years, with 85.82 per cent of the agricultural population covered. Usually the account unit is the village. Every person who joins a co-operative medical service should pay 3 to 4 yuan each year. The peasants are entitled to free consultations with the doctor in the village clinics but can get some compensation only when they receive medical treatment in the township or county hospitals. In recent years experimental health insurance systems have been running in 13 towns in different conditions to meet the needs of the masses. The health insurance scheme is supported by the Government. County and town governments with other relevant departments and health units constitute the management committee. They manage and practise the health insurance systems and bear economic risks together.

Jin Tan County tests various health insurance systems, apart from the co-operative medical service, as follows:

(a) *Peasant health insurance:* More than 10,000 of the agricultural population have joined this system. The township hospital undertakes the health insurance work. Every village in this town joins the insurance collectively. Every person should pay a premium of 10-15 yuan, with 15 per cent paid by individuals and the rest provided by the village from the public welfare fund. The peasants are given medical care and drugs free of charge, but 50 per cent has to be paid for ancillary examinations in the village and township medical service. Half of the drug charge is free in the county hospital. The insurance fund settles the accounts at the end of the year with villages. If the expenditure is exceeded, the township hospitals will bear 60 per cent and the villages 40 per cent. Furthermore, if it is balanced, the insurance fund will be shared in the same way as overspending. The range of health insurance benefits includes child immunisation, health education, common diseases and infectious diseases. Treatment of congenital diseases, injuries from fighting and cases of attempted suicide are not free. The wages for village health workers are determined according to the village economic conditions. Some villages pay the salary from the insurance fund, but other villages do not. The following table shows the revenues and expenditures of Shanshan village in recent years:

Year	Population of the village	No. of members	Income (yuan)		Others	Total
			Personal payment	Village payment		
1986	4 037	4 037	0	10	0	40 370
1987	4 046	4 046	0	10	0	40 480
1988 (1-10 months)	4 039	4 039	0	12	0	50 488

Year	Expenses (yuan)					Balance
	Out-patient	In-patient	Transfer	Other	Total	
1986	21 000	858	3 615	14 575	40 048	321
1987	26 249	1 135	3 027	15 615	46 026	−5 546
1988 (1-10 months)	27 344	1 740	1 078	–	–	–

As shown in the table, the insurance fund was in deficit in 1987. The main reasons were: the increased costs of drugs; poor management and control; and the premium was not quite scientifically determined and the influence of some social factors was neglected. This health insurance system faces certain difficulties:
— the fact that the village public welfare fund comes mainly from village enterprises means that if the village enterprises have inadequate profits, the village will be unable to pay the insurance fees for peasants;
— because most of the health insurance fee was paid by villages from the public welfare fund but not by the peasants themselves, the phenomenon of wasted drugs is not controlled effectively;
— as the introduction of new equipment or new techniques increases expenditure, financial constraints restrict the development of the township hospitals.

(b) *Children 0-14 year-old health insurance:* 2,800 children of He Tou and Cheng Xi towns joined this insurance programme in 1987. The premium is 20 yuan for a year. The township hospital is responsible for the children's health. The range of insurance benefits includes regular physical examinations and common and infectious diseases. It does not cover congenital diseases or extraordinary damage. Unless the insured children go to the local township hospitals and village clinics, the expense of medicine and check-ups is all free. Those transferred to county level and test hospitals are compensated by 60 to 80 per cent of drug expense, while the insurance is responsible for all excess expenditure. In 1987 in He Tou 1,455 persons were insured, the insurance revenue was 28,900 yuan, and the total cost was 27,884 yuan, in which clinic visits occupied 47.28 per cent, in-patient 16.45 per cent, transfer 8.72 per cent. The surplus at the end of the year was 1,016 yuan. On the basis of 1987, in 1988 the ceiling compensation at county level hospital is 200 yuan, with 50 per cent of drug expense paid at county level hospitals. The salary and bonus of countryside doctors are paid out of the insurance fund.

(c) *Children's immunisation insurance:* About 2,000 children in nine villages have joined the insurance. Children between 0.7 years old pay 2 yuan every year or 14 yuan for the whole period, 20 per cent of which is the reward for countryside doctors, and 80 per cent for purchase, repair, management and compensation (vaccines are provided free by the State). The insurance covers inoculation against infantile paralysis, measles, pertussis and diphtheria and tetanus, BCG, encephalitis B, and epidemic meningitis. The insured after being inoculated with the above "six vaccines" but who still contract the diseases may receive free treatment, and the injury and death caused by such diseases will be compensated by 200 to 700 yuan. The development of planning immunisation insurance aroused the enthusiasm of countryside doctors and children's parents and raised the inoculative rate and quality, so it is popular among the public. Because of the very few cases of sickness after inoculation and the payment rate 10 per cent lower, the insurance fund has a surplus.

(d) *Maternity insurance:* Newly married couples can go to the countryside hospitals and join the insurance with a 36 to 46 yuan payment, the scope of which includes antenatal care on more than six occasions, normal delivery in hospital, the treatment of complications during pregnancy and delivery, and more than three postnatal care consultations. The expense of treatment of diseases before, during and after delivery is implemented in the light of the relevant regulations, the collective medical system or the peasants' health insurance system. Thirty per cent of the whole drug cost and delivery expenses will be compensated for those who need to be transferred to the hospitals above county level. In case of maternal mortality, the family would be compensated by 1,000 yuan. After being tried out, it strengthened the systematic management of pregnancy and decreased maternal mortality effectively.

(e) *Health insurance for workers in township enterprises:* Recently, with the fast development of township enterprises, a proportion of the labour force in the countryside has been transferred to these factories. How to protect them and accomplish the job of industrial hygiene and epidemic prevention become the important tasks of health insurance for township enterprise workers. In this insurance scheme township hospitals are the insurers, and township enterprises pay the insurance premiums. The standard of insurance based on the economic conditions of each township is 30 to 40 yuan per worker per year generally, which is offered by the factories, and the workers present their ID cards when they visit the doctor. The expenses, except for registration in the township hospitals, are borne by the scheme. It does not cover tonic drugs, artificial limbs for the injured, severe accidents, and the operation, complication and sequelae of family planning. Fifty per cent of the drug expense is compensated for those transferred to hospitals above the country level, and the rest is paid by the employers or the workers themselves. The fund accounts are settled at the end of the year. The insurers are responsible for 60 per cent and insured for 40 per cent of any deficit. The insured get 40 per cent, and the insurer 60 per cent of the surplus. At present more than 70 per cent of workers in township enterprises are taking part in this scheme. It has shown some advantages:
— decreased medicine waste and cost (according to statistics, 20 to 30 per cent has been saved compared with the past);
— more patients are effectively and reasonably controlled; and
— increased funds for the township hospitals.

(The insurance provided 40 per cent of the income of the township hospitals in 1986.) The financial situation of the scheme is as follows:

Year	No. of participants	Total income	Total expenditure (yuan)			Balance
			Out-patient	In-patient	Trans-ferred	
1986	1 451	52 236	29 777	1 013	1 108	20 338
1987	1 603	57 708	35 015	2 470	3 561	16 662
1988 (1-10 months)	1 873	67 428	39 832	1 588	2 187	23 820

It is summarised that the five insurance schemes mentioned above of Jin Tan County bring most of the rural areas into the scope of insurance, providing a foundation of medical service for Health for All by the year 2000. However, there are still some problems and difficulties.

(a) *Difficulties in fund collection:* Since most of the insurance fund relies on the support of township enterprises, and has little connection with the individual, the enterprises are reluctant to pay and the patients are inclined to waste the resources. On the other hand, it is not advantageous for the development of township hospitals.

(b) *Universal overspending:* Determination of the premium ignored the effect of commodity prices and other factors. In Jin Tan County they calculated the medicine expense from past expenditure, and did not consider the risk factor, management expenses, price increases, and so on. So overspending was to be expected. On the other hand, thought must be given to the stimulative or restrainable effect of the medical needs at the beginning of the insurance scheme practice. The period of insurance should not be too long, and the premium should be regulated every year.

(c) *Lack of special management institutes and efficient management systems:* Because the management of the collective medical service is concurrently undertaken by persons of the related institutes, omissions and deficiencies are commonplace. These include delays in disseminating information and statistics, lack of scientific analysis of materials, limited controls and checks, "gift prescriptions" by doctors in the hospitals, not strictly observing the medical rules, etc., although some money may be saved in management.

Conclusions

1. *The feasibility of health insurance in rural areas of China:* Production has increased more rapidly during the reform of the economic system in Chinese rural areas. As a result, the net income of peasants increased 1.7 times in eight years. This situation provides an economic basis for increasing the possibilities of implementing various health insurance programmes. But China is still a developing country with the commodity economy undeveloped. To implement health insurance systems in all the counties will take a long time and can be accomplished only step by step.

2. *Different health insurance systems will be required:* As the economic situations are very different from province to province in China, peasants' needs for medical and health care are different too. It is helpful to offer voluntary participation and various models of health insurance so that peasants can select models that are feasible in their specific situations.

3. *Various sources of financing should be utilised:* The main insurance fund comes from individuals and the collectives (including the public welfare funds of residents' committees, the profit of village and town enterprises), and the Government (town government finance) gives some support to health insurance. Government support is used to build county and town medical units, which ensures a better infrastructure for schemes. The amount of funds collected for health insurance and the rate of medical and drug charge compensation must be determined by means of a scientific method. The rate of medical and drug charge compensation must be decided according to the paying ability of the peasants.

4. *Health insurance is a part of social security:* Health insurance must be supported and co-ordinated by local government to perform smoothly. For example, in some counties the leading group had as members the vice-county magistrate, the director of the Bureau of Public Health, the manager of the insurance company and the director of the sanitation and anti-epidemic stations. Similar leading groups were also founded by towns and villages with effective results.

5. *There should be an administrative organisation made up of skilled persons to manage health insurance work:* It may be an independent administration system, a unit belonging to the health department, or a part of the overall social security system. There are only a few county insurance companies participating in the management of health insurance to increase the ability to bear the risk of diseases. Health insurance is non-profit-making and free of tax, but its reserve funds should allow reasonable increases in value to subsidise and support this cause.

6. *Strengthening the propaganda of health insurance:* Social insurance is still new to the Chinese peasants. The Government should help them to understand health insurance through propaganda. The extent of the propaganda will determine whether health insurance may develop successfully or not. Medical and health institutions should undertake the work of medical care, and they also have a duty to improve and disseminate knowledge of health insurance.

FIJI

DEMOGRAPHY AND HEALTH DATA

Fiji's population was about 720,000 in 1988. The average annual population growth rate for the decade 1976-86 was 1.97 per cent, but this rate was only 0.5 per cent for the year 1988 as a result of emigration. The last census in 1986 showed 38.7 per cent of the population living in urban areas. The per capita GNP in 1987 was US$1,810, after an annual average growth rate of 2.8 per cent in the previous decade. Following a steep decrease in 1987 and 1988, the projected average annual increase for 1989 is 3.0 per cent.

The infant mortality rate in Fiji was 27 and the child mortality rate was 33 deaths per 1,000 live births in 1987. The average annual reduction rate in child mortality was not available. Life expectancy was 71 years in that year. Adult literacy rates were 90 per cent for males and 81 per cent for females in 1987.

HEALTH SERVICES

The Ministry of Health is responsible for the delivery of health services, from nursing stations to community-based primary health care centres at the village level and hospitals in urban areas. The government services are supplemented by two government-subsidised hospitals as well as private doctors, dentists and chemists. The government services are not all provided free of charge, as patients pay a fixed daily hospital ward charge. Children under the age of 15 are exempt from these charges. In 1985, 3.7 per cent of the GNP was spent on health care, with 90 per cent of the funds coming from government general tax revenues.

HEALTH INSURANCE

The Government of Fiji has been actively studying health insurance options over the past year, following recognition of the necessity to reduce government spending and the spread of private commercial health insurance in Fiji. A working group set up by the Ministry of Health has drawn up an outline for a compulsory health insurance system, based on low-rate contributions, government subsidies mainly for hospital care, and user charges. Whether or not this evolves as the financing formula adopted for such a scheme, the Fiji National Provident Fund, which is the major social security institution in the country, has expressed willingness to extend its operations to administer a medical care scheme. The study of the various options for financing, benefits, health care delivery and provider payment methods is currently being assisted by consultants from international organisations.

INDIA

DEMOGRAPHY AND HEALTH DATA

The population of India had reached 802 million by 1987, with an annual growth rate of 2.2 per cent for the preceding six years. Some 27 per cent of the population were in urban areas in 1987. The per capita GNP for that year was US$290, with an average annual growth rate of 2.2 per cent over the preceding period.

In 1987 the infant mortality rate was 100 and the child mortality rate 152 per 1,000 live births. The annual average reduction in child mortality was 2.39 per cent between 1980 and 1987. Life expectancy was then 59. The adult literacy rate was 57 per cent for males and 29 per cent for females in 1985.

HEALTH SERVICES

Health services are in general provided by state governments under the supervision of the federal Ministry of Health. At the smallest peripheral level a network of primary health centres is being developed to serve populations of 20,000 or 30,000, depending on the type of area. These centres, staffed by a Medical Officer and various types of paramedics, also serve subcentres. Villages with small populations (1,000) are served mainly by voluntary health guides, trained through government programmes. In cities and large urban areas the delivery of health care is undertaken by municipal corporations, which have also developed a network of primary health care centres for low-income areas. National voluntary and charitable organisations, some subsidised by government grants, play a significant part in the delivery of care, particularly in urban areas. The private sector also supplements the delivery system, and has contributed significantly to the development of secondary and tertiary hospitals in the past decade.

Responsibility for the health care of persons covered by the two major government insurance schemes, for state employees and central government employees, lies with the Ministry of Health, in which separate departments have been established. The health care of persons working in defence is taken care of by the Defence Ministry, while the Railway Ministry is responsible for the health care of railway workers.

In 1986 India spent 2.1 per cent of its GNP on health care, with most of the expenditure coming from government sources. The central Government assists the states in the implementation of specific programmes, such as maternal and child health, infectious disease control and medical education. State governments finance the remaining costs, with charges levied on patients according to their income group and the type of services given in government and government-assisted institutions.

HEALTH INSURANCE

The description of social security health insurance in India is based on a paper prepared by Mrs. Kusum Prasad, the Director-General of the Employees' State Insurance Co-operation, New Delhi.

The introduction of health insurance in India

Following the introduction of the Workmen's Compensation Act, 1923, and maternity benefits legislation, the defects of employers' liability schemes became apparent. This led to consideration of the social insurance approach based on the principle of the pooling of risks and finances. In this context, the question of health insurance came up from time to time from 1928 onwards at different forums but no headway could be made. The Third Conference of the Labour Ministers, in 1942, examined a tentative scheme of sickness insurance for factory workers, and decided that the scheme should, in the first instance, cover only the cotton, jute, textile and heavy engineering industries. The Indian Government appointed in March 1943 Professor B. P. Adarkar to draw up a full health insurance scheme for industrial workers.

Prof. Adarkar submitted a scheme in August 1944 which was to cover all perennial factories in the three major groups of industries, namely, textiles, engineering and minerals and metals, exemption being contemplated for employment in the armed forces, in public departments and public utility concerns where the sick pay and medical facilities were not inferior to those under the scheme, and in the case of factories in sparse areas where medical facilities could not be provided. The fundamental principles of the scheme were that (i) it must be compulsory; (ii) it must be contributory as far as possible; (iii) it must not be too ambitious in the beginning; (iv) it must be financially sound, economical in its working and actuarially balanced; (iv) it must be workable in the peculiar circumstances of Indian labour and industry; (vi) it must be in conformity with international labour Conventions. Prof. Adarkar had also concluded that medical services organisation under the health insurance scheme could not be entrusted to the outside authority of state governments, but should be fully controlled by the insurance institution itself in the interests of correct and reliable certification and should make special efforts to reduce morbidity incidence by taking constant preventive measures. He had also made out a strong case for merging maternity benefit and Workmen's Compensation laws into a unified and integrated scheme of health, maternity and employment injury insurance.

The report submitted by Prof. Adarkar was considered by the Government, in consultation with the state governments and other interests concerned and it was also examined by two International Labour Office experts, Messrs. M. Stack and R. Rao. These experts suggested certain modifications in the light of social insurance principles and practices obtaining in other countries of the world. While agreeing with the fundamental principles enunciated by Prof. Adarkar in respect of coverage of contingencies and the financial participation of the State, the ILO experts suggested the following important modifications:

(a) separation of the administration of medical and cash benefits;

(b) integration of maternity benefits and workmen's compensation in the health insurance scheme; and

(c) extension of the scheme to all perennial factories covered by the Factories Act and also non-manual workers.

They had suggested that the administration of medical benefit under the scheme should be entrusted to the state governments, the state governments being required to bear about two-thirds of the cost of medical benefit and the cost of additional cash benefits over and above the normal expected rates, which would serve as a positive guarantee of efficiency of these services in the administration of medical benefit.

A Workmen's State Insurance Bill was introduced in the Legislative Assembly in 1946, based on the scheme prepared by Prof. Adarkar and the modifications suggested by ILO experts. This Bill was passed in April 1948 as the Employees' State Insurance Act, 1948. This Act marked the beginning of social insurance in India.

The scheme was to be implemented in a phased manner throughout the country, as implementation required a great deal of preparatory work and the setting up of medical services. It was, therefore, decided to launch the scheme initially in the two industrial cities of Delhi and Kampur during 1950. However, the employers required to contribute in these two areas opposed such selective implementation, on the grounds that this would place them under a competitive handicap vis-à-vis employers in non-implemented areas. The force of the argument was conceded and the Act was amended in 1951 to introduce transitory provisions requiring payment of employers' special contributions by all employers in lieu of the employers' contribution levied on employers in the areas where the benefit provisions of the scheme were brought into force. The rate of employers' contribution payable by employers in implemented areas was slightly higher than the rate payable by employers in non-implemented areas. A few other minor amendments were also made. (The transitory provisions of Chapter V.A were repealed from 1 July 1973 and the original provisions of the Act restored from that date.)

In the light of practical experience of the scheme, various modifications were considered necessary. Meanwhile, the working of the ESI scheme was reviewed by the various committees which made certain recommendations for amendment of the ESI Act. Keeping in view the recommendations of various committees and experiences, the ESI Act was further amended by the ESI (Amendment) Act of 1966 (Second Amendment), 1975 (Third Amendment) and 1984 (Fourth Amendment).

General structure of social security health insurance

The Employees' State Insurance (ESI) Scheme of social security health insurance under the Employees' State Insurance Act, 1948, which was begun in 1952 covering 120,000 industrial workers, today covers over 6.9 million workers in the country. The scheme is compulsory and contributory and provides medical care and cash benefits in the contingencies of sickness, maternity, employment injury and death.

The scheme provides a full range of medical benefits (out-patient services, specialist treatment and hospitalisation), through a network of dispensaries, specialists centres and ESI hospitals.

The cash benefits provided are:
(i) sickness benefit;
(ii) maternity benefit;
(iii) employment injury benefit; temporary disability benefit; permanent disability benefit; dependants' benefit; and
(iv) funeral benefit.

Administration of the scheme

Though health comes under the purview of the Ministry of Health in the Government of India and the state governments, the Ministry of Labour, Government of India, is the administrative and co-ordinating Ministry for the provisions of the Employees' State Insurance Act, 1948.

At the national level, the ESI scheme is administered by a statutory body called the Employees' State Insurance Corporation, which consists of representatives of employees, employers, the central Government, state governments, the medical profession and the Parliament. A Standing Committee constituted from amongst members of the Corporation acts as the executive body. There is also a Medical Benefit Council to advise the Corporation on matters connected with the provision of medical care. At the regional level, Regional Boards have been constituted in each state and at the local level, local committees have been formed which function as advisory bodies.

For the day-to-day administration, the Corporation has set up a Regional Office in each state and for the disbursement of cash benefits, which is the direct responsibility of the Corporation, there is a network of local offices all over the country. The administration of medical care is the statutory responsibility of the state government. The Corporation may assume responsibility for providing the medical care in any state, subject to the condition that the state government will have to continue to contribute a one-eighth share towards the cost of medical care. The Corporation has, however, so far taken over the responsibilities for administration of medical care in the Union Territory of Delhi, from the Delhi Administration.

In-patient treatment is given through ESI hospitals and annexes and reservation beds in other government hospitals. Out-patient medical care is rendered through a network of full-time ESI dispensaries, part-time, mobile and employers' utilisation dispensaries and clinics of insurance medical practitioners.

The extension of the social security scheme to the areas which have not so far been brought under the purview of the ESI scheme depends upon the Corporation and the state government, who are mainly responsible under section 58(3) of the Act to create the necessary infrastructure of medical benefits for the workers of the factories and establishments and their families. After these infrastructures are created, the extension of the scheme to other areas and new types of establishment become possible.

Coverage

The Act applies in the first instance to non-seasonal factories using power and employing 20 or more persons. It is being extended area-wise by stages. The Act contains an enabling provision under which the "appropriate government" is empowered to extend the provisions of the Act to other classes of establishments, industrial, commercial, agricultural or otherwise. Under these provisions, most of the state governments have extended the provisions of the Act to the following new classes of establishments:
(i) small power-using factories employing ten to 19 persons and non-power-using factories employing 20 or more persons;
(ii) shops, hotels, restaurants, cinemas, including preview theatres, road motor transport and newspaper establishments employing 20 or more persons;
(iii) beedi manufacturing establishments employing ten or more persons in the implemented areas; and

Health insurance in developing countries

(iv) slate-pencil manufacturing establishments employing one or more persons.

The employees of the foregoing establishments in receipt of wages not exceeding Rs.1,600 per month are covered under the Act. The wage ceiling for coverage under the ESI Act was enhanced from Rs.1,000 to Rs.1,600 per month by the ESI (Amendment) Act, 1984, from 27 January 1985. The rate of contributions from employees and employers is fixed at 2.25 per cent and 5 per cent respectively of the wages payable to the employees. Employees in receipt of average daily wages below Rs.6 are exempted from payment of the employees' contribution.

The ESI scheme now covers workers in organised industry mostly in urban and semi-urban areas, all over the country with the exception of the states of Jammu and Kashmir, Sikkim, Nagaland, Tripura, Arunachal, Pradesh, Mizoram and Manipur and the Union Territories of Andaman and Nicobar Islands, Lakshdweep, Dadar and Nagar Haveli and Daman and Diu. It was in force in 551 industrial centres in the country covering about 7 million employees as on 31 March 1988. The total number of beneficiaries including insured persons entitled to medical care as on 31 March 1988 was 27 million.

Coverage under the ESI scheme is shown in the table below:

Year (as on 31 March)	Centres	No. of insured persons	No. of beneficiaries
1986	520	7 152 000	27 751 700
1987	537	7 123 000	27 637 300
1988	551	6 960 000	27 004 800

Organisation and delivery of medical care

The Employees' State Insurance scheme provides comprehensive medical care in the form of medical attendance, treatment, drugs and injections, specialist consultation and hospitalisation to insured persons and also to members of their families where the facility for specialist consultation and hospitalisation has been extended to the families. For the families, this benefit has been divided into three categories as below

Restricted medical care

This consists of out-patient medical care at dispensaries or panel clinics. In these institutions facilities for consultation with Medical Officers and supply of drugs are available; pre-natal and post-natal care, family welfare, immunisation and maternity child health services are also available. The beneficiaries are also entitled to call a doctor to their house to see a serious case.

Expanded medical care

This consists of consultation with specialists and supply of special medicines and drugs as may be prescribed by them in addition to the out-patient care. This also includes facilities for special laboratory tests and X-ray examinations.

Full medical care

This consists of hospitalisation facilities and includes specialist services, drugs and diets as required for in-patients.

Apart from the curative services provided through hospitals and dispensaries, the Corporation also provides the following facilities including family welfare services.

Immunisation

The Corporation has embarked upon a massive programme of immunisation of young children of insured persons. Under this programme preventive inoculation and vaccines are given against diseases such as diphtheria, smallpox, polio, tetanus, measles and tuberculosis.

Family welfare services

Along with the immunisation programme, the Corporation also provides family welfare services to the beneficiaries of the scheme. The Corporation has organised these services in 180 centres besides reserving 200 beds in hospitals for undertaking tubectomy operations. So far 408,838 sterilisation operations, viz. 131,940 vasectomies and 276,898 tubectomies, had been performed up to 30 November 1987. The ESI has also extended additional cash incentives to insured persons to promote acceptance of sterilisation by providing sickness cash benefit equal to full wages for a period of seven days for vasectomy and 14 days for tubectomy. The duration of the cash benefit may be extended if any complications occur. The Corporation had incurred an expenditure of Rs.241,311,351 on this account up to 30 November 1987.

Supply of special aids

Insured persons and members of their families are provided with artificial limbs, hearing aids, artificial dentures, spectacles and artificial appliances such as spinal supports, cervical collars, walking calipers, crutches, wheelchairs and cardiac pace makers as a part of their medical care entitlement.

Methods of delivering the medical care

Medical care has been organised in three sections, namely:
— out-patient service;
— specialist service; and
— hospital service.

Also provided are ambulance services and drugs and other appliances.

Out-patient care: Out-patient treatment is provided both under the service system as well as under the panel system. Under the service system, separate State Insurance dispensaries have been set up exclusively for the beneficiaries. The doctors and other staff working in these dispensaries are full-time employees of state governments. They are generally drawn from the State Medical Services and are transferable from ESI dispensaries to other state government dispensaries and hospitals and vice versa. The doctors under the scheme are not permitted to engage in any private practice and, due to this, there has been reluctance to accept postings under the ESI scheme in spite of the non-practising allowances attached to these posts. In order to make postings under the ESI scheme more attractive, the Corporation granted a special ESI allowance of Rs.100 per month, recently raised to Rs.200 per month, to Medical Officers in ESI dispensaries. In order to attract doctors to the ESI scheme, the Corporation is also persuading the state governments to set up a separate cadre of ESI Medical Officers with better pay scales and promotional avenues. Some of the state governments have already constituted separate ESI cadres and others are actively considering the proposals.

Full-time dispensaries are established with medical and para-medical staff where the number of insurable employees' family units is about 1,000 and above. The patients do not have a free choice of doctors in a dispensary but female patients may choose a woman doctor in dispensaries having two or more Medical Officers. If the number of insurable employees family units at any centre is fewer than 1,000 but not fewer than 500, which does not justify opening of a dispensary with full staff admissible for even a one-doctor dispensary, a mini-ESI dispensary is established with a minimum staff of one Medical Officer, one staff nurse, one pharmacist and a junior clerk. Dispensaries belonging to governing and local bodies or Primary Health Centres are also utilised on a part-time basis for ESI beneficiaries in areas where the residential concentrations of insured persons are not sufficient to justify full-time dispensaries. The Medical Officer and other para-medical staff of such part-time dispensaries receive remuneration according to the number of insured persons' family units attached to them. Mobile dispensaries are provided for rendering medical treatment where residential concentrations of beneficiaries are in small pockets scattered over a wide area. The ESI dispensaries are also provided with equipment and auxiliary staff for minor surgery, routine laboratory tests and the distribution of drugs and medicines.

Under the panel system medical practitioners are appointed on the panel after selection by an "Allocation Committee". A panel doctor is required to have his own consulting room and dispensary and to maintain certain minimum standards in respect of these which are verified by authorised inspectors before selection. The insured persons have the choice of registering themselves with any panel doctor of their liking. Their terms and conditions of service have been prescribed and include the range of services to be rendered, clinic hours, conditions regarding domiciliary visits, etc. The panel practitioners are paid a capitation fee recently raised from Rs.40 to Rs.50 per insured person family unit per annum and in return are expected to provide ambulatory and domiciliary care and ordinary medicines. Other drugs and dressings are obtained on prescription by panel practitioners, from approved panel chemists or at ESI Aushdalyas (medical stores) established on the direct pattern. For diagnostic aids the panel doctor refers patients with a written note to one of the diagnostic centres which are set up under direct pattern, and, where necessary, refers the patient to a specialist for advice and for prescription of more costly patent medicines. Each panel doctor is permitted to have up to 750 family units on his list.

At some places the ESIC also utilises the employers' dispensaries on the indirect pattern, on payment of a capitation fee, on the following broad conditions:

(a) these medical facilities are at least of as good a standard as provided by the state government to beneficiaries in State Insurance dispensaries;
(b) the employers' dispensaries will be open to inspection by the state government and the ESIC to ensure maintenance of the requisite standards;
(c) the employees of the employer will have the option to receive medical treatment at the employers' dispensary or at any other ESI dispensary and employees of other employers may also be assigned to receive medical treatment at that dispensary;
(d) the conditions similar to those laid down for panel doctors will be applicable to the employer and his medical staff and the employer will be entitled to payment of a capitation fee at the same rate as payable to panel doctors, for outdoor treatment, domiciliary visits and costs of all ordinary drugs and dressings. For the supply of drugs and medicines included in the specialists list, payment of Rs.15 per insured person will additionally be made.

The figures for the service dispensaries, Medical Officers, panel practitioners and doctors in employers' utilisation dispensaries functioning under the scheme for the past three years are as below:

Year (as on 31 March)	No. of dispensaries	ESI dispensaries (Direct system)		Panel practitioners (Indirect system)	
		No. of Medical Officers sanctioned	in position	No. of panel practitioners	No. of doctors in employers' utilisation dispensaries
1986	1 224	5 273	4 522	4 365	102
1987	1 249	5 286	4 411	4 356	97
1988	1 265	5 082	4 338	4 187	92

Specialist service: Specialist service is provided in all branches of medicine and surgery. Ambulatory specialists' care and services are provided in a hospital out-patient department or at separate specialist/ diagnostic centres set up for the purpose. These services are organised in different centres depending upon the extent of the area to be catered for. It is not necessary to appoint specialists in all specialities at all centres. Specialists in medicine, surgery, tuberculosis, obstetrics and gynaecology, pathology, paediatrics, eye, ENT, skin and sexually transmitted diseases, radiology, orthopaedics and physiotherapy are provided on a centre-wise basis. Specialists in psychiatry, leprosy, dentistry, cardiology, neurology, urology and plastic surgery are appointed on a zonal basis while specialists in malignant diseases, cardiac surgery, neurosurgery and thoracic surgery are appointed at state level. The idea behind setting up these specialists centres is that costly equipment such as X-ray and pathological equipment is provided only at one specialist centre, thus eliminating the need to have more X-ray and laboratories spread out at various places in the same centre. The total number of specialist centres functioning under the scheme is 307. The specialists are appointed either as full-time salaried specialists or on a part-time basis on payment of an "honorarium" for attending for prescribed hours each week. Full-time specialists are not permitted to have private practice inside or outside the hospital and specialist centre. The number of full-time and part-time specialists for the past three years are as below:

Year (as on 31 March)	No. of specialists	
	Full time	Part time
1986	735	2 189
1987	750	2 153
1988	818	2 216

Hospital services: Hospitalisation is provided in ESI hospitals as annexes to government or public hospitals specially built for exclusive use of the beneficiaries of the scheme. In areas where there are no ESIC hospitals or annexes or where the number of beneficiaries is smaller and does not justify a separate hospital, care is provided in reserved beds in existing government and public hospitals on payment of a fixed per diem rate. Hospital beds are provided on a scale of four beds per 1,000 employees' family unit. As on 31 March 1988 a total of 19,930 beds had already been provided in 103 ESI hospitals and 42 annexes constructed exclusively for insured persons and 4,445 beds were reserved in government hospitals and others.

With a view to securing maximum economy in planning, construction and development of ESI hospitals, schematic plans for hospitals of different sizes ranging from 50 to 500 beds have been drawn up and norms and standards of equipment, furniture and other appliances and staffing have been prescribed to ensure uniformity of standards. New hospitals are equipped with the latest modern equipment and in the case of old hospitals, new equipment is being installed to modernise facilities for diagnosis and treatment. Even the smaller hospital with 50 beds is provided with specialists in medicine, surgery, obstetrics and gynaecology, while the biggest hospitals with 500 beds are staffed with specialists in medicine, surgery, obstetrics, gynaecology, paediatrics, orthopaedics, ENT, eye, anaesthesia, radiology, pathology, skin and sexually transmitted diseases, chest diseases, dentistry and psychiatry. Special units for cardiology, burns and intensive care are set up in all bigger hospitals. For highly sophisticated and super specialities such as heart surgery, cancer treatment, kidney transplant, etc., the beneficiaries of the scheme are referred to specialised government and other institutions in the country at the cost of the scheme.

A uniform scale of diet based on caloric value of ingredients has been prescribed for all ESI institutions and as such any rise in prices does not dilute the standard of diet. The net daily costs of hospital facilities are much higher in ESI hospitals than the per diem payments made to government and other hospitals for reserved beds for care of beneficiaries. For these higher costs the ESI hospitals provide a much higher quality of service through larger staffs, better diets and more individual attention to patients.

Ambulance services: Free ambulance services are provided to beneficiaries for specialist consultation, investigation or admission to hospitals if the patient is so ill as not to be able to travel by other modes of conveyance. One ambulance is provided for centres having 10,000 or more employees' family units, two for 30,000, three where there are 60,000 and, for centres with 100,000 or more employees' family units, four, with one extra ambulance for every 50,000 employees' family units.

A small type of ambulance is provided for a minimum of 7,000 employees' family units. In a smaller area where no ambulance is provided the beneficiaries are paid conveyance charges at prescribed rates. The number of ambulances provided was 242 in 1986, and 248 in 1987 and 1988.

Drugs and other appliances: The distribution of drugs to ambulatory patients follows both direct and indirect patterns in different areas. In direct service areas drugs are provided at ESI dispensaries, ESI hospitals and Central Medical Stores. In panel areas, where panel practitioners paid by capitation give out-patient care, the common drugs are dispensed directly by the panel doctor from his clinic and are covered in his capitation fee. Special and more expensive drugs, or drugs which may be prescribed by specialists, are supplied to the patients at private pharmacies on the approved list or at Medical Stores Depots established on the direct pattern. All drugs and medicines are provided free to the beneficiaries. The private pharmacists and chemists on the approved list are paid their bills for each prescription directly by the Administrative Medical Officer of the scheme for the area, according to the pricing formula included in the agreement between the ESI authorities and the pharmacists and chemists. The scheme has its own drug formulary classifying three types of drugs by their generic names: *(a)* common drugs which are expected to be stocked and supplied by even private practitioners included on the panel of the scheme; *(b)* drugs including special and more expensive drugs which can be prescribed by Medical Officers working in ESI dispensaries and hospitals and also by private practitioners included in the panel; and *(c)* drugs which can be prescribed only by a specialist. The pharmacopoeia is reviewed periodically to include all the latest modern and efficacious drugs of approved therapeutic value. With a view to ensuring supplies of quality drugs and medicines at a uniform rate throughout the country, the ESIC have entered into rate contracts at the central level with the reputed drug manufacturers for the bulk supply of drugs.

A wide range of artificial aids and appliances which are necessary for treatment and rehabilitation are provided free of cost to the beneficiaries.

Remuneration and paying medical providers

As already mentioned, under the service system the scheme is served by the full-time Medical Officers and specialists who are directly appointed or taken on deputation by the ESI Corporation or the state government. Under the panel system the doctors and the specialists are paid on the basis of an agreed capitation fee and lump-sum remuneration fixed by the ESI Corporation.

Methods of control and documenting standards

The day-to-day supervision and quality control of medical care under the scheme are the responsibility of the regular government health services administering medical care in each state and of the ESIC in the Union Territory of Delhi where medical care is administered directly. The routine supervision and inspection at the technical level by the Director of ESI medical services of each state government and of the ESIC in Delhi, affect the day-to-day operations and functioning of the medical institutions and services. There are also tripartite Regional Boards and local committees with representatives of workers, employers, the state government and of the ESIC. These committees make periodical reviews and inspections and look into complaints.

At the central level the Director General and the Medical Commissioner of the ESIC frequently visit and inspect the ESI medical institutions in the states in performance of their statutory functions and responsibilities. The ESIC has also appointed a number of Inspectors called Medical Referees, who are qualified Medical Officers in each state, who carry out routine periodical inspections of ESI dispensaries and clinics and other medical institutions. In addition, senior medical personnel are appointed as Regional Deputy Medical Commissioners on a zonal basis function under the control and supervision of the Medical Commissioner. Above all, there is a high-powered Subcommittee of the ESIC called the General Purposes Sub-Committee, consisting of medical experts and representatives of the workers and employers on the Corporation. This Sub-Committee periodically visits medical institutions in different states for an in-depth inspection and review of the working of the medical institutions. It makes a thorough review of manpower requirements, equipment, availability and stocking of drugs and medicines, facilities in operating theatres, laboratories and X-ray units, etc. The shortfalls and excesses are taken note of and remedial steps are taken quickly. These exercises have brought about considerable improvements in the working of the ESI scheme.

The scale of medical benefit, the kind of service to be rendered, the standard norms and yardsticks for establishment of hospitals and dispensaries, their staffing, equipment and provision of specialists and other facilities, etc., are specified by the Corporation on the advice of a statutory professional body called the Medical Benefit Council, on which every state government is represented. These norms and standards are designed to provide medical care of a uniform standard throughout the country. As a further measure to achieve uniformity and simultaneously to exercise a degree of budgetary control over the cost of medical care to be applied uniformly in all states, the ESIC has prescribed ceilings on expenditure on medical care which are reviewed and enhanced from time to time to meet the price rises.

As regards the norms for staffing the dispensaries the number of family units to be attached to each dispensary is taken as the basis. Experience has shown that, since the incidence of sickness is not uniform in a large country like India, the number of employees' family units does not serve as an appropriate criterion and instead the workload based on the number of attendances in a dispensary is the more appropriate basis. On an average, a Medical Officer is expected to examine about 60 cases per day which can be bifurcated into 20 new and 40 repeat cases. This system ensures that more doctors and staff are assigned in areas where the incidence of sickness is higher and also that the allocation of excessive numbers of doctors and staff in the areas of lower incidence is avoided.

Personnel: The Employees' State Insurance Scheme employs 5,286 Medical Officers, 818 full-time and 2,216 part-time specialists, 12,716 (excluding principal officers) administrative staff and 2,682 personnel for administration of medical benefit in the Territory of Delhi (being directly administered by the Corporation).

Advantages and disadvantages of the delivery methods of medical care

The relative merits and demerits of the panel and service system in India have been discussed on a number of occasions by the ESIC and also by various ad hoc committees. The preponderantly held view has been that the service system provides more satisfactory care to workers than the panel system. The merits and demerits of the two systems in India are shown below.

Merits

(a) Medical Officers under the service system are more amenable to control by the authorities and the standard of treatment is superior, as no element of profit is involved. Under the panel system a tendency has been noticed on the part of doctors to prescribe costly medicines.

(b) Specialist advice, advantages of para-medical staff, facilities for diagnostic and laboratory tests, etc., are readily available in the service system, while in the panel system patients have to be referred to diagnostic/specialist centres or to out-patients departments of the hospital even for minor examinations or for the prescription of drugs from the specialist's list.

(c) More satisfactory arrangements for the supply of costly and special medicines are made under the service system by storing them at every dispensary.

(d) More effective checking on lax certification is possible in the service system, as there is no incentive for the Medical Officer to issue unwarranted certificates. Panel practitioners are willing to oblige patients by readily issuing certificates, for fear of the insured persons changing to another doctor.

(e) Though the panel system is expected to offer better scope for development of the doctor-patient relationship, in actual experience it is found that panel doctors do not attend their clinics regularly, pay greater attention to their private patients, do not examine insurance patients properly, and so on.

Demerits

(f) The non-practising nature of ESI assignments make service doctors reluctant to accept postings in ESI dispensaries. Often raw and inexperienced doctors are posted in service dispensaries.

(g) The service doctors are subject to frequent shiftings and cannot develop a continuing personal contact with patients. This adversely affects the standard of diagnosis and treatment.

(h) In sparse areas setting up of separate service dispensaries is not economically viable. It is also difficult to get enough Medical Officers to serve in sparse areas.

(i) Service dispensaries are located at a few selected centres and in some cases the patients have to travel long distances, as it is not possible to provide a dispensary at the door of every insured person.

Every effort is being made by the ESI Corporation to switch over to the service system in the areas where the panel system is in vogue.

Financial aspects

The ESI scheme is mainly financed by contributions from employers and employees. Employers contribute 5 per cent of the wages payable to insured employees and employees contribute 2.25 per cent. Employees who are in receipt of wages below Rs.6 per day are not required to contribute. However, employers contribute in the prescribed manner for such employees also. The state governments share one-eighth of the expenditure on medical care. The contributions collected are utilised for providing medical and cash benefits to insured persons and their families as well as for meeting the administrative expenses of the ESI Corporation. The income and expenditure of the ESI scheme over the past three years is given overleaf.

Health insurance in developing countries

	Years (as on 31 March)		
	1986 (Rs. in millions)	1987	1988
Income	3 644.52	3 792.10	3 953.47
Expenditure			
(a) Medical benefit	969.80	1 156.08	1 107.10
(b) Cash benefits	826.94	1 033.42	1 042.23
(c) Other benefits	2.25	2.63	2.97
(d) Administrative expenses	290.31	344.13	402.28
(e) Other expenses (including reserve funds)	470.43	228.53	220.83
Total	2 559.73	2 764.79	2 775.41

Collection of social security contributions

Under the provisions of the ESI Act, employers are liable to pay contributions—both employers' as well as employees' contributions. As the contributions from employers and employees are payable by employers of covered factories/establishments, etc., by the 21st of the following month to which the wages relate as dues under the Statutes (ESI Act), the flow of income from this source is automatic in respect of each calendar month. The contributions are paid by employers directly into the specified branches of the authorised banks which are channelled into a central account. By this arrangement a sum deposited anywhere in the country reaches the central account in about one to two weeks' time. However, a few instances of delayed credits have sometimes been noticed due to negligence on the part of the banks or due to delay in transmission of messages through communication networks, as these are manually handled.

The main problem in realisation of contributions arises in cases where the employer commits a default or coverage is disputed by them in courts of law or where a factory or establishment has been closed after remaining in default for some time. In such cases the recourse is to legal action, including panel action under the provisions of law, and where the courts so order, the contributions are paid by the employers. The contributions are recoverable as arrears of land revenue.

The administrative cost for the past three years as percentages is indicated on the facing page:

India

	Years (as on 31 March)		
	1986 (%)	1987 (%)	1988 (%)
Contributions	9.31	10.64	12.41
Expenditure on revenue account	11.34	12.45	14.49
Benefits	16.13	15.70	18.69

Note: The 14.49 per cent (1988) administrative cost of total expenditure on revenue accounts is within the acceptable limits for the scheme.

Methods of monitoring expenditure

The scale of medical benefits, the kind of service to be rendered, the standard norms and yardsticks for establishment of hospitals and dispensaries, their staffing and equipment and provision of specialist and other facilities, etc., are specified by the ESI Corporation on the advice of the Medical Benefit Council. The norms and standards are designed to provide medical care of a uniform standard throughout the country. As mentioned earlier, the ESI Corporation has prescribed ceilings on expenditure on medical care which are reviewed and enhanced from time to time to meet rises in prices and increasing overall costs of providing medical care. The initial and the current ceilings are as below:

	Initial (Rs.)	Current (Rs.)
Restricted medical care	50	70 per insured person family unit per annum
Expanded medical care	54	85 per insured person family unit per annum
Full medical care	64	190 per insured person family unit per annum

Further, expenditure on drugs, medicines and dressings, exceeding Rs.30 but not exceeding Rs.70 (effective from 1 April 1988) per employee per annum is allowed over and above the ceiling. In addition, expenditure on rents for ESI hospitals and dispensaries and on initial equipment in new hospitals is provided outside the ceiling at Rs.15,000 per bed in hospitals having up to 150 beds, Rs.12,000 for each additional bed from 151 to 300 beds, and Rs.8,000 for each additional bed over 300 beds subject to a minimum of Rs.1.5 million. Apart from the above, additional expenditure up to Rs.0.6 million is allowed outside the ceiling for replacement of costly equipment for an existing department or for new equipment in a department added to an already commissioned hospital.

Purchases are made by inviting open tenders and entering into rate contracts. The procedure followed is according to the General Financial Rules.

Trends in expenditure and strategies for cost containment

The per capita margin in the income from expenditure after meeting the expenditure on cash and medical benefits alone was Rs.212, R.165 and Rs.175 during the years 1986, 1987 and 1988 respectively. The increase during 1987-88 was due to savings effected in cash benefits through controls over lax certification.

The margin of surplus (excess of revenues over expenditure on revenue account) was 1,084 million rupees, 1,027 million rupees and 1,178 million rupees during the years 1986, 1987 and 1988 respectively. This works out to a per capita margin of Rs.174, Rs.163 and Rs.190 during those years. This margin of surplus was not available up to the year 1986, as the wage ceiling for coverage under the scheme was Rs.1,000 per month until raised to Rs.1,600 per month from 27 January 1985. The ESI Corporation had in fact experienced a deficit position in respect of its revenue receipt and expenditure on revenue account during the years 1981 and 1984 (31 March), i.e. prior to the raising of the wage ceiling as mentioned above. The situation of having annual revenue surpluses is, however, likely to change on account of expenditure on medical benefits and falls in revenue income due to employees going out of coverage. To meet the situation a proposal to further enhance the wage ceiling for coverage is under consideration by the central Government.

Assessment of financial viability of the scheme

The ESI Act requires the ESI Corporation, at intervals of five years, to have a valuation of its assets and liabilities made by a Valuer appointed with the approval of the central Government. All the benefits under the ESI scheme, except the permanent disablement and dependants' benefits, are financed on the "pay-as-you-go" system, in that the benefits that are likely to be disbursed during a certain future short period should match with the corresponding contributions likely to be received during the same period.

Review of progress

As an integrated and unified scheme of medical care and cash benefits for sickness, maternity and employment injury, necessary arrangements for providing medical care have to be made before the scheme can be extended to a new area or to a new class of establishments. This involves setting up both out-patient and in-patient facilities, siting of accommodation for dispensaries/clinics, securing services of medical and other staff and their training. Out of three common methods of coverage, namely area-wise extension, industry-wise extension or extension by wage groups, the ESI scheme had to adopt the first-named method and the extension of coverage including extension to new classes of establishments has been on a geographical basis from area to area. This enabled the ESIC to acquire and build up experience gained in implementation of the scheme as it proceeded from one area to another. The administration of medical care under the scheme being the responsibility of state governments, the extension of its coverage in an area or to new classes of establishments in an area depends on the agreement of the relevant state government and the speed with which it is able to build up the requisite medical facilities. The pace of extension of the scheme, therefore, has not been altogether easy and has not progressed according to the phased programmes due to the non-availability of adequate physical resources, including suitable land and buildings for ESI hospitals and dispensaries in the area, shortages of medical and para-medical staff in the state, limited medical and hospitalisation facilities in government hospitals to cater for the additional needs of persons to be covered under the scheme and financial constraints of the state government to meet its share of costs. Thus, the extent of implementation of the scheme and widening of its coverage are beyond the control of the ESIC and, unless the state government provides medical benefits at a particular place, cash benefits for sickness, maternity and employment injury also cannot be provided. Thus the extent of implementation and the standard of medical benefits provided varies from state to state.

The ESI Corporation launched a massive programme of acquiring land, with the help of the state governments from the year 1960 onwards, and the construction of buildings. This programme put a great financial burden on the Corporation with the result that it was in deficit between 1967 and 1970, when it was decided to (i) prescribe a ceiling of expenditure on medical care, as mentioned earlier; (ii) to set up a Contingency Reserve Fund for meeting unexpected increases in expenditure on benefits; (iii) to set up a Capital Construction Reserve Fund to which a part of the income (10 per cent from 1974 to 1981/82 and 5 per cent thereafter) from contributions is earmarked every year. The ESI Corporation has since constructed 103 hospitals and 42 annexes and 1,250 dispensary buildings. The problem of constructing more buildings as per the norms fixed by the Corporation still remains. It requires a capital outlay of 3,704 million rupees at the present reckoning. The financial resources to achieve this target are not as big a problem as the non-availability of physical resources, such as suitable plots of land at fairly reasonable prices, construction agencies in the government sector to execute those projects, and raw materials such as cement and steel. Even when these buildings are ready, shortages of medical and para-medical personnel stand in the way of their working as hospitals, as the concerned state governments at times find it difficult to recruit staff or to meet their share of additional expenditure due to constraints in their own finances.

Although the per capita expenditure of about Rs.200 per annum on medical care under the ESI scheme is almost four times the per capita expenditure incurred on public health and family welfare programmes by the various state governments, there is dissatisfaction among the beneficiaries about the quality of medical care they receive. Perhaps their expectations are the greater since they are required to pay social security contributions. The ESI scheme is getting criticism from various sections on account of non-performance or lack of performance of the state governments.

Various alternatives are being evaluated to provide satisfactory services to the beneficiaries One of the proposals is that the ESI Corporation should take over the responsibility of administering medical benefits to the beneficiaries from the state governments. However, there is a reluctance on the part of the state governments to accept the proposal. Another suggestion is to entrust the administration of the medical benefit to a committee on which representatives of the various interests including the Corporation and the state governments are represented. This committee will function as an independent body.

The existing financial resources and the present financial position of the ESI Corporation for administering the benefits admissible under the ESI scheme on the scales and levels in force are sufficient and likely to remain so during the foreseeable year in the light of the free reserve of about 5,258 million rupees (31 March 1988) supported by annual surpluses of about 1,000 million rupees. The problems are those of an effective and efficacious machinery and dual control by the ESI Corporation and state governments on the medical care front, which is already engaging the attention of the Corporation, central and the state governments.

Future developments

The wage ceiling for coverage was last enhanced to Rs.1,600 per month in January 1985. The decrease in coverage is resulting in shortfall in the revenue income of the Corporation. There is a proposal to enhance the wage ceiling for coverage from Rs.1,600 to Rs.2,500 per month.

As already mentioned, constraints in the financial position of the state governments hamper the progress in the implementation of the scheme in new areas. A proposal is under consideration to bear the cost on account of new implementation by the Corporation for the first three years. This could help in extending coverage to more new areas at a faster pace.

There is a pressing demand for extending coverage under the social security scheme to those sections of workers who do not enjoy any social security benefits at all at present. Two such categories of workers who are proposed to be brought under coverage are those employed in seasonal, especially sugar, factories and those in the unorganised building construction industry. The seasonal industries are presently excluded from the purview of the ESI scheme. The ESIC has recently decided on, and recommended to the Government, the extension of the scheme to workers in the sugar industry and the necessary amendments are under consideration. About 65 per cent of the workers in the sugar industry are seasonal workers who are employed at the factory during the crushing period of sugar-cane, which varies between two to six months depending upon the crop yield of sugar-cane during a year. These workers reside in their native villages far away from the factories and come to the factories only for the duration of the crushing period, after which they go back to their villages. While there will be no difficulty in extending the existing scheme to permanent workers of the sugar factories and organising medical care facilities for them near to their place of work or residence on the existing direct pattern by establishing service dispensaries, problems will arise in providing medical care for seasonal workers and their families and following them to their villages scattered over a wide area, in view of difficulties in organising medical facilities in rural areas. Arrangements for out-patient medical care may have to be made for them either through the primary health centre situated near to their village or through mobile vans. These arrangements may also be unsatisfactory. Similar problems are likely to arise in providing medical care for construction workers who are migratory, having no fixed residential dwelling and frequently moving from one construction site to another. The extension of the medical care under the ESI scheme to workers in the sugar and building construction industries will extend the area of operation of the scheme, which has been hitherto confined within urban limits, to the rural areas.

As mentioned earlier, about 80 per cent of the Indian population lives in villages. A sound and efficient system of providing medical care for them under the social security system, therefore, assumes great importance and will have to be devised in such a manner as can ultimately merge with the national health service as and when a national health service comes into being in India.

INDONESIA

DEMOGRAPHY AND HEALTH DATA

Indonesia had a population of just over 172 million in 1987, growing at an annual rate of 2.2 per cent over the previous six years. Of the total, 27 per cent were then in urban areas. The per capita GNP in 1987 was US$490 and had been increasing by an average of 2 per cent over the period 1980-86.

In 1987 the infant mortality rate was 85 and the child mortality rate 120 deaths per 1,000 live births. The average annual rate of reduction in child mortality from 1980 to 1987 was 2.67 per cent. Life expectancy at the end of that period was 57 years. Adult literacy rates were 83 per cent for males and 65 per cent for females.

HEALTH SERVICES

The health care system is mainly run by the Government, which has developed a network of hospitals, health centres and integrated health posts with active community participation. While health centres have been developed for every 30,000 people, health subcentres, each with a midwife, have been built in villages to provide limited preventive and curative services. Mobile teams with two to three nurses and a doctor cover people in remote areas. By 1986 the Government had developed over 5,000 health centres and 10,000 subcentres. The private sector also maintains health centres and hospitals, all of which are supervised by the Ministry of Health. In 1985 more than half the hospitals were owned by the private sector, most of them operated by religious organisations. National non-government organisations also play a very significant role in the health services of Indonesia.

The central Government of Indonesia spent 1.9 per cent of its total expenditure on health in 1987, with an increasing share of the expenditure shifting from central to provincial and district levels over the past decade. Government health services are not free, except for a limited number of patients, and direct cash payments are the largest source of revenue. Approximately 65 per cent of total health care expenditure in

Indonesia is privately funded, with up to 50 per cent of this expenditure going to drug purchases.

HEALTH INSURANCE

The description of social security health insurance in Indonesia is based on a paper prepared for the Seminar by the Joint PKTK Coordinating Committee of the Ministries of Health and Manpower in Indonesia. The PKTK is the pilot voluntary health insurance system launched in January 1985 in Jakarta and subsequently expanded to eight provinces. The paper deals with the policy issues of establishing health insurance in Indonesia within its health development plans, and with the current scope and potential of the system.

Health policies

All government policies in Indonesia are founded upon the Basic Laws of 1945 and the National Pancasila Philosophy. A National Health System (SKN) was developed in 1982 which established the constitutional basis for all health activities, government as well as community and privately sponsored. An outgrowth of the SKN was the Long Range Plan for Health Development which formulates the policies, strategies and specific objectives for the health sector until the year 2000. The objective of the SKN is to enhance the capability of each person to live healthily and care for his or her own health in order to achieve an optimal level of health of the community.

The SKN affirms health as a basic right of every Indonesian citizen and establishes the Government, through its Ministry of Health, as the guarantor of that right. Consequently, the SKN directs the Government's health system to make health services available to all citizens. The SKN does recognise, however, that community participation is a necessity in order to achieve the general objectives of national development and self-reliance in health. Community participation is interpreted broadly, meaning community involvement in identifying problems and needs, planning health programmes, delivering health services, and financing health care. In the delivery and financing of health services the SKN clearly identifies the private and social financing schemes, as long as they maintain standards of quality, effectiveness and efficiency.

The Government has developed through its Five-Year Development Plans a basic network of health facilities, delivering health services to the general population. At the lowest administrative level the Puskesmas (Health Centre) is the health system's most peripherally situated non-hospital clinic facility, staffed with medical, dental and paramedical personnel, and provides technical support for the community-based health and family planning system. There were 5,472 Puskesmas in August 1988.

The Puskesmas are backed up by regional and provincial hospitals with various specialities available.

Government health expenditure constitutes 35 per cent of all yearly expenditures on health, while 65 per cent is contributed by private and community sources. The private sector's financing potential needs to be co-ordinated and directed towards promotion and prevention, and reaching national health objectives as stated in the SKN.

Social security systems in health

Two social security health plans are prominent in Indonesia, the ASKES plan and the PKTK plan. ASKES is a popular name for the compulsory health insurance system covering civil servants, active and retired, and retired military personnel, and their dependants. The plan was introduced by the Government in 1968 and since then has undergone several reorganisational changes. In 1984 ASKES was reorganised as a parastatal company, Perum Husada Bhakti, or PHB, which is technically responsible to the Minister of Health, but requires the joint approval of the Ministries of Health and Finance for its budget. As a Perum (public corporation) the organisation has greater flexibility in management than a government agency.

As of August 1988, ASKES had enrolled 3,872,437 subscribers. Including their dependants, the total number of ASKES members was 15,489,748. Contributions are set at 2 per cent of monthly income, which entitles members to free use of government health centres, including basic drugs. Members are entitled to free use of government hospitals and to a class of accommodation in accordance with their respective ranks in the civil service.

The experience with the ASKES system led the Ministry of Health to consider the extension of the principles of the system to other groups in the population. The DUKM (Dana Upaya Kesehatan Masyarakat) concept was developed and introduced to the private sector, consisting of pre-paid managed health care systems, including the delivery of comprehensive health care and capitated financing. It is intended to be the policy framework which will encompass all health insurance activities in Indonesia. Implementation of DUKM will ultimately involve drafting national legislation and the establishment of a DUKM supervisory body.

The current ASKES system is implementing most of the principles of DUKM and is gradually striving towards a complete model of DUKM implementation. Based on the same DUKM principles, the PKTK plan was developed and can be considered as a private sector analogue of the ASKES plan.

Health insurance in developing countries

Health insurance for private employees

In 1985 a Joint Decree was signed between the Minister of Health and the Minister of Manpower, which formed the basis for the development of a health insurance programme for private employees based on DUKM principles. This voluntary programme eventually became known as the PKTK programme (health care programme for private employees). The objective of the programme is to provide basic health care of good quality which is financially affordable. The reason behind the signing of the decree was the recognition that health care is one of the most important factors in the promotion of the productivity of private workers and that the costs of health care may post a heavy financial burden on employees. With the decrease in government resources to financing the health sector, due to the world economic recession, it becomes imperative for employees' health care to be financed through contributions from employers and the employees themselves.

In the Joint Decree it was stated that the Minister of Manpower is responsible for collecting the contributions and the Minister of Health for the delivery of health services on the basis of an agreed upon budget. The general policies for implementing the programme are to be laid down by a Joint Committee installed by both ministers. The Joint Committee comprises eight members, four of whom represent the Ministry of Health and the other four the Ministry of Manpower and ASTEK. The chairmanship rotates between representatives of the two Ministries.

On the basis of the Joint Decree, a joint decision was made regulating the amount of contribution as 7 per cent of the monthly payroll. A decision of the Minister of Manpower stipulates that Perum ASTEK would be responsible for the administration of membership, the collection of contributions and the allocation of the budget to finance the scheme. Perum ASTEK is a parastatal company under the Ministry of Manpower which provides social security insurance for private workers.

PKTK offers comprehensive health care to participating firms' employees and their dependants, which includes curative as well as preventive and promotive care. Health care is delivered through government health facilities or appointed private facilities. The members are entitled to an expanded basic drug list and a higher class category in hospitals than ASKES members. Members have to be officially referred by a primary care doctor in order to be entitled to in-patient care in hospitals. PKTK reimburses the primary doctor or the Puskesmas on a capitation basis.

The programme started in 1985 as a pilot project in Jakarta, but was quickly followed by other provinces. In 1988, 16 cities in eight provinces' were participating in the programme with a total membership of about 80,000 people. Several reasons were behind the slow progress, among others the voluntary character of the programme and the fact that many of the bigger companies already have good health care programmes running for their employees. Most of the companies joining the programme are of the middle or smaller size.

At the local level two implementation units are established. These are the BPKD, formed by ASTEK and responsible for the membership administration and the collection of contributions, and the BPPK, formed by the Regional Health Office and responsible for arranging the delivery of care and payment to the providers of care. Collected funds are divided as follows: 2 per cent to the PKTK Joint Committee, 8 per cent to BPKD (ASTEK) for administration, 10 per cent for the reserve fund, 10 per cent for BPPK (Health Department) for administration and 70 per cent for BPPK (Health Department) for providing health services.

Although the PKTK programme is still facing many problems, financial as well as managerial and organisational, it certainly fulfils a great need amongst the private workers. Very few of the enrolled companies have left the programme. The two ministries involved, therefore, are determined to face these challenges together and are constantly trying to overcome the problems and find new alternatives to make the programme worth while and more attractive to the private employees.

Conclusion

In view of the declining financial resources for health care financing, it is imperative for efficiency in the use and allocation of existing funds to be increased, and for additional funds to be mobilised in an organised manner. Social security health schemes are programmes which will foster this viewpoint. The Government of Indonesia is determined to expand the social financing schemes in health care on the basis of insurance principles.

JORDAN

DEMOGRAPHY AND HEALTH DATA

The population of Jordan was 3.8 million in 1987, following an annual average growth of 3.7 per cent in the preceding six years. Some 66 per cent of the population are in urban areas. The per capita GNP in 1986 was US$1,540 following a period of negative growth of −0.2 per cent as average for the preceding years.

The infant mortality rate was 45 and the child mortality rate was 60 deaths per 1,000 live births in 1987. The average annual reduction in child mortality for the preceding years was 4.03 per cent. In 1987 life expectancy was 67 years, and adult literacy was 87 per cent for males and 63 per cent for females.

HEALTH SERVICES

The Ministry of Health is responsible for the delivery of health services, while policy and legislation are primarily determined by a Supreme Health Council, headed by the Prime Minister. The Ministry of Health has attempted to shift resources to community care and has developed a network of village clinics, health centres in urban areas and maternal and child health centres to strengthen primary and preventive care. Two-thirds of the hospital beds are owned by the Ministry of Health, while the rest are privately owned and operated. A major problem is the maldistribution of health care resources by region on the one hand and duplication of curative services in the public and private sectors in urban areas on the other.

HEALTH INSURANCE

Social security health insurance is still very limited in Jordan. Special sickness insurance schemes have been developed for public sector employees, with a very low flat rate contribution. The scheme is considered inadequate and expansion of the system is now being considered.

REPUBLIC OF KOREA

DEMOGRAPHY AND HEALTH DATA

In 1987 the Republic of Korea's population was 42.1 million, after a declining growth rate in the preceding period. The annual average population growth rate for 1980-86 was 1.4 per cent. The percentage of the population in urban areas was 68 in 1987. In that year per capita GNP was US$2,370, following an average increase of 6.8 per cent in the previous six years.

In 1987 the infant mortality rate was 26 and the child mortality rate was 34 deaths per 1,000 live births. The latter had shown an average annual decrease by 3.30 per cent in the preceding six years. In 1987 life expectancy was 70 years. The adult literacy rate in 1985 was 81 per cent for males and 66 per cent for females.

HEALTH SERVICES

The Republic of Korea's health care system is predominantly private, particularly in urban areas, with about 85 per cent of all hospital beds in the country owned by the private sector. The Government operates health centres, clinics and general as well as specialised hospitals. The Government also operates a rural network of primary health posts, health centres and subcentres, and maternity and child care centres. The Government has thus attempted to counterbalance the spread of private hospital-based services in urban areas with affordable community services for the rural population.

In 1986 total health expenditure was about 4.3 per cent of the GNP, with the public sector accounting for about one-third of the amount spent. At that time, the central Government allocated 1.5 per cent of its budget to health care. In recent years the role of Government has grown through the expansion of medical assistance and the introduction of the social insurance scheme, which covers the entire population as of July 1989.

HEALTH INSURANCE

The experience of the Republic of Korea on social security health insurance is based on a paper presented by Professor Chong-Kee Park, Professor of Economics at the Inha University in Seoul and an ILO consultant.

Socio-economic development and its implications for health

In the early 1960s the Republic of Korea was a poor farming country. Already overcrowded, the country was experiencing a population growth rate of 3 per cent per annum, and there was widespread unemployment and underemployment. With a per capita income of less than US$100, the nation's domestic savings were negligible, and the country had no significant industrial base.

In spite of these unfavourable conditions, the country achieved its remarkable economic success by adopting an export-oriented growth strategy, which focused on the promotion of highly labour-intensive industries. This development strategy provided a steadily expanding pool of job opportunities to the unemployed and the underemployed, as well as to the growing labour force.

Available statistics show that total employment increased at an average annual rate of 4 per cent during 1963-80, compared with 3 per cent for the potential labour force. Some 6 million new jobs were created between 1963 and 1980. The extent of the structural change is highlighted by the sharp increase in the share of manufacturing in total employment from only 8 per cent in 1963 to 22 per cent by 1980, while the share of agriculture decreased from 63 to 34 per cent. Thus, the Republic of Korea's outward-looking development strategy, based on rapid growth of labour-intensive manufacturing combined with a strong "trickle-down" effect, has measurably improved the employment situation and thereby helped to increase the level of income. Between 1963 and 1980 real GNP grew at an average annual rate of 8.7 per cent, with nominal values of manufactured output and exports increasing by 19.2 and 37.8 per cent per annum respectively.

Rapid growth of the economy has been accompanied by improvements in social welfare. The reduction of the fertility rate has contributed significantly to improved social and economic conditions in the country. With effective family planning programmes, the country was able to bring down the growth rate of population from nearly 3 per cent in the early 1960s to 1.6 per cent by 1980. There were parallel improvements in other indicators of social progress, such as life expectancy, the infant mortality rate, calorie intake, supply of clean water, and school enrolment. Furthermore, the Korean income distribution in the 1960s was considered relatively less concentrated than in other countries at similar stages of development. The major factors in maintaining low income concentration were the early land reforms and widespread education. The initial relative equity in the distribution of land and human resources has had favourable effects on income distribution.

It has been generally accepted that the Republic of Korea's successful performance during the two decades of the 1960s and 1970s has a great deal to do with human resource development. The efficiency of Korean human capital was credited as one of the most important sources of the rapid economic growth during the 1960s. The labour force was characterised by a high level of literacy and education, adaptability, and industriousness. The achievement of a high literacy rate and universal access to primary education provided people with a chance of fully developing their own skills and potential in their work. Thus the secret of "Korean success" was the appropriate use of efficient human capital.

The Republic of Korea's human resource based economy, however, began to show signs of weaknesses during the 1970s. Urban-oriented, rapid industrialisation led to a gradual deterioration in the distribution of income. As the industrial structure shifted toward "second generation" industries with more capital-intensive technologies, the old human resources base rapidly evaporated and primary level education became less relevant than higher levels of education. A growing emphasis on skill-intensive, heavy industries rapidly increased the demand for highly skilled and educated manpower, resulting in sharp rises in wages, which in turn exacerbated the worsening income distribution. An ever-increasing role of large business conglomerates led to further concentration of wealth and assets, aggravating the inequality in income. There was also a deterioration in the distribution of farm income in the 1970s. A government price support programme, introduced in the 1960s, widened the gap in income differentials between small and large farm households, since large farms benefited relatively more from the high price of rice.

Emphasis on industrial expansion has also created problems arising from rapid urbanisation. Over-concentration of population in a few large cities and a corresponding strain on the resources of these urban centres was one result. The extent of urbanisation is illustrated by the statistical fact that in 1960 Korean cities comprised only 28 per cent of the population. By 1980, however, this percentage had increased to more than 57 per cent. Seoul, the nation's largest city, alone accounted for over 22 per cent of the total population in 1980.

The rapid migration of rural people, seeking economic opportunities in the urban sector, has resulted in an imbalance in the distribution of labour between the rural and urban areas and consequent aggravation of the already existing disparities in the development of the two sectors. Another problem arising from rapid urbanisation was the heavy strain on schools, hospitals, housing, transport, recreational facilities, water supply, sanitation and other urban facilities.

It may be appropriate to note here that the past improvements in social welfare could be attributed not so much to an expansion of social welfare expenditures *per se*, as to development strategies that resulted in expanding employment opportunities and to increased level of income. Between 1963 and 1980, in terms of both share in total expenditure and absolute level, government spending on social welfare remained relatively low by international standards. Throughout this period social welfare policy received for the most part a low priority from decision-makers in the Government. Growth and efficiency had remained the Government's primary objective.

In the light of the growing income inequality and the widening disparity between certain segments of society, social welfare became an increasingly important issue in the late 1970s. Motivated by social pressures, such as urbanisation and rising expectations of the educated population, the Government consequently took measures to improve social welfare, particularly through the implementation of various health and social security programmes.

One of the important social welfare policy initiatives taken by the Government in the second half of the 1970s was the enactment of the Medical Insurance Law on 22 December 1976. During the mid-1970s the Government identified health as a priority area, and health became a focal point of the social development component of the Fourth Five-Year Development Plan (1977-81). Its significance to socio-economic development was the recognition that health is a fourth basic necessity of life along with food, clothing and shelter. Health was also considered as contributing importantly to national economic progress through the improvement of the quality and productivity of the labour force by reducing absenteeism, debility and disability of individual workers.

The background of the health insurance programme

With increasing emphasis on equity and social welfare, the Republic of Korea witnessed a major change in concern about the health of the people during the second half of the 1970s. There was a growing awareness among policy-makers and economic planners of health as a critical element of development strategies for basic needs. The President stressed the importance of expanding the accessibility of health care services to the underprivileged people, by stating that health care is the "fourth basic necessity of life".

Thus the Fourth Five-Year Plan began to place increasing emphasis on equity and on development in the health sector, and this represented a significant departure from the previous five-year plans, which had assigned lopsided priority to the achievement of rapid economic growth as a primary objective. The growing emphasis on health was also manifested in a five-year health sector loan agreement signed between the Government of the Republic of Korea and the United States Agency for International Development in September 1975. One of the major purposes of this agreement was to strengthen the capability of the Government to plan, implement and evaluate a low-cost health delivery scheme directed primarily toward under-served communities.

For the first time, the Republic of Korea became actively engaged in major planning aimed at improving the organisation, delivery and financing of health care services. A new health development strategy was incorporated in the creation of a tripartite body made up of the National Health Council, the National Health Secretariat in the Korea Development Institute and the Korea Health Development Institute. The ultimate objective of these sector-planning efforts was to provide access to adequate medical care for the population, regardless of income, age or place of residence. A related objective was the provision of quality health care with reasonable efficiency.

During this period there was also a major change in the focus of world-wide concerns about health in developing countries. This change was manifested in a resolution adopted by the 1977 World Health Assembly that the main social target in the coming decades should be "attainment by the citizens of the world by the year 2000 of a level of health that will permit them to lead a socially and economically productive life". The 1978 Alma-Ata Conference on Primary Health Care also underscored the change in health perspectives by declaring that "primary health care is the key to attaining this target as part of development in the spirit of social justice".

It was in this spirit and context that the Medical Insurance Law of 1976 was adopted and the primary health care approach was introduced. Community health programmes, the Korean version of primary health care, were developed and tested by the Korea Health Development Institute in the mid-1970s and subsequently incorporated into the national health plan. Major features of this innovative programme included the improved coverage of basic health services, the mobilisation of financial resources, the deployment of middle-level health workers, the maximum utilisation of public health centres and posts, and community participation. Implementation of primary health care programmes called for a major reorientation of policies and perspectives in the way health is perceived, protected, promoted and delivered.

In its coverage and impact, the new medical insurance law represented the first comprehensive social security programme in the nation. Its enactment was thus a landmark in the history of the country's social legislation. The beginning of the fragmented social insurance medical programmes, however, can be traced back to the early 1960s, with the adoption of the Medical Insurance Law in 1963.

The 1963 Law was the basis for operating 11 government-sponsored pilot insurance programmes, four of which were employer-sponsored insurance associations while the remaining seven were non-profit community insurance co-operatives primarily for self-employed workers. As of 1976, only 15,300 workers and 51,700 dependants in 11 groups were covered by this insurance scheme. In addition, there were 17 other medical insurance associations operated independently without government approval and subsidies. These 17 associations had a total of over 160,000 members.

On 22 December 1976, however, the Government enacted Law No. 2942 which drastically amended the original Medical Insurance Law of 1963. In order to make use of the available medical resources, the Law established a new social insurance scheme aimed at pooling the resources of a wide segment of the population. The ultimate objective of this programme is to improve national health and enhance social security by facilitating access to medical care in the event of illness, injury, childbirth or death. With the enactment of this Law, the Government of the Republic of Korea has taken a major step towards enhancing the welfare and the productivity of its people. The Law itself provided the promise of further improvement.

The new Law established a two-part medical insurance programme including: (i) a plan requiring employers with 500 workers or more to offer specified medical insurance for their employees and their dependants (employed workers); and (ii) a voluntary community-based health insurance plan providing medical insurance for all others (mainly self-employed workers). The insurance programme is administered by the health insurance associations established for the workers in enterprises and industrial parks, and in the case of self-employed and others by the administrative districts of countries, cities and towns.

Mobilising economic support for the health sector

The absence of a well-co-ordinated mechanism for planning and allocating resources in the health sector attested to the low priority that this sector had been accorded in previous development plans. One important consequence was that the provision of health services depended too heavily on private organisations, which made investments of scarce health resources without specific reference to the socio-economic development goals and an overall national health development strategy. This meant that investment projects were not assigned priorities in accord with their expected benefits and impact on the equity.

At the same time, fragmentation of responsibilities and authority among government ministries and agencies has often resulted in inefficiency and waste in the management of health services. The Ministry of Health and Social Affairs has responsibility for broad health policy co-ordination throughout the nation. The programmes that substantially affect health, however, are scattered over several other ministries as well. The Ministry of Home Affairs, for instance, is responsible for financing and operating a network of provincial hospitals and health centres. The Ministry of Education has the administrative responsibility for universities and other institutions training medical professionals and other types of health manpower. Finally, the Economic Planning Board has the overall responsibility with respect to national development planning and resources allocation policies for the nation.

To provide a co-ordinating mechanism among the health programmes of the various operating agencies, the National Health Council was established in 1976 at the cabinet level. The membership of this council was composed of the Deputy Prime Minister (concurrently Minister of the Economic Planning Board) as chairman, the Minister of Health and Social Affairs as vice-chairman, the Minister of Home Affairs, the Minister of Education and three private citizens. The council was to provide an effective forum for policy co-ordination, resource allocation decisions and implementation for the health sector.

The National Health Secretariat was set up within the Korea Development Institute (NHS/KDI), which is operated under the aegis of the Economic Planning Board, to provide inputs and resources to the council for sound planning and operation. The Korea Health Development Institute (KHDI) was also created under the supervision of the Ministry of Health and Social Affairs to develop low-cost health delivery schemes and to engage in micro-level health planning research.

Although the National Health Council has been criticised as being inactive or indifferent in the face of mounting health problems, the institutional set-up creating a tripartite body itself has produced some positive end results.

The institution provided a new opportunity for the NHS/KDI staff economists to participate in a wide range of inter-disciplinary research dealing with critical health policy issues and to interact with health professionals in the academic community, medical organisations and the Ministry of Health and Social Affairs officials at the working level, through various activities of the NHS/KDI. The active involvement of the NHS/KDI in inter-disciplinary health research and policy planning has not only facilitated co-operation (which had previously been lacking) between researchers and policy-makers, and between economic planners and health planners, but also made a significant contribution to the design and implementation of a number of important health policy measures.

With regard to the delivery capacity of the health system, the nation's health resources were unduly concentrated in the urban sector. It was estimated that in the mid-1970s almost 87 per cent of physicians and 90 per cent of medical facilities were concentrated in urban areas, although only about half of the nation's population resided in those areas. Furthermore, there was little organised delivery of primary health care services within the system. Too much was being spent on curative care in expensive hospitals in urban centres, while health care services in the rural areas were totally inadequate. The direction of expansion in the health delivery system has been in the traditional pattern of emphasising a high degree of specialisation in the training of physicians, thus limiting the number of physicians available for primary care.

Although innovations of less traditional, low-cost alternative approaches to the delivery of health services to the rural and urban poor have been widely discussed, their use has been substantially limited because of the influence of organisations with vested interests in preserving the traditional methods. There was, however, a growing feeling in the mid-1970s that the climate at the time was suitable for the gradual introduction of these innovative methods. Thus the Korea Health Development Institute was created in April 1976 to demonstrate and test these innovative approaches, often referred to as a community-based primary health care system.

The basic purpose of the Korea Health Development Institute demonstration project was to improve the delivery capacity of the public rural health system so that it would provide curative as well as preventive and promotional services to at least two-thirds of the rural residents. Such a system made maximum use of new types of health personnel, such as community health practitioners (CHP), community health aides, and village health agents, who would operate at different levels in the community.

Throughout the mid-1970s much attention was focused on the rising costs of medical care and their effects on consumers and on society as a whole. The cost of medical care has been rising rapidly, and this dramatic increase has placed such care beyond the reach of many individuals, especially rural residents and disadvantaged groups in the urban sector. The cost barrier has thus emerged as one of the major factors in preventing a large segment of the population from receiving adequate medical care. The role of Government in financing health care was very limited, as there were no commercial insurance carriers. Direct spending by individual consumers was the major source of financing health services.

Therefore, it was not surprising at the time to find a consensus that a medical insurance scheme would play an important role in overcoming the cost barrier through spreading the risks and the pooling of financial resources, and that it was necessary to introduce such a scheme without further delay. The passage of the Medical Insurance Law on 26 December 1976 was the major accomplishment of the Fourth Five-Year Plan so far as social development programmes were concerned. The objectives of the Law were to improve national health and to enhance social security by

Republic of Korea

facilitating access to medical care and eliminating the financial hardship of large medical care bills.

One of the important advantages of a medical insurance system is that it ensures the flow of financial resources to the health sector and channels them into organised services. Hence a medical insurance programme, even if the coverage is initially limited to a small segment of the population, has the effect of mobilising additional financial resources for the whole health sector. By facilitating access to health care services, medical insurance can have, over the long run, a favourable effect on its scope, on the type of financial mechanism, and on the manner in which the medical benefits are provided.

Development of health insurance programmes, 1977-87

The enactment of the Medical Insurance Law on 22 December 1976 has been one of the early efforts in the Republic of Korea's social security development. Since its implementation on 1 July 1977, the medical insurance scheme has played an important role in promoting health care to meet more effectively the health needs of the growing population.

As stated earlier, one of the important advantages of a medical insurance system is that it ensures the flow of funds to the health sector and channels them into organised services; therefore, a medical insurance programme, even if the coverage is initially limited to a small group of population, has the effect of mobilising additional financial resources for the whole health sector. Obviously much depends on its scope, on the type of financing mechanism, and on the manner in which the medical benefits are provided.

Although a latecomer in the field of social security health insurance, the Republic of Korea is one of few developing countries where the extension of population coverage has progressed at an exceptionally rapid rate. On 1 July 1977 the country embarked on a new medical insurance programme requiring employers with 500 or more workers to provide specified medical insurance benefits to their employees and dependants. The new scheme allowed firms employing fewer than 500 workers to participate on a voluntary basis. The scheme also included a voluntary-based plan providing medical insurance for all others.

The compulsory coverage requirement was later expanded to include firms with at least 300 workers in 1979, 100 workers in 1981, 16 workers in 1983, and finally all firms with at least five workers in 1988. In addition, government legislation in 1979 made medical insurance compulsory for all government officials and teachers and workers in all educational institutions. In 1980 further legislation extended coverage to all military dependants and in 1981 to pension recipients and their dependants.

In 1981 the Government undertook experimental medical insurance programmes for farmers and other self-employed persons in three designated areas. Three additional areas were brought into experimental programmes in 1982. Another development in 1982 was the organisation of medical insurance programmes for persons engaged in some self-employed occupations such as barbers, taxi drivers and artists. The regional medical insurance scheme was expanded in 1988 to cover self-employed workers in all rural areas.

As a result of these modifications, health insurance coverage expanded dramatically over the past 11 years. The number of persons covered by medical insurance increased from only 3.2 million in 1977, the year the scheme was introduced, to 28.3 million in 1988. While only 8.8 per cent of the population had medical insurance in 1977, over 66 per cent were covered by 1988.

Presently, the medical insurance scheme in the Republic of Korea is broadly divided into four major types. They are:

(i) employed workers in industrial and commercial enterprises (53.2 per cent of total coverage);

(ii) government officials and private school teachers (15.4 per cent);

(iii) self-employed occupational groups such as hairdressers, novelists, and medical doctors (4.1 per cent); and

(iv) self-employed persons in rural areas (27.3 per cent).

In 1977 the Government introduced the Medical Assistance Programme which organised medical services for those unable to pay for medical care services. At present, over 4 million persons, or some 10 per cent of the population, are covered by this programme. Recipients of benefit under this programme are divided into those unable to work and persons with low income. Persons unable to work include those aged 65 and over, children and adolescents below 18 years of age, pregnant women, the disabled, the physically handicapped and other relief recipients under the Livelihood Protection Law of 1961. Low-income persons include those whose income is below the minimum cost of living and are annually identified by local government authorities.

Under this programme all medical services are provided free of charge to those below the poverty line or unable to work. For those low-income persons who are able to work, the programme pays for 50 per cent on hospital costs and all out-patient expenses. Moreover, the Government provides interest-free loans for the remaining 50 per cent of costs. This provision of low-cost or free health services is extremely important in upgrading the status of the poor in view of the fact that high medical costs caused by illness in the family has been a major reason for the perpetuation of poverty and for the fall of middle-income persons to the poverty level.

The total number of persons covered by the social security health care programme, including both the medical insurance and medical assistance programmes, reached 32.6 million in 1988. This number represents 76.5 per cent of the population, compared with a 14.5 per cent coverage in 1977. Thus, three out of four persons are now covered by some kind of government-sponsored health care programme. It is expected that the goal of universal coverage will be achieved by the middle of 1989 when self-employed workers in urban areas and all employed workers are protected by the social security health care programmes.

The growth in the number of persons entitled to medical insurance benefits is reflected in increased revenues and benefit payments of the system, but the disproportionate increase in the latter also reflects sharply increased utilisation rates and increased treatment costs since 1977. For medical insurance programmes covering employed workers in private industries and government officials and private school teachers, total expenditure increased at a much faster rate than revenue, so that expenditure as a proportion of revenue rose sharply, from 43.1 per cent in 1977-78 to 79.5 per cent in 1986. During the 1978-86 period revenue rose 15.3 times, from less than 50 billion won in 1978 to over 746 billion won in 1986. In comparison, expenditure grew 23.5 times, from 25 billion won to 593 billion won over the same period.

Expenditure for medical care benefits usually accounts for roughly 90 per cent of total expenditure. During the entire period between 1977 and 1986 a total fund of about 3,746 billion won has been mobilised through the medical insurance system, and approximately 2,948 billion of that amount has been channelled into organised medical services to improve the health and welfare of the people.

Lessons from the Republic of Korea's experiences

The experience of the Republic of Korea clearly shows that even if rapid growth of the economy is achieved and the overall standard of living is improved, a point is soon reached when it becomes necessary to increase emphasis on social development. By then, the growth of inequities in income and wealth, in conjunction with rising aspirations throughout society, accounts for many of the frictions and instabilities with which social development planning must cope. The Government, as a dominant force in Korean society, is able to influence the ownership of wealth and the pattern of income distribution. This ability could be used to formulate policies leading to more widely based participation in the prosperity than society has been enjoying.

There is a growing awareness among economists and planners that the goals of equity and social justice could be better achieved if more social development policies were enunciated from a broader perspective to parallel and complement economic growth. These policies, translated into well-conceived, concrete programmes and services, could then be incorporated into national development plans.

In health there is a need for a rational plan based on the equitable distribution of health services and the efficient utilisation of health resources.

Health has been identified by the Government as a priority area, and it has been a focal point of the social welfare component of development plans since the Fourth Five-Year Plan (1977-81). Its importance to socio-economic development is indicated by the recognition the development plan gave to health as a fourth basic necessity of life. Government investment in health has been relatively small, and private medical care has been beyond the means of most Koreans. The resulting situation has been further aggravated by a shortage and maldistribution of medical facilities and personnnel. The social security health insurance scheme has been a major policy instrument for overcoming the cost barrier, which prevented a substantial number of people from receiving adequate medical care. The non-contributory medical assistance programme has played an important role in promoting medical care to meet more effectively the health needs of the underprivileged group. In addition, the primary health care programme substantially increased the accessibility and use of modern health facilities in rural areas.

KUWAIT

DEMOGRAPHY AND HEALTH DATA

The population of Kuwait was close to 2 million in 1987, with half of this population registered as foreign residents. It is not clear therefore to what extent the average annual population growth rate of 4.4 per cent for the period 1980-86 represents a real population growth, or an increased influex of foreign residents. By 1987, 95 per cent of the population were classified as residing in urban areas. The per capita GNP was US$13,890 in that year.

The infant mortality rate was 19 and the child mortality rate 23 deaths per 1,000 live births. For the preceding six years there had been an average annual reduction in child mortality of 5.43 per cent. Life expectancy in 1987 was 73 years. In 1985, 76 per cent of adult males and 63 per cent of adult females were literate.

HEALTH SERVICES

The Ministry of Health has developed a network of health care facilities, based on community clinics for every 40,000, polyclinics for 100,000 and a regional hospital for every 500,000 residents. One tertiary care hospital serves as a national referral centre and patients who require more sophisticated care are sent abroad. The government services are provided free of charge to all residents. The Government spent 7.1 per cent of its total expenditure on health in 1986, and given the rise in health care costs, this is increasingly considered a heavy burden on the Ministry of Health.

HEALTH INSURANCE

The Government of Kuwait is reviewing proposals for the creation of a Health Insurance Institute to administer health care through a compulsory social security scheme. The main purpose is to find other and more stable sources of funds for health care. It is also generally felt that the current free government system is abused and that a contributory mechanism would be preferable. The problems now being tackled include how the health services could be improved, who will be responsible for the collection of contributions, what effect will the instability of at least half the population have on regular contributions, and how the income should be invested.

MALAYSIA

DEMOGRAPHY AND HEALTH DATA

Malaysia had a population of 16.2 million in 1987, with a slightly increasing average annual growth rate of 2.7 per cent for the preceding six years. In 1987, 40 per cent of the population resided in urban areas. In that year the per capita GNP was US$1,830, with the average annual growth in GNP at 1.1 per cent between 1980 and 1986.

In 1987 the infant mortality rate was 24 and the child mortality rate 33 deaths per 1,000 live births. The average annual reduction in child mortality between 1980 and 1987 was 3.39 per cent. At the end of that period life expectancy at birth was 70 years. Adult literacy was 81 per cent for males and 66 per cent for females in 1985.

HEALTH SERVICES

The Government provides most health services in Malaysia, mainly through the Ministry of Health but also through health care delivery networks of the Ministries of Defence, Home Affairs and Education. A referral system has been developed, beginning with the rural dispensaries and health centres, through cottage, district and regional general hospitals and ending with the National Referral Centre General Hospital in Kuala Lumpur. The scope of functions of each level has been defined by the Ministry of Health to ensure uniformity of available services and avoid duplication.

All the government services provided at the rural level are currently free of charge, and hospital patients pay minimal charges, with exemptions for the medically indigent. The private sector has been expanding in recent years, from mainly ambulatory care in the cities to services in the rural areas and to in-patient facilities for general, maternity and nursing care in state capitals. Private employers also provide services for their employees, outside the government network. Traditional healers still play a significant role, with over 1,000 Chinese and 2,000 Malay practitioners occupied full time and some 20,000 part time among the different types of traditional healers in urban and rural areas.

In 1984 the Government spent 1.8 per cent of its expenditure on health care. This source accounts for about 76 per cent of all health care expenditure with the rest coming from the private sector.

HEALTH INSURANCE

The chapter on Malaysia is mainly a description of the planning for social security health insurance. These remarks are extracted from a report presented at the Seminar by Dr. James Jeffers, Asian Development Bank Consultant to the National Health Security Fund Feasibility Study for the Government of Malaysia.

Background of the study

The Fourth Malaysia Mid-Term Plan Review called for a study of ways in which the health services delivery system could be made more efficient and equitable, and to look into the possibility of developing an alternative way of financing health services delivery in Malaysia. The Government of Malaysia commissioned the Health Sector Financing Study with the financial support of the Asian Development Bank. This study was completed by September 1985 and was reviewed favourably by the National Development Planning Council (NDPC).

The most significant recommendation of the study in terms of its impact on the future of the financing of the health sector was the proposed merger of SOCSO and the EPF in the formation of an agency that would establish the National Health Security Fund (NHSF). The NHSF would be responsible for developing a national health insurance programme that would finance the delivery of curative medical services (including both in-patient and out-patient services) while at the same time shifting the burden of finance away from government towards consumers who can afford to pay directly for curative medical services.

The Government of Malaysia then commissioned the assessment of the feasibility of the NHSF with the financial support of the Asian Development Bank. This study was conducted by the Government of Malaysia in two phases with financial support from the Asian Development Bank. Phase I was initiated in April 1987 and the analysis showed that the NHSF is a feasible concept in the context of Malaysia; however, time and resources available were not sufficient to address all issues pertaining to the form of organisation of the NHSF most appropriate for implementation. Phase II was initiated on 22 September 1988 and was designed to refine the analysis undertaken during Phase I, develop a privatisation option as an alternative organisational form of the NHSF, provide more details concerning all optional organisational forms worthy of consideration, and to develop a strategy for implementation of the NHSF.

Objectives of the NHSF

The NHSF was planned to meet specific objectives. The NHSF would reduce further government expenditure and commitment by establishing a national health insurance programme under which those who can afford would be required to pay insurance premiums regularly and co-payments at the point of service to finance the operating costs involved in the provision of curative medical services. Sources of finance would include Government, and private sector employers and employees, and the self-employed who can afford to pay for services. The Government would continue to subsidise the receipt of curative medical services received by the poor and public sector employees following historical precedents, and would continue to finance public medical sector development costs, as well as the costs of medical education and training and illness prevention and health promotion programmes.

The savings to the Government as a result of establishing the NHSF would be spent on rapidly accelerating the development of public health sector infrastructure in order to increase accessibility to services. In addition, savings would be spent on improving the quality of health services delivered. The NHSF, in co-operation with the MOH, would also develop and implement a certificate of need and right to practise programmes designed to equalise access to privately delivered curative medical services throughout the nation.

The NHSF would reduce inequity by extending access of the entire population to medical services rendered in the private medical sector which is currently restricted to rich and higher-income segments of the population. Efforts will be made to reduce the tendency of private providers to be located only in large urban areas of the nation.

The NHSF would develop and implement programmes to contain costs and assure reasonable quality of services. In co-operation with the MOH, the NHSF would develop and implement utilisation review and quality assurance programmes designed to contain costs and to assure that a reasonable standard of medical care is maintained in the nation. Introduction of new and expensive medical technologies would be allowed, based on considerations of their effectiveness relative to cost, and the capacity of the nation to afford their introduction. Every effort will be made to eliminate duplication and waste of medical resources.

In addition, NHSF would "harness" the private and public medical sectors together in attaining the health development goals of the nation. Under the NHSF private providers would be eligible to receive the same rate of reimbursement for delivering the same medical service of equal quality, with adequate provision for a "fair profit". The private and public medical sectors would be encouraged to work together in planning the future development of the health sector; and would share facilities, manpower and other resources in delivering the maximum quantity of quality medical services at minimum costs.

Experience rating and community rating

The report presented by Dr. Jeffers deals extensively with the concepts of experience rating and community rating. As it relates to the optimal solutions in planning a national health insurance system in a developing country, this section of the report is particularly important.

Experience rating is a concept in group insurance that is similar to the concept of individual equity in individual insurance. Experience rating as a generalisation of the concept of individual equity is often applied to group insurance. Under experience rating each group is treated like an individual. The premiums charged to the group are based on the actual past experience of the group. If the group is small, its experience is combined with that of other small groups in order to get enough experience so that statistical fluctuations are minimal. If the group is sufficiently large, the premiums for the group are based solely on the experience of the group. Just as with individual premiums, some groups would experience a low cost and thus be charged a low premium. These groups would be those with young healthy workers in non-hazardous occupations. Other groups would have high cost experience and be charged a high premium. These groups would be those with older workers in hazardous occupations.

The financing philosophy of group insurance applies more readily to social insurance than does that of individual insurance. The premiums charged in social insurance programmes are based on the experience of the programme. Under the NHSF programme, there are four large groups that could be treated somewhat differently: government employees, private employees, the self-employed, and the poor (including in each case their respective family members). If the NHSF programme were to use the experience rating financing philosophy, each of these groups would be charged a separate premium that, in each case, was based solely on the experience of that group. This would not make a great deal of sense in the case of the poor who by definition can not afford to pay for services. Thus there is a need for a subsidy to be paid on behalf of all who cannot pay a premium that would be adequate to defray the costs of their probable utilisation of medical services.

The truly poor must be subsidised directly by a third party, usually the Government. However, given the rather wide distribution of after-tax income that exists in a society in which income tax is not a very large portion of total revenues available to the Government, the latter is unable to subsidise all the people who are not poor and therefore can afford to pay for at least part of costs of the services that they need, but cannot meet all the finance of needed health services. Thus a means must be devised to accomplish "cross subsidisation" within private sector population segments which are above the poverty line, i.e. not poor.

The most equitable way to achieve the needed cross subsidisation is to base premium payments on a percentage of income, with or without a ceiling on the base of income on which premiums are paid, depending on the total costs of medical services that are needed by the aggregate society. Because cross subsidisation is required, high-income people end up paying for some of the services consumed by lower-income people, all of whom are paying something for the health services that they consume, except those who genuinely are too poor to pay. Many higher-income people, however, tend to think in terms of individual equity; therefore they resent paying for part of the services of others and would refuse to do so if their contributions were solicited on a voluntary basis. In view of this, premium subscriptions in the case of national health insurance programmes which involve substantial cross subsidisation within private sector contributors must be compulsory, and some element of government subsidy is required to make the programme generally acceptable.

The implication of building cross subsidisation into the premium structure as a result of basing premiums on income and not on calculations of expected utilisation by various population groups is that risk management classification has shifted from an experience rating approach to a "community rating" approach. Community rating is like experience rating in that it uses past experience to set premium rates. Under community rating, however, the experience of groups is aggregated, and the premium base of all groups is combined, so that everyone is charged virtually the same rate, thus providing for cross subsidy.

When designing a national social health insurance programme involving universal entitlement, the community that must be "rated" in order to establish an appropriate premium is the entire population. Thus the national experience in the consumption of health services, restricted to curative medical services in the case of Malaysia, must be aggregated and projected forward, and premium rates to be charged in the case of those above the poverty line must be set in terms of an equal percentage of income. Approaching matters in this way achieves a measure of social equity (everyone pays the same percentage of income as a premium), and allows for adequate cross subsidisation to ensure solvency without excessive government subsidy.

From this perspective, a compulsory social insurance programme can not place much emphasis on the concepts of individual equity or experience rating. Because of its compulsory nature, the concept of community rating thought of as the nation's population as a whole generally is the appropriate approach.

Existing maldistributions in medical resources geographically lead to variations in actual health utilisation and costs. The consequent medical care cost experience of individual regions and states or even smaller subdivisions of the nation can be taken into account and reflected in charging different premium rates to members of the private sector. The premium rates, however, must remain as levies of a percentage of income. In addition, when weighted by the percentage of projected national medical services costs, the weighted average percentage premium must equal the "unweighted national average" in the interests of maintaining solvency of the programme.

Thus under the NHSF, if premium rates vary by region or state, it does not mean that these groups have no concern for the rest of the nation, or that their members are not part of a cross-subsidising scheme. The situation would reflect a refinement of the concept of social equity, i.e. high-income earners subsidise low-income earners in the NHSF scheme. High-income earners in states and regions who currently do have as much access to consume medical services as is true on average, should not "subsidise" as much as high-income individuals enjoying greater access to services living elsewhere.

There may be merit and/or necessity for some groups, i.e. civil servants, to be kept separate, and have their expenses and premiums be accounted for separately and pay less for the package of benefits they receive. At first sight this may be seen to be very unfair. More correctly, however, it reflects a "topping up" of the basic package of benefits by their employer, namely the Government, and that same employer, the Government, is subsidising the rest of the nation in many other ways. A separate accounting for Public Sector Employees (PSE) under the NHSF is not as unfair as it may seem at first inspection when it is realised that the Government assumes the entire responsibility for paying the costs of all the services utilised by the poor which lowers the premium that would have to be paid by the private sector, if they had to pay for the costs of the poor as well.

Separate accounting could lead to unequal premiums, with the civil servants paying less on the average than private sector contributors. But it must be remembered that any employer has a right to top-up the benefits or subsidise the benefits received by their employees, and this will occur in the private sector as well.

Further, it must be emphasised that in the NHSF the costs that are being financed are the operating costs of curative medical services provision only. The Government will continue to pay for the costs of development of the public system infrastructure, and the bulk of the costs of illness and disease prevention, training and health promotion.

Recognising this, the NHSF with all the underlying elements of government subsidisation, represents a programme that adheres to the philosophy of social adequacy, and which in the main follows the community rating approach, with the nation as a whole constituting the community. Given the large element of government subsidy constituting roughly a third of the entire health bill of the nation, health care in Malaysia will remain as an outstanding "value for the dollar".

The NHSF is designed to be a truly national health insurance programme. The proposed programme can properly be called a Nation Health *Insurance* Programme, as opposed to just a National Health Programme, because it contains the following distinguishing features:

(a) coverage, although mandatory and universal, is prescribed by law and requires a contribution either by or on behalf of each individual in order to attain insured status;
(b) benefits are enumerated and provided as a right by law to each insured individual;
(c) the financing of the programme is entirely out of the contributions, and interest thereon, paid by or on behalf of the insured population;
(d) the financial transactions of the programme are made through a separate fund with no other purpose than to collect the specified contributions of the insured and to pay the specified benefits and associated administrative expenses.

Because the only source of funds to provide for the benefits prescribed to the insured population is the NHSF, it is imperative for the continued functioning of the programme that the fund remain solvent. A fund of sufficient size and adequate income to ensure its solvency is said to be "actuarially sound". A fund with more than sufficient reserves and a significant excess of projected income over projected outgo is said to be in "actuarial surplus".

A fund with insufficient reserves or inadequate projected income to insure its continued solvency is said to be actuarially unsound or to be in "actuarial deficit". A fund with the appropriate level of reserves and with projected income and projected outgo sufficiently matched is said to be in "close actuarial balance". It is the purpose of this report to determine the financing necessary to place the NHSF in close actuarial balance.

One note of caution concerning implementation. It is imperative not to divide up occupational groups or subgroups (industrial, agricultural, commercial, etc.) and use experience rating premium setting.

The costs of the basic package of medical services (illness prevention, health promotion, development, training, and overall health administration costs are not to be financed by the NHSF) were projected under best case, most realistic, and worst case scenarios involving differing assumptions concerning probable rates of utilisation, incremental costs of medical technologies, "induced demand" and other factors, all in connection with the possible effects of constructive policy interventions such as greater restriction over hospital admission rates, greater use of day care centres, etc.

Conclusions and probable impact

It is probable that health care costs will rise over time due to secular factors in Malaysia, but not much due to the introduction of the NHSF. In fact, it is most likely that the rate of escalation in medical costs will be ameliorated due to introduction of certificate of need, greater control over the rate of introduction of new but expensive medical technologies and utilisation review. The NHSF is a package of constructive interventions designed to improve many aspects of health services in Malaysia. Security enhancement, improved equity and cost containment are the major goals of the NHSF.

Quality of care should become more uniform and will rise due to the continued if not accelerated development of quality assurance programmes, and the greater scrutiny of medical inputs and outcomes that will accompany the introduction of the NHSF. Both the public and the private medical sectors, however, will have to work together in order for this to occur.

Final consumer prices of non-health commodities will increase very little as the result of the NHSF. There is no evidence that Malaysia's export position will be harmed in the international market-place as the result of the payment of premiums.

It is anticipated that the balance of service provision between the private and the public medical sectors will change somewhat, more in favour of the private medical sector (3 to 5 percentage points), and more on the out-patient side than on the in-patient side. To the extent that the private medical sector is able and willing to provide services of equal quality at the same prices or less than costs in the public sector, this is all for the good, except for the matter of the distribution of medical resources. Strong efforts must be made to equalise incomes in the public and private medical sector and to encourage the private medical sector to shoulder a bigger burden of achieving social equity in access to services than has been demonstrated in the past.

From this description it is clear that the NHSF is more than just a health financing scheme. It is truly a national health insurance scheme that offers security to individuals in terms of accessibility to services, regardless of where they live and of their economic circumstances. The approach appears feasible in all respects, but the issue of the appropriate organisational form remains to be resolved, as well as many issues of implementation.

MYANMAR

DEMOGRAPHY AND HEALTH DATA

In 1987 Myanmar had a population of 39 million, with a declining average annual growth rate of 2 per cent from 1980-86. By 1987, 24 per cent of the population were in urban areas. The per capita GNP was US$200 in 1986, with average annual growth of 2.7 per cent for the six previous years.

The infant mortality rate was 71 and the child mortality rate 98 deaths per 1,000 live births in 1987, with an average annual reduction in this rate of 2.62 per cent between 1980 and 1987. Life expectancy was 61 years in 1987. Recent literacy figures were not available, but the rates were over 85 per cent for males and 60 per cent for females in the 1970s.

HEALTH SERVICES

Health services are generally provided by the Ministry of Health, mainly through hospital based services. The over 600 hospitals serving peripheral townships range from station hospitals, through hospitals with 16, 25, 50 , 100, 150 and 200 beds. A referral system has been introduced between these facilities and the general and specialised hospitals at the central level. The Ministry of Health also operates primary care rural health centres, urban health centres and maternal and child health centres. All these services are free, but substantial funds for the construction of these facilities come from the community, which also provides voluntary health workers. Several other Ministries provide health services: the Ministry of Labour provides care to covered workers in the Social Security Board Clinics, and the Ministries of Transport and Communications, Mines and Industry operate clinics through quasi-public corporations for their workers and families. The clinics operated for its workers by the Ministry of Co-operatives also provides services to the general public on a payment basis. In the private sector over 5,500 general practice clinics are owned by about half the practising doctors in the country. There are no private hospitals in Myanmar. Under the current structure the public sector covers only 40 per cent of the expenditure on health care, and 60 per cent is borne by private sources.

HEALTH INSURANCE

Social security health insurance was first implemented in Myanmar in 1956, two years after legislation. It established the Social Security Health Insurance System, operated by the Social Security Board under the Department of Labour. Workers in the public and private sectors in enterprises with over five employees are covered, and around 407,000 workers are now insured. About 83 per cent of those insured are public sector workers and the rest from private or co-operative enterprises. Dependants and pensioners are not covered.

Implementation has been gradual, by region, beginning with Yangon and Mandalay and now covering 59 other districts. The number of insured persons has doubled over the past decade.

The scheme provides benefits in cash and in kind for the insured workers. The cash benefits include:

— sickness benefit: giving 50 per cent of previous earnings, for up to 26 weeks, with eligibility conditional on 17 weeks of contributions in the last 26 weeks;
— maternity benefit: two-thirds of previous earnings, with a fixed minimum amount, for six weeks before and six weeks after confinement, after 26 weeks of contributions in 52 weeks before the confinement;
— funeral benefit: providing a lump sum, with no qualifying period.

For the insured workers with current coverage, the medical care benefits include:

— general practitioner and specialist physician care for as long as medically necessary;
— hospital care, including room and board and medical care for as long as medically necessary;
— pharmaceuticals and supporting laboratory services without limitation.

For employment injury cases, physiotherapy, prostheses and appliances are also provided by the scheme. Preventive care, such as immunisations against infectious diseases, are not currently covered, as is the case with dental care. There are no patient co-payments for the medical care benefits provided in the scheme.

The method of providing services is a combination of both the direct and indirect method: general practitioner and specialist services are provided in Social Security Clinics, which also provide pharmaceuticals.

There are currently about 85 clinics and five mobile units. Hospital care is given in the one Social Security Hospital, a second hospital is now being constructed, and in Ministry of Health hospitals. The Government hospitals also provide out-patient care.

The funds for the scheme derive mainly from contributions, with employers paying 2 per cent of payroll and workers contributing approximately 1 per cent of wages, according to six wage classes but with a defined ceiling. The State subsidises the scheme with an annual grant of approximately 1 per cent of total wages.

The scheme is administered by the tripartite Social Security Board, in the Ministry of Labour, and headed by a Chairman who serves as Chief Executive Officer. In addition to administrative personnel, the Board employed 132 doctors and 424 other health care staff at the beginning of 1989. The scheme co-operates with the Ministry of Health in overall planning and in the delivery of services, and all health care activities are supervised by the Ministry of Health. The general goals are codified in the Socialist Party's development programme.

NEPAL

DEMOGRAPHY AND HEALTH DATA

Nepal had a population of 17.8 million in 1987, with a fairly steady average annual growth rate of 2.6 per cent in the preceding six years. Only 9 per cent of the population were in urban areas. The majority of the population live in mountainous areas, which account for 63 per cent of the total land area of the country. The per capita GNP was US$150 in 1987, after an average annual growth of 0.8 per cent in the period from 1980 to 1986.

The infant mortality was 129 and the child mortality rate 200 deaths per 1,000 live births in 1987, with an average annual reduction of 1.48 per cent in the latter in the previous six years. Life expectancy was 52 years in 1987. Adult literacy was 39 per cent for males and 12 per cent for females in 1985.

HEALTH SERVICES

Health services are provided by the Government, which now operates over 820 health posts in the 75 districts, 20 health centres, 52 district hospitals with between 15-25 beds, eight zonal hospitals with 50-100 beds, one regional hospital with 150 beds and five central hospitals with over 300 beds. An additonal 24 mission hospitals supplement this network but there are still 18 districts without any in-patient facilities. Not all the health posts provide basic primary care, and the current plan is to establish a sub-health post at the village level, as an extension of the health post, to provide minimal medical care, particularly maternal and child care. Nepal has a large number of traditional healers, estimated at about 400,000, or one practitioner for every 20 persons in the country.

In 1987 the Government allocated 5 per cent of its budget for health care, and this was the major source of financing for current costs. Foreign assistance provided more than half the resources for the development of health care facilities. User charges in hospitals are limited to a small number of hospitals, some of which also operate paying beds.

HEALTH INSURANCE

Nepal has no social security health insurance system, but an interesting voluntary scheme has developed over the past decade. In 1978 the United Mission to Nepal initiated a health insurance scheme in five health posts in one district. Although it was set up to provide cost recovery for drugs in excess of the government contribution to the health post, the scheme entitles members to free services and drugs at the health post, free registration to the district hospital, first priority to see a physician at the hospital and a deduction from any out-patient and in-patient hospital fees. Irregularity in the payment of premiums and reluctance of the health post committees to increase the premiums over time have prevented these schemes from becoming self-sufficient. However, the principle is seen as being workable, and as having future potential in Nepal.

PAKISTAN

DEMOGRAPHY AND HEALTH DATA

The population of Pakistan reached 111 million in 1987, following a steady average annual increase of 3.1 per cent over the preceding six years. Thirty-one per cent of the population reside in urban areas. The per capita GNP was US$350, with an average annual growth of 3.4 per cent over the period 1980-86.

In 1987 the infant mortality rate was 110 and the child mortality rate 169 deaths per 1,000 live births, with an average annual decrease of 1.81 per cent since 1980. Life expectancy was 58 years in 1987. The adult literacy rate was 40 per cent for males and 19 per cent for females in 1985.

HEALTH SERVICES

Most health services are provided by the Government's public health system, operated by the Federal Ministry of Health, Provincial Health Departments and local agencies. The services provided range from basic health units, sub-centres, maternal and child centres, dispensaries, rural health centres and hospitals. The community network is supplemented by some 12,300 private traditional birth attendants' clinics, and about 15 per cent of the hospital beds are privately owned.

In 1986 the Government of Pakistan allocated 1 per cent of its total budget for health. Currently about 50 per cent of total health expenditure is borne by the private sector, paying through user charges for drugs, hospital out-patient and in-patient treatment. Altogether, expenditures on health accounted for 2.8 per cent of the GNP in 1986.

HEALTH INSURANCE

Pakistan has had a social security health insurance scheme for over 20 years. The development of the first scheme and subsequent expansions are described in the following extraction from the papers submitted to the Seminar by the Labour Division of the Ministry of Labour, Manpower and Overseas Pakistanis.

Health insurance in developing countries

General structure of social security health insurance in Pakistan

A social security health insurance scheme was launched in Pakistan through the Provincial Employees' Social Security Ordinance, 1965. After promulgation of this Ordinance, the West Pakistan Employees' Social Security Institution was set up and preparatory work was undertaken. The law was put in actual practice on 1 March 1967 when it was applied to the textile industry in Karachi, Hyderabad and Faisalabad. It was gradually extended to other areas and industries.

The Ordinance provides medical care and cash benefits for secured workers and their dependants in the event of sickness, maternity, employment injury, invalidity or death. Section 2(8) of the Ordinance extends coverage to any person working for at least 24 hours per week in any notified industry, business, undertaking or establishment for wages not exceeding Rs.1,500 per month (US$1 = Rs.18.6) or Rs.60 per day. All types of workers whether employed on permanent, temporary, part-time, casual, seasonal or probationary basis are liable to be covered under the scheme. Although the law provides no limit, for administrative convenience the Ordinance was applied initially to establishments employing 20 or more workers. Later on, the minimum limit for the coverage of establishments was reduced from 20 to ten workers. The Ordinance excludes the following from its purview:

(a) persons in the service of the State, including members of the armed forces, police force and railway servants;

(b) persons employed in any undertaking under the control of any defence organisation or railway administration;

(c) persons in the service of a local council, a municipal committee, a cantonment board or any other local authority;

(d) any person in the service of his father, mother, wife, son or daughter, or of her husband;

(e) any person employed on wages exceeding Rs.1,500 per month or Rs.60 per day.

Health insurance schemes are organised at the provincial level. At present the schemes are in operation in the provinces of Punjab, Sind and North-West Frontier Province. The scheme is likely to be launched in the Baluchistan province in the very near future. At the federal level, the Ministry of Labour, Manpower and Overseas Pakistanis deals with the legislative aspects of the schemes. The provincial Labour Departments control and supervise these schemes in their respective provinces. On the tripartite Governing Bodies of the Social Security Institutions, a representative of the Health Department is included. This helps in co-ordination between social security institutions and provincial health authorities. The Health Departments in the provinces cover the entire population, while the social security institutions cater to the requirements of only a small segment. The facilities available with the social security institutions are not sufficient in terms of hospital beds, laboratories and specialist services. In case of need, they draw upon the facilities available with public health authorities on payment. They also have similar arrangements with the private sector.

The social security administration has a three-tier organisation. At the apex is the provincial government, which determines the broad policy of the institution and exercises control at the highest level. The day-to-day administration of the schemes is entrusted to autonomous Social Security Institutions in the provinces. The general direction of the affairs of the Institution rests in a Governing Body which, with the assistance of the Commissioner of these institutions, exercises all powers and carries out the functions of the institution.

The Governing Body consists of the members to be appointed by the Government through notification, including Provincial Labour Ministers or the Provincial Labour Secretary (Chairman), four persons to represent the provincial government, one each respectively from the Department of Labour, Industries, Health and Finance, three persons to represent employers, three persons to represent insured workers, the Commissioner and the Medical Adviser, ex-officio.

The Governing Body gives approval to the budget of the institution, its annual activity report, and the audit report. The Governing Body also frames regulations. Some of the important regulatory aspects include the following:

(i) the manner in which medical practitioners shall be authorised to give certificates required under any of the provisions of this Ordinance, the form of such certificates and the duties of medical practitioners in this regard;

(ii) occupational diseases which may cause employment injury;

(iii) qualifications for appointment as medical practitioner under this Ordinance;

(iv) duties of the Medical Adviser in connection with medical care;

(v) powers, functions, fees and allowances of medical practitioners and medical boards;

(vi) methods of recruitment, pay and allowances, superannuation benefits and other conditions of service of officers and staff of the Institution;

(vii) powers of the Commissioner with regard to appointment, transfer, promotion, dismissal and other matters affecting the staff of the Institution;

(viii) conditions of entitlement to receive sickness, maternity and injury benefit, disablement pension, disablement gratuity, death grant, survivors' pension and medical care;

(ix) the manner in which medical care shall be provided;
(x) the manner in which, and the times and places at which, payment in respect of benefit shall be made.

The provincial governments have powers to make rules to further the objectives of the scheme. The important aspects on which rules can be framed include the following:

(i) the manner in which the Governing Body may be appointed, its powers and functions and fees and allowances of the members;
(ii) the percentage of the amount by which contributions and special tax in arrears may be increased;
(iii) the manner in which security reserves shall be established and invested;
(iv) the time at which and the manner in which *(a)* the budget shall be prepared and submitted to the government; and *(b)* the accounts of the Institution shall be audited by the external auditors;
(v) the time within which claims for benefits shall be made;
(vi) remuneration and conditions of service of officers to be appointed by the government.

The Ordinance applies only to such areas, classes of persons, industries or establishments from such date as may be notified by the provincial government. The insured persons registered under this Ordinance are employees drawing wages less than Rs.1,500 per month. The total number of secured employees on 30 June 1987 was 448,894. The wife or a needy invalid husband of the insured worker and any unmarried children under the age of 16 years are covered by the Ordinance. The number of dependants on the same date was 1.80 million.

Organisation and delivery of medical care

The provision of medical care to the insured workers is the most important function of the social security institutions in Pakistan. It accounts for the bulk of their resources. It is delivered largely through the direct system under which each Institution has established a network of hospitals, dispensaries and injury treatment centres. On a limited scale medical care is also provided through the indirect method involving a system of retainer doctors. These retainer doctors provide treatment to the workers and receive payment for the services from the social security institutions.

Social security institutions provide medical care which consist of the following:

For insured workers:
(i) examination by the medical practitioner, including domiciliary visits;

(ii) specialists' care in hospital for in-patients and out-patients and such other specialists' care as may be required outside the hospital;
(iii) essential laboratory tests such as X-ray, blood, urine, sputum, etc.;
(iv) indoor treatment in hospital for all ailments according to need;
(v) essential pharmaceutical supplies as prescribed by a medical practitioner;
(vi) pre-natal confinement and post-natal care either by a medical practitioner or by a qualified midwife;
(vii) provision of artificial limbs (in Punjab);
(viii) medical rehabilitation (in Sind);
(ix) in case of need, a worker can even be sent abroad for treatment;
(x) ambulance service in case of accident or emergency.

For dependants:
(i) medical examinations at dispensaries and the provision of medicines;
(ii) essential laboratory tests from the Institution's laboratories;
(iii) in-patient treatment in the hospital only in cases of operation and in case of wives of insured workers for delivery purposes;
(iv) ambulance service in case of accident or emergency.

The scheme is not restricted to curative care only. It provides such comprehensive health care as immunisation against six preventable diseases (viz. diphtheria, pertussis, tetanus, poliomyelitis, measles and tuberculosis), child care, midwifery and provision of artificial limbs to workers in case of disability (especially in Punjab) and medical rehabilitation (in case of Sind) and insures fully primary health care.

For the delivery of medical care, the social security institutions have a network of their own hospitals, dispensaries, injury treatment centres and maternity and child health centres. Workers are attached to one of these units and in case of need they visit these units for treatment. For the purposes of identification, the insured workers and their dependants are issued registration cards. At the dispensary or hospital, medical history books are supplied and with these they are examined by the medical officer or lady medical officer, who prescribes treatment. If the illness is serious, the medical officer refers the patient to the senior medical officer who examines the patient himself and, if necessary, refers him or her or the dependants to a hospital or to a specialist for further treatment. The dispensaries of the Institution are adequately staffed and equipped to provide primary medical care and out-patient treatment. The medicines prescribed by the doctor are supplied free and, in case the medicine is not available, its cost is reimbursed to the workers on production of receipts.

There is a prescribed procedure for the appointment of doctors and para-medical staff. Vacancies are advertised in newspapers. The applicants are called for interview by the competent selection board and the candidates are selected on the basis of merit. The doctors and the para-medical staff are allowed similar salaries, allowances and fringe benefits as are available to their colleagues in the government service.

The greater reliance of the social security institution on the direct delivery method through their networks of hospitals, dispensaries, medical aid posts and injury treatment centres is by and large appreciated by the insured workers and their dependants:

(i) the system has developed a sort of personal relationship between the doctor and the insured person;
(ii) the workers of a particular industry tend to show symptoms of a particular ailment. This facilitates diagnosis and treatment as well as the implementation of preventive programmes;
(iii) the system has helped the institutions to add infrastructure facilities in the shape of buildings for dispensaries, hospitals and injury treatment centres;
(iv) it has also been a source of employment for medical professionals and para-medical staff;
(v) it permits cost containment and better services for the workers and their dependants in the shape of consultations, pharmaceutical supplies and laboratory tests;
(vi) a satisfactory doctor-patient ratio can be maintained;
(vii) most of the employers, especially of smaller units employing ten to 100 workers, are in favour of the social security hospitals and dispensaries because they can never either run these medical units themselves or give the benefits which a social security scheme can offer.

Among the major disadvantages of the system, the following can be listed:

(i) in Pakistan many workers move to other provinces in search of work, leaving behind their family members in their home towns. Since the social security scheme is operated at the provincial level, the family members of such workers are thus deprived of the medical benefits;
(ii) dispensaries are located in many cases away from the place of residence of the secured workers and they have to incur heavy expenditures on transport to reach these dispensaries;
(iii) the doctors complain that the insured workers occasionally demand costly medicines and complain when effective but less costly substitutes are prescribed. They also occasionally force the doctors to grant leave when not justified on medical grounds;
(iv) the workers demand examination by specialists even when this is not needed;

(v) the working conditions and standard of medical care provided are not uniform in the three provinces. The weakest institution, both financially and organisationally, is that of the North-West Frontier Province compared with the Institutions in Punjab and Sind.

Financial aspects

The main source of income of the schemes is the monthly contribution paid by the employers. At the time of launching the scheme in March 1967, the employers' contribution was 4 per cent and the workers' was 2 per cent of wages. In February 1972 the workers' contribution of 2 per cent was abolished and the employers' contribution was raised to 6 per cent. In January 1976 the employers' contribution was further raised to 7 per cent of the wages of the insured workers. The term "wages" means all remuneration for services paid or payable in cash or in kind. However, it should not be less than the wages declared under the Minimum Wages Ordinance, 1961. The term "wages", however, does not include payments for overtime, any sum paid to defray special expenses entailed by the nature of employment, a gratuity payable on discharge, or any sum paid as bonus by the employer.

The Government and the employees pay no contribution. However, in case of the Social Security Institution of NWFP, the provincial government allowed a grant of Rs.150,000 during the 1985-86 period to tide over its financial difficulties.

The Ordinance provides that in case an employer fails to observe rules of safety or hygiene prescribed under any enactment, the Commissioner of the social security institution may increase the employer's rate of contribution up to 20 per cent. However, this power has not been invoked by any of the social security institutions so far.

The provincial government, in consultation with the Institution under section 70 of the Ordinance, is empowered to impose special taxes, not exceeding 5 per cent of the wages paid by the employers of any group of industries or area to be utilised for capital expenditure towards building and improving the medical facilities available for the provision of medical care under this Ordinance. During the 1985-86 period this provision was invoked by the Punjab government which received Rs.75,377 from the Multan area.

The entire cost of medical care is borne by the social security institutions. The insured workers are not required to share any element of the cost. In addition to the contribution income, the institutions also earn a small amount as interest on their investment of the surplus funds.

Methods of collecting contributions: The employers are required to submit to the contribution section of the local directorate of the respective institution each month a contribution schedule, showing names and registration numbers of the employer, name, social security numbers, designation, wages, number of days worked, etc., of the employees. This schedule also shows the contribution being paid in respect of an individual worker. These schedules are duly checked and the employers are asked to rectify any errors or omissions before making payment. The contribution for a particular month is required to be paid by the end of the following month. In case of delay in the payment of contribution by the due date, the amount of contribution payable increases at the rate of half percentum per day, subject to a maximum increase of 50 per cent of the amount due.

Internal audit department: Social Security Institutions have an audit department which ensures that the provisions of the Ordinance, rules and regulations, code of staff instructions and circulars issued by the head office from time to time are observed properly. The audit department is specifically responsible for the correct receipt of contributions, maintenance of books of account and also supervises the work of local audit officers at the dispensary and payment of cash benefits by pay offices. The audit department is required to submit periodical reports bringing out the position of collection of contribution compared with budgetary provision, the estimated expenditure and point out irregularities, if any. The audit staff checks the record of covered establishments to ensure correctness of contributions paid by them. The internal audit also examines the best avenues for the investment of surplus and reserve funds.

The audit department also checks the receipt and issue of medicines from the central medical stores and subsequent receipt in different dispensaries and hospitals. Discrepancies, if any, are reported to the higher authorities.

In addition, there is a tripartite Governing Body at the head office level, tripartite committees at the level of local directorates, dispensaries and hospitals to keep close watch on the activities of the institution, sort out problems, if any, and redress the grievances. These administrative measures have helped on the one hand in better service to the insured workers and on the other have helped the institution in its varied activities.

Financial viability: The provincial Social Security Institutions have no uniform income base. The institutions in the Punjab and Sind are better placed in terms of resources. As such, these institutions have over the years constructed their own hospitals, dispensaries and injury treatment centres. They are also allowing better cash benefits in case of sickness, maternity and work injury. The institutions in these provinces are facing financial constraints in view of the rising cost of medicines and the pay rises of the medical and other employees. These institutions are constantly demanding increases in the contribution rate.

The financial condition of the Social Security Institution in the North West Frontier Province is not satisfactory. This is evident from the fact that all the dispensaries of this Institution are still housed in rented premises. The rates of benefits in case of sickness and maternity are lower than in Punjab and Sind. The Social Security Institution has been constantly urging the provincial and the federal Government to extend financial assistance to tide over their difficulties.

Review of progress

The social security health care programme has been in operation for over 20 years. Medical cover was available initially only to the secured workers and that too when they had at least contributed for 90 days towards the social security fund. This was relaxed and the employees have been made eligible to medical treatment without any condition. Now they are entitled to full treatment from the very first day of enrolment in the notified units. The dependants were first made eligible for surgical treatment but now they are entitled to full medical care at the dispensary level, in-patient treatment in the hospital in case of surgery and ambulance services.

In 1967 the Ordinance was applied to the employees of textile units in three cities only. In the same year, the Ordinance was extended to three more cities. At present, the Ordinance is applicable to the industries and establishments where ten or more workers are employed. The wage limit for the coverage of the workers was in the beginning Rs.500 per month. This was raised to Rs.1,000 per month in 1976 and to Rs.1,500 per month since July 1985.

Health is a neglected sector in Pakistan and needs far larger inputs. The social security health care programme has helped in mobilising resources for the health sector. It has facilitated expansion of infrastructure facilities such as new hospitals, dispensaries, maternity homes and also employment opportunities for medical and para-medical personnel. The social security institutions in the country have developed the following health facilities:

	Punjab	NWFP	Sind	Total
1. Hospitals/polyclinics/mini-hospitals	12	—	4	16
2. Dispensaries	68	15	50	133
3. Injury treatment centres	22	—	—	22
4. Medical aid posts	50	—	—	50
5. Maternity home	—	—	1	1

These hospitals and dispensaries have 956 beds. In addition, they employ 602 qualified doctors, 114 specialists and 1,942 para-medical staff. The medical facilities available to the workers and their dependants are much better compared with what is available to the general public through public hospitals.

However, the organisation of the scheme at the provincial level has also given rise to a number of problems and denial of facilities to a large number of persons, otherwise eligible for medical benefits. The migratory workers leave behind families and dependants who are not able to avail themselves of the medical facilities. Moreover, the standard of medical care is not uniform in all the provinces. It varies according to the infrastructure facilities and financial resources of a provincial social security institution.

Future developments

Amendments in the existing Ordinance are under active consideration by the Government. The present condition imposing a wage limit is likely to be removed. This will facilitate coverage of all the workers irrespective of their wage. However, a wage limit will be prescribed for contributions by the employers. This will contain the financial burden on the employers. There are other suggestions for improving the rate of cash benefits and also the eligibility conditions for these benefits.

The Seventh Five-Year Plan (1988-93) has placed great responsibilities on the Social Security Institutions for mobilising resources for medical care. This is proposed to be done by extending health care to non-industrial workers and to workers employed in establishments where two or more workers are employed. This will pose a great challenge for the Social Security Institutions in the coming years.

PAPUA NEW GUINEA

DEMOGRAPHY AND HEALTH DATA

Papua New Guinea had a population of 3.7 million in 1987, after a period of decrease in the annual growth rate, which averaged 2.1 per cent between 1980 and 1986. In 1987, 15 per cent of the population were in urban areas. The per capita GNP in that year was US$720.

The infant mortality rate was 61 and the child mortality rate 85 deaths per 1,000 live births in 1987, with an average annual reduction in the child mortality rate of 3.74 per cent since 1980. Life expectancy was 55 years in 1987. The adult literacy rate was 55 per cent for males and 35 per cent for females in 1985.

HEALTH SERVICES

Health services are the responsibility of the Government, with decentralised responsibility for the development and delivery of care by province. The National Department of Health is responsible for national functions such as policy formulation and planning, legislation and medical education. The provincial Health Departments are responsible for a range of services, classified as aid posts, health sub-centres, health centres, home medicine and self-care, ambulance services, family health services and infectious disease control. This includes responsibility for the hospitals which have been built in each province. These services are supplemented by rural health services organised by the churches, subsidised in part by the Government and currently accounting for 30 per cent of the health services in the country. The two large mining companies provide free health care to their employees in company-run clinics and hospitals. There is one private hospital, with only 15 beds and an out-patient department.

In 1986 the Government allocated 9.6 per cent of its total expenditure to health care, with funds derived from general revenues. This expenditure constituted 3.4 per cent of the GNP in 1986, and over half the funds went to primary health care. Papua New Guinea also has considerable assistance in funds for health care from external sources, mainly multilateral and bilateral programmes, or loans and grants. There are user charges for hospital care but these are minimal and contribute only 2.5 per cent of the hospital operating costs. The collection of fees for community care in government or church-operated health centres is not standard and remains very limited.

HEALTH INSURANCE

Public health insurance is currently limited to a scheme for about 10,000 Public Service Association members. The scheme could be extended to other workers, and this is currently being considered. A major problem would be the extension of coverage to rural populations.

PHILIPPINES

DEMOGRAPHY AND HEALTH DATA

The population of the Philippines reached 58 million in 1987, after a period of slightly decreasing growth. The average annual population growth rate between 1980 and 1986 was 2.5 per cent. In 1987, 41 per cent of the population resided in urban areas. The per capita GNP was US$560 in 1987. The average annual change in GNP for the total period 1980-86 was 4 per cent, but there has been a positive upswing over the past two years.

In 1987 the infant mortality rate was 46 and the child mortality rate was 75 deaths per 1,000 live births. The annual decrease in child mortality for the period from 1980 was an average of 1.94 per cent. Life expectancy was 64 years in 1987. The adult literacy rate in 1985 was 86 per cent for males and 85 per cent for females.

HEALTH SERVICES

Health care in the Philippines is provided by a mix of public and private sectors. The Government provides a range of preventive and curative services in community health centres and hospitals, and these are expected to cater to the lower-income groups. The private sector, which owns and operates over half of the hospitals, and an increasing number of clinics, generally caters to the middle- and upper-income groups. The government services at the smallest level are the village health stations and rural health units. Patients needing hospital services are referred from this level to the district hospital, usually with 25 to 50 beds. The next level is the provincial hospital with 100 to 150 beds, then the regional hospital with 200 to 250 beds, and the medical centres, located in the larger towns and cities, have over 250 beds. These government hospitals have limited charges, according to the individual patient's ability to pay.

In 1986 the Government allocated 6 per cent of its expenditure to health care, yet government funds financed only 25 per cent of the total health care expenditure in the Philippines in 1985. The next largest sector is the household out-of-pocket expenditure on health. Company and community generated resources are also significant private sector sources.

HEALTH INSURANCE

The Philippines implemented health insurance into its social security system in 1971. The description of the two current schemes is extracted from the paper prepared for the Seminar by the Philippines Medical Care Commission.

The Medicare Programme

The Philippines has two social security health insurance programmes: the Medicare Programme and the Employees' Compensation Programme. Poverty affected a majority of Filipinos in the 1960s as much as it does in this decade. This fact and the high cost of medical care conspired to make adequate health care services way beyond the reach of the average Filipino. Republic Act 6111, or "The Philippine Medical Care Act of 1969" was enacted into law on 4 August 1969 to partly correct this situation. This Act created the Philippine Medical Care Plan, a social security health insurance scheme whose basic aim was to extend medical care to all Filipinos in an evolutionary way and by providing the people with a viable means of helping themselves pay for adequate medical care. In this scheme people and their employers would contribute according to the former's income to a fund called the Health Insurance Fund. This fund would be used to provide benefits equivalent to a certain percentage of a member's hospital care cost.

The Medicare Programme seeks to cover the entire population. Its implementation was divided into two stages or programmes. *Programme I* covers the formally employed sectors of the population. The implementation of this stage in 1971 was facilitated by the existence of two social security institutions already covering the formally employed— the Social Security System (SSS) for the privately employed and the Government Service Insurance System (GSIS) for public employees. Programme I also covers the legal dependants of its members. *Programme II*, which seeks to cover the self-employed professionals, agricultural workers, unemployed, etc., is still non-operational for lack of a feasible administrative and funding mechanism.

The Philippine Medical Care Commission was created to implement the administration of the Medicare Programme. It is an attached agency of the Department of Health, with the Secretary of Health serving as chairman of the Commission. The other members of the Commission are: An Undersecretary of Health designated by the Secretary as Vice-Chairman; the Administrator of the SSS; the President and General Manager of the GSIS; Secretary of Finance; Secretary of Local

Government; Secretary of Labour and Employment; and four other members representing the beneficiaries, private employers, physicians and hospitals.

The Commission is largely a supervisory body and is responsible for policy formulation, the accreditation of health care providers into the programme, and the adjudication of administrative cases. However, the administration of the Health Insurance Fund, a function that includes the collection of contributions and the payment of benefits, is the responsibility of the two social security agencies.

There are currently about 21 million Medicare Programme I beneficiaries, broken down as follows:

(a) 15 million private sector employees and their dependants; and

(b) 6.7 million public employees and their dependants.

The Employees' Compensation Programme

The Employees' Compensation Programme was established by Presidential Decree No. 626 on 27 December 1974. The Programme provides sickness, disability and death benefits for work-related injuries and ailments. The Programme covers all employees covered by the SSS and GSIS who are not over 60 years of age.

The objective of this programme is to help workers in the event of employment related injury, sickness, disability or death to promptly receive meaningful and adequate income benefits, medical and rehabilitation services.

This programme is implemented by the Employees' Compensation Commission, a government corporation attached to the Department of Labour and Employment. The latter provides policy co-ordination and guidance. The State Insurance Fund, which consists of all contributions collected from employers and all its accruals, is administered by the GSIS (for public employees) and the SSS (for private sector employees).

The Commission is chaired by the Secretary of Labour and Employment. Other members are the GSIS President and General Manager, SSS Administrator, Chairman of the Philippine Medical Care Commission, Executive Director of the ECC Secretariat and two appointive members representing the employees and the employers.

Organisation and delivery of medical care

The Medicare Programme provides hospital-based in-patient care benefits to its beneficiaries by covering a certain portion of their hospital care cost. The amount Medicare shoulders is automatically deducted from the total amount that the hospital bills the patient. The rest of the bill is paid by the patient. This feature of the programme is known as co-payment.

The insured can receive Medicare benefits only upon admission to an accredited hospital. The benefits that they are entitled to are limited to a schedule set by the Philippine Government. In 1988 these benefits supported, on the average, 33 per cent of a beneficiary's total hospital care cost. When this programme began in 1971 the proportion covered, or support value, was 70 per cent. The services covered are hospital room and board, medicines, X-ray and laboratory tests, operating room and physician consultations.

The medical practitioners are reimbursed an amount equal to the Medicare share by the SSS or GSIS on a fee-for-service basis.

In 1987 claims were submitted for 1.5 million members who occupy 19 per cent of total hospital beds in the accredited hospitals.

The Medicare Programme does not employ its own doctors nor does it operate its own hospitals. The Commission merely accredits the health care providers, i.e. licensed doctors, dentists, hospitals and clinics, who want to participate in the programme. As of 23 November 1988, 1,528 facilities and 6,000 medical practitioners have been accredited.

The Commission, the SSS and the GSIS conduct random inspections to monitor compliance with the standards and rules set by the Commission. Violations of Medicare's rules and regulations are filed with the Commission, which also hears and decides on these cases.

The major advantage of the Medicare scheme, as in any insurance scheme, is the guarantee that the beneficiaries get their benefits whenever they need them and the providers are assured of the payment for their services. Moreover, beneficiaries are given the flexibility to choose from any accredited service provider they prefer.

The disadvantage of this method is the tendency toward unnecessary hospital care, since benefits can only be used for in-patient care. There is likewise no incentive for service providers to be efficient, since they are reimbursed for the cost of services rendered.

The Employees' Compensation Programme provides both curative (benefit in kind) care and cash benefits to employees. The employees' dependants are also provided some cash benefits in case of disability or death of the member. Just like the Medicare Programme, this Programme accredits practising doctors and licensed hospitals who are also reimbursed for the services they provide. It has its separate scheme of accrediting providers and has approximately the same number of accredited hospitals and physicians.

Financial aspects

The source of financing of the Medicare Programme is the Health Insurance Fund, which consists of the contributions collected from members and the investment income of the fund.

The contribution rate is set by law and is currently pegged at a minimum of 2.5 per cent of an employee's base salary. The contribution, however, is shared equally by the employee and his employer, i.e. one-half of the amount is paid out of the employee's salary and the other half is paid by the employer. The total amount due to Medicare is remitted monthly by the employer to the appropriate social security agency.

The SSS and GSIS, as fund administrators, can use as much as 12 per cent of the fund for their administrative costs. The Commission monitors the funds through the financial reports submitted by the two agencies. In 1987 the Medicare Programme paid out 69.7 per cent of its revenue for hospital claims.

The main source of financing for the Employees' Compensation Programme are the contributions collected from employers, equivalent to a maximum of 1 per cent of their employees' base salary. The method of collection of contributions and monitoring of its operations are similar to the Medicare Programme.

Review of progress

The Medicare Programme's aim is to provide Filipinos with a viable method of helping themselves pay for adequate medical care. We can consider two parameters when assessing the effectiveness of the programme: the extent of coverage and the level of benefits provided.

The coverage of the programme has never extended beyond the formally employed sector largely because the administrative and funding needs of an expanded scheme have never been fully addressed. The current programme covers only 37 per cent (as of 1988) of the total Philippines population. The non-insured sector includes the lower-income groups (e.g. farmers, fishermen) who are in the greatest need of Medicare protection. Various pilot projects, however, are being conducted in earnest to test the feasibility of two schemes that have been proposed for the coverage of the non-insured. The schemes are:

(a) a community-based health insurance programme which is similar to the Medicare set-up wherein the local government acts as both supervisory body and fund administrator;

(b) a sectoral/occupational group insurance plan which targets specific occupational associations as beneficiaries.

The level of benefit support has been declining since 1971. In that year, the support value was 70 per cent. Inflation, however, had eroded this value to 39 per cent by 1980. Last year, this value further went down to 33 per cent. This was despite the fact that benefit ceilings were raised several times between 1971 and 1988. This trend points to the lack of an adequate cost-containment mechanism in the current set-up. Paradoxically, the benefit ceiling increases that were enacted to counter increasing costs have also adversely affected the funds' viability.

It is worth taking note, however, that these increases were accomplished without any increases in contributions. This is important since the majority of Medicare beneficiaries can ill-afford any deductions in their wages. As a result, the Commission's efforts to expand benefits must be achieved with a minimal increase in contributions. This has led to the search for alternatives to the current set-up.

The Commission is currently experimenting with subcontracting the delivery of benefits to private Health Maintenance Organisations (HMOs). This scheme is optional for Medicare members and will not entail any additional contributions. The efficiencies inherent in these private organisations will allow them to provide a greater level and range of benefits than Medicare provides at the current level of contribution.

Future developments

The current efforts to expand existing benefits and coverage are still in the experimental or planning stages. The most likely results of these undertakings include:

(a) an increase in contributions in order to restore the support value to 70 per cent;
(b) inclusion of out-patient benefits;
(c) the implementation of an alternative system of delivering medical care benefits such as contracts with private Health Maintenance Organisations (HMO);
(d) expansion of pilot projects under Programme II using various models; and
(e) development of alternative modes of payment for hospitals and doctors.

The system is currently under extensive review to find the optimal means of achieving these results. In the short term, decisions are already being implemented to increase the support value for hospital care.

SRI LANKA

DEMOGRAPHY AND HEALTH DATA

Sri Lanka had a population of 16.6 million in 1987, following a period of significant decrease in its annual growth rate. The average annual growth from 1980 to 1986 was 1.5 per cent. In 1987, 21 per cent of the population resided in urban areas. Per capita GNP was then US$400, and had increased by an average of 2.5 per cent over the preceding six years.

The infant mortality rate was 34 and the child mortality rate was 45 deaths per 1,000 live births in 1987. From 1980 the average annual reduction in child mortality was 3.56 per cent. Life expectancy was 71 in 1987. Adult literacy was 91 per cent for males and 83 per cent for females in 1985.

HEALTH SERVICES

Sri Lanka has established a National Health Development Network (NHDN) as a co-ordinating body for the various ministries and agencies responsible for health care, with a National Health Council serving as the policy-making body. Both Western and ayurvedic medicine are provided free of charge by the Government. Western medical services are operated by the Ministry of Health and the Ministry of Women's Affairs and Teaching Hospitals. The latter is responsible for the hospitals in the capital and the four provincial teaching hospitals. The Ministry of Health manages the other hospitals, and the preventive services provided through 108 medical officers, as well as the infectious disease control programmes. All these services are provided free of charge, but the larger government hospitals enable patients to pay for a doctor of choice and services in private wards. These exist only in the large cities, and revenues from this source generated only 0.6 per cent of the cost of government services.

In addition to these national health services, some individual employers operate limited medical schemes for their employees. The number of employers undertaking this responsibility has declined in recent years.

The recent growth of private care was encouraged by a shift in demand for out-patient care from government hospitals to private practitioners. This trend has been encouraged by the Government as a means of decreasing its own burden and maximising the use of available manpower. The private sector is currently limited to ambulatory care and nursing homes.

In 1986 the Government spent 5.7 per cent of its total expenditure on health. The amount spent accounted for 58 per cent of the total expenditure on health, with 39 per cent coming from private sources.

HEALTH INSURANCE

The ILO held a National Tripartite Seminar in Sri Lanka in 1987 to review the development of social security protection in that country. From the report of that seminar, we learn that social security programmes were first developed in the 1930s. The changes implemented after the country's Independence in 1948 now provide a relatively diversified range of old age, invalidity, survivor, employment injury and maternity benefits. Despite such a well-established social security system, medical care and sickness benefits have not been introduced, following a national policy that the availability of free health services provided by the State should not be dependent on the fact of employment. Up to the present, the Health For All programme developed by the Ministry of Health has called for a reorganisation of the health care delivery system, mainly aimed at strengthening primary care, rather than seeking legislation that would provide a compulsory and regular contribution to obtain health services.

THAILAND

DEMOGRAPHY AND HEALTH DATA

Thailand had a population of 53.3 million in 1987, following a period of slightly decreasing growth. The average annual population growth from 1980 to 1986 was 2 per cent. In 1987, 21 per cent of the population were in urban areas. The per capita GNP in that year was US$810, with an average annual increase of 2.8 per cent from 1980.

In 1987 the infant mortality rate was 40 and the child mortality rate 51 deaths per 1,000 live births. From 1980 to 1987 the average annual reduction in child mortality was 3.82 per cent. Life expectancy was 66 years in 1987. The adult literacy rate was 94 per cent for males and 88 per cent for females in 1985.

HEALTH SERVICES

The Ministry of Public Health has taken major responsibility for the delivery of health services in Thailand. The Government owns and operates 70 per cent of the hospitals, and the 30 per cent in the private sector have fewer beds and are located mainly in urban centres. A very significant shift to community care was achieved through the implementation of the Fifth Five-Year National Health Development Plan (1982-86). This entailed converting the Ministry of Health midwifery centres to health centres and there are now over 7,800 such facilities throughout the country. The lowest level of public services, however, are community health posts and drug co-operatives which had been established in 58,612 villages by 1987. In urban areas the scope of hospital out-patient care is increasing but the private sector still provides most ambulatory care in clinics and pharmacies.

Thailand currently spends about 5.5 per cent of its GNP on health care, with about two-thirds still coming from private sources. This proportion has grown slightly in recent years, due to the limitations on government spending. A significant part of the private expenditure on health is on drugs purchased over the counter from private pharmacies.

HEALTH INSURANCE

Thailand has recently made very significant progress in the legislative process towards implementing a social security health insurance system. The Social Security Law now in its final stages of passage will in fact be the first social security programme in the country, and will cover medical care services and cash sickness benefits, as well as maternity, disability and funeral allowances.

The development of health insurance and related schemes are described in the following extracts from the paper prepared for the Seminar by Dr. Damrong Boonyoen, Chief Medical Officer for Policy Analysis and Planning, of the Ministry of Public Health of Thailand.

Historical background

The development of health insurance, amongst other forms of health care financing in Thailand, is reviewed in the light of various initiatives, political actions and responses made by both public and private sectors in their attempt to ensure accessibility to better health services through some system of prepaid, risk-sharing, or government subsidies as parts of social security and public assistance. The Thai Parliament first passed a Social Security Law in 1954 but it has not yet been successfully put into practice due to several political reasons. On this initial basis, different proposals have been made many times since then to submit alternative versions to the Parliament. To date, no social security system nor health insurance scheme has been implemented to cover the entire country.

However, there are a number of activities and projects currently providing health insurance or health insurance related schemes for particular subgroups of the population. Interestingly, some people can be under the coverage of more than one scheme while a large proportion of them are not covered by any single scheme. The rationale for initiating or expanding each of these schemes differs. One of the schemes is compulsory, whereas many others are either voluntary or classified as state welfare. Among the total population of 53 million, the active labour force account for 24 million including independent self-employed workers (31 per cent), employers (1.5 per cent), household workers (36.2 per cent), government employees (8.5 per cent), and employees of private firms (22.8 per cent). When the activities and projects providing health insurance and health insurance related schemes are taken into consideration altogether, the coverage of the schemes account for around 39 per cent of the total population or approximately 21 million.

It is important to note that the existing activities or projects are different from each other in terms of not only objectives and target population but also the scope of medical benefits such as types of illness, level of reimbursement for the cost incurred, types of services to be provided, and conditions regarding utilisation of health care facilities. Government interventions on these schemes vary from direct budgetary provision to subsidisation and co-payment. Surprisingly, government responsibility in health care financing is proportionately much lower than the public at large unless the capital expenditures on health are taken into account.

The major schemes and their present coverage are described below.

The Government Free Medical Care Project

The Free Medical Care Project was introduced through the first budget allocation made specifically for it in the fiscal year 1976. As part of the Government's proposals for helping the poorer sections of the population, the project was initiated and the objectives were spelled out as follows:

(a) create more equitable opportunity in receiving government health services among the people;
(b) increase accessibility to health services and improve the health status of the poor, especially in rural areas;
(c) pave the way for National Health Insurance for the poor; and
(d) stimulate positive attitudes among the poor regarding government health services.

Initially, the project had three components: free medical care, mobile health service units, and medical care through radio communications – the first being by far the largest, as indicated by the budget allocations for the first years. When the project was first introduced, eligibility cards were to be issued in Bangkok to those who were classified, according to a set of criteria based mainly on monthly income, as poor. This practice was later discovered to be too rigid or unrealistic and had to be relaxed by giving the government hospital director or persons in charge of the health centres the responsibility of deciding who qualifies for free care, on the basis of various criteria which define poverty.

Subsequently, a policy decision was made to reintroduce the cards under a decentralised scheme which gives the district officers of the Ministry of the Interior the responsibility of issuing the cards while village headmen and *kamnans* (formal leader of a group of villages) act as screeners for the eligible poor. Since the project is aimed at helping the poorest or the real medically indigent, the number of free medical care card holders cannot be too excessive. Several practical problems were encountered with the income criteria and the difficulty of reaching and granting the cards to all who are qualified. Questions have been raised on whether it is possible to establish a criterion which is not dependent on calculating personal or household income. Unfortunately, it remains too difficult to find any other practical criterion that correlates closely with poverty and hence suitable for substituting the income criteria. With this weakness, the present coverage of a free medical care project for approximately 7.7 million people deserves critical evaluation, especially in terms of geographical equity and major changes in income over time due to economic fluctuation, natural disasters, etc.

The Government Medical Care Welfare or Sickness Benefits

The military personnel, policemen, civil servants, including retired officials, and employees of public enterprises are provided with fringe benefits part of which is medical care. This benefit is provided in addition to the salary they receive monthly and is extended to include eligible persons in their family such as father, mother, spouse and children (up to the age of 20) but not more than three dependants. The government medical care welfare scheme also covers some other groups of people as specified by law or ministries' regulations such as veterans and their families, teachers in private institutions, village headmen and *kamnans*, village health volunteers and village health communicators.

It appears from the records of the Department of Comptroller General, Ministry of Finance, that during the years 1983-87 the medical care expenditure payable as sickness benefits to the civil servants, military personnel, permanent employees of government agencies, retired officials, and all eligible persons from their families, almost doubled in current prices. A similar trend is seen from estimates of the medical care expenditure payable to the employees of the 19 public enterprises during the same period. Based upon the figures and the rate of annual increase during this period, it is possible to make a statistical projection for both cases up to the year 2000. It is evident from this projection that the future escalation of financial burden of the Government which will be required to pay for the sickness benefits for these two groups of people may become a serious issue. To ease this financial burden, a more appropriate scheme may have to be devised to counter the inefficient spending or at least to contain the costs.

Workmen Compensation Fund

The initiative of establishing a Workmen Compensation Fund dates back to 1972 when it was imposed by law that employers must be responsible for their employees' illness and injury resulting from work or work-related activity. However, it was observed during the first years after enforcement of this law that there were many inefficiencies and disputes, and in most cases the employees had to bear the disadvantages. The most common issues were the level of compensation, whether the illness was work-related or not, and when the employers would agree to pay the compensation. These disputes were definitely detrimental to the employer-employee relationship and undesirable from the national social security standpoint.

It was therefore decided that the Workmen Compensation Fund should be established and expanded gradually step by step. Beginning in 1973 with private firms with more than 20 employees and located in Bangkok and in the subsequent periods which followed, the fund was gradually expanded to cover a similar size of firms in five more provinces around Bangkok, in 12 provinces by 1977, and eventually reaching 56 provinces in 1985. At present, the fund covers private firms in all provinces of the country and is being planned to extend to include smaller firms which employ ten employees or more by 1990. However, the capacity to implement the scheme still depends to some extent on the availability of budget and manpower.

While the Workmen Compensation Fund is expanding its coverage, those firms which have not yet joined the scheme are supposed to provide sickness compensation directly to the employees. Under the circumstances, it can be anticipated that labour disputes will remain. Moreover, several studies reveal that although there is a legal provision which requires employers to register with the Workmen Compensation Fund when their firms meet the criteria, there are still many employers who do not do so. These firms may employ much more than the minimum number of employees stipulated but they do not comply with, or in some cases the employers themselves do not really understand, the requirements of the Labour Act, especially those on the Workmen Compensation Fund. It is left solely to the employers to decide how much they would be financially responsible for the illness of the employees. The usual alternative for those employees who can hardly afford to pay the medical bill is to seek free or heavily subsidised care from government health facilities. This is considered undesirable since it violates the principle of social justice and equity as laid down by the Labour Law and has implications on government health care expenditures.

The Community-based Health Card Project

The Community-based Health Card Project constitutes another new initiative begun by the Ministry of Public Health in 1983 to influence and structure effective demand for health services among the rural self-employed population. The original idea behind the project is inventive and conceptually sound. In principle, the project serves to:

(a) encourage and strengthen community organisation and involvement in the management of the fund for maternal and child health, other preventive or promotive activities, as well as curative purposes;

(b) increase the use of Tambon Health Centres, most often by-passed by rural families in favour of district or provincial hospitals;

(c) reduce congestion and waiting time for those referred to hospitals;

(d) ensure accessibility to services through voluntary purchasing of the health care or prepaid health insurance; and

(e) raise capital, and with loans or other income generating activities increase it further to finance health services and other community development efforts.

At present, there are approximately 2,500,000 health card project members in around 19,000 villages, 4,500 tambons and 680 districts of every province except Bangkok. Although the coverage seems to be countrywide, only 5 per cent of Thailand's population is covered by this project. To become a member of the project, or to withdraw from it, is a voluntary decision of the individual. Purchasing of the health card then depends mainly on the individual's purchasing power and his expectation regarding the risk of illness. According to a general observation, health card holders are more in the middle-income group than in the lower-income bracket. From past experiences, active local leaders and well-organised communities are found to be good promoting factors of the project. However, any increase in the card price, any adjustment in the benefits, or the manner in which health service providers react to the project members, are always critical to the growth or reduction in the demand for the health card.

Regardless of the original purposes of the Health Card Project and all of the observable problems, the project can be regarded as a scheme of voluntary health insurance. A notable advantage of this project is the provision for community participation in management of the fund. Besides, the Health Card Project on its voluntary basis serves rural communities and individuals to gain access to health and medical services in a more equitable manner. Improved efficiency of rural health centres may or may not be very significant, but there is always a tendency for health centres to become more fully utilised through the designed referral system under the Health Card Project. And wherever such a system is in practice, the project definitely helps recover the costs of health services rendered by the lowest level of health care facilities which are otherwise provided free of charge.

A decisive issue is now confronting the project, as it has gone on an experimental basis long enough. Instead of rigidly maintaining its community-based framework with the objective of intensifying primary health care development at village level, the project may have to adopt a clearer concept and more prominent practices of more comprehensive voluntary health insurance.

The private insurance business

There are four different types of private insurance in Thailand, including: life insurance companies; general insurance companies; health insurance companies; and re-insurance companies.

Thailand

Companies of the first three types offer the services of health insurance. For life insurance companies it is customary that health insurance is offered in the form of supplementary contract. Insurance on medical expenses due to illness or accident originates as one among a total of 17 types of contract offered by the general insurance companies.

Two types of private health insurance contracts are currently available. The first is individual health insurance which may pay the medical expense either to insured persons only or include also their spouses and children as beneficiaries. The second and by far more popular is group health insurance where the majority of clients are employees and sometime include their spouses and children. Private group insurance plans are usually in the form of general hospitalisation and clinical benefits which cover injury or illness not related to work. For cost control reasons, some insurance companies will only pay for clinical treatment performed in designated clinics. A list of conditions, diseases, and specific types of service is agreed as exempt from the benefit package. The premium or health insurance rates offered by the companies are usually flexible, depending on the details of the arrangement concerning benefits, but basically they are calculated on a risk-sharing basis.

According to the available figures on the number of individuals and employees buying their own health insurance, it may be concluded that private health insurance in Thailand has not been significant in its market share. The rate of expansion of this business is very slow. Most of the private health insurance companies have to run a relatively small-sized business which make overhead costs unusually high and as a result they are struggling with deficits since 1978. The future prospect for these companies is not promising, although the number of target clients is larger every day due to the sustained high level of economic growth and rapid industrialisation of the country.

Strengthening the performance of existing health insurance and related schemes

Based upon knowledge of the problems and the level of progress and achievement each existing scheme is now experiencing, there is agreement on the necessity for the country to establish a National Health Insurance system. In July 1989 the Parliament passed an amended Social Security Law, providing for medical care and cash sickness benefits, disability cash benefits, maternity benefits and a funeral allowance. This Bill will shortly be presented to the Upper House of Parliament, and then hopefully prepared for implementation. It is drafted to cover workers in private sector enterprises with over 20 employees in all provinces of the country. The present Government also now plans:

(a) to strengthen the performance of some selected schemes such as

the Workmen Compensation Fund and private insurance business particularly for group contracts;

(b) to adjust or improve the operation of government welfare schemes like medical sickness benefits, for officials and employees, and also the free medical care project for the poor, by exerting more control measures on identification of qualified dependants of the schemes, resource allocation and financial management;

(c) to modify the concept and even administrative organisation and management, especially of the community-based health card project; and

(d) to evolve a collateral scheme for wage earners by annexing additional compulsory health insurance into the existing scheme under the Workmen Compensation Fund through a tripartite agreement aimed at covering sickness and death of individual workers unrelated to work.

Beyond all these steps, there is a need to harmonise actions and future plans of each of the existing schemes under an umbrella of a National Health Insurance System. This national system refers more to its function than its organisation in a strict sense. The major consideration is efficiency, which will be gained if various existing activities and future projects for expansion or development are better co-ordinated. Given the prevailing social and political factors, a multiple scheme of National Health Insurance System consisting of the existing activities and projects may be the most appropriate system for Thailand. The possibility is apparently promising, since the system will serve the various interest groups, several authorities and agencies, and can cater for potential targets of each of the existing schemes.

Future health care financing, health insurance and related schemes based upon Health For All perspectives

The providers of health services in Thailand can be categorised broadly as public and private. Among the public health services, the Ministry of Public Health operates a large number of health centres in every tambon (group of villages), a district hospital ten to 90 beds in every district, a provincial hospital of medium or large size with specialised care in every province including Bangkok, and specialised clinics and hospitals for tuberculosis, venereal diseases, leprosy and psychiatric patients in a number of provinces scattered all over the country. Besides the facilities of the Ministry of Public Health, the university hospitals, military and police hospitals and hospitals under the responsibility of some public enterprises and the Bangkok Metropolitan Administration provide a considerable share of patient care for the general public. It is noteworthy that all of these public hospitals and clinics recover their maintenance costs by applying user charges. In most cases, this becomes a major source of income for the hospitals, which they in turn use for operational expenditures. With regard to capital formation or investment cost, it is customary for every medical and health facility to get direct financial support from the government budget. However, public donations and part of the hospital's income do serve as a considerable source of financing capital.

As an outcome of the health care financing practices already described, the Government of Thailand has during the past decade and a half been able to expand its services dramatically in terms of the number of institutions, beds and manpower. Despite the successful expansion and improvement of public health care facilities, a significant part of unmet demand for health services remains to be filled by private health care facilities of various types. It is also interesting to note that even though private hospitals and clinics always charge a higher level of fees than government health facilities, they still account for a significant share of health service utilisation over the past decade and a half.

Total health care expenditures have been increasing steadily in real terms since 1979, from 31,725 million baht or US$1,269 million in 1979 to 54,100 million baht or US$2,164 million in 1985. This increase is from 3.5 per cent of GNP or 633 baht per capita in 1979 to 5.1 per cent of GNP or 1,060 baht per capita in 1985. The annual rate of increase in per capita expenditure on health care is approximately 7.5 per cent, which is very high. If the same trend continues through 1991, expenditure on health care will reach 5.9 to 7.3 per cent of GNP (depending on different assumptions with regard to the growth of the economy) or about 1,663 baht per capita and account for a total of US$3,734 million.

However, public expenditure on health services has proportionately declined while the private share showed a slightly rising trend. As of 1983 around 69 per cent of total health care expenditure was financed by households and other private sources while the Ministry of Public Health's share accounted for about 19 per cent and the other government agencies provided the balance. From 1983 up to the present fiscal year of 1989, the Ministry of Public Health has increased its budget at a consistently low percentage of around 4.1-4.4 of the total government budget per annum. In this light, it can be concluded that the major source of health care finance has been and will remain to be the household contribution. It has also been observed that the household expenditure on health would be one of the fastest rising items as compared with other goods and services whenever there is a significant increase in income. This phenomenon might reflect a change in consumption behaviour where drugs for self-treatment are substituted by professional health services. In addition, the disease pattern is definitely shifting towards more chronic degenerative and severe illnesses such as accidents, cancer and heart diseases where the cost of treatment is relatively much higher than communicable diseases caused by poor sanitation and nutrition in the past.

Today less than 40 per cent of the population are at present covered by some forms of health insurance or related scheme. Among this population, around 1.5 million workers of private firms are still not at all insured for the sicknesses proved to be unrelated to work. With regard to individual or group health insurance organised by private insurance businesses, the market share in terms of number of members is relatively very small and highly fluctuated. Hence, for these businesses to become financially viable the opportunity of increasing membership is very crucial for them. As for the Community-based Health Card Project, although the total number of members may seem to be adequate, this voluntary scheme is operating in a large number of villages each of which retains its own independence. Accordingly, many villages in which the number of members are too small will not be in a position to pool adequate resources. The principle of risk-sharing on financing of health care among health card holders can be longer be sustained when the resource is far less than the cost to be recovered by providers.

In order to ensure accessibility to health services for everyone there is evidently pressure to enhance insurance and related schemes that can supplement financial support for health care. A more effective management of cost recovery through the existing system of user charge would be desirable, since hospital income might be diverted to subsidise those who can hardly afford to pay the full expense. An initiative could be taken in areas of compulsory insurance of high priority, such as third party insurance for motor vehicles and motorcycles, which could be diverted to payment for medical services for a large number of traffic accident cases. Enhancing the Workmen Compensation Fund through labour inspection and law enforcement should provide increased revenues, since the responsible organisation has already taken steps to ensure coverage of all eligible employees. In this connection, the fund will be better prepared to provide an increasing amount of medical compensation and in some cases rehabilitation expenses also. At the same time, it is interesting to note that the Workmen Compensation Fund has almost 3 billion baht available for spending and two-thirds of this amount derives mainly from bank interest.

As far as modification or adjustment in the concept and management of the Community-based Health Card Project is concerned, the health card price may have to be standardised or re-estimated on a cost-recovery and risk-sharing basis. The size of membership of each health card fund, which is at present based on a single community (or village) needs to be reconsidered. Larger community-based health card funds at district or even provincial level should be explored. The project also requires a critical look at the feasibility of handing over management responsibility in some project areas to more appropriate institutions or organisations.

Continuation of the scheme on a voluntary basis is a major requirement for the success of the health card project. However, the many operational difficulties have to be dealt with by systematic evaluation and action, and it is highly questionable whether the project will be politically viable in the long run.

ANNEX I

GLOSSARY
HEALTH INSURANCE AND HEALTH CARE TERMS

HEALTH INSURANCE

Benefits in kind
Health services provided to insured persons which are delivered, paid or reimbursed in full or in part by the scheme.

Cash benefits
Cash payments made by the scheme to compensate for loss of income in case of illness, accident or maternity, or for additional expenditures in case of maternity or death.

Catastrophic insurance
Reimbursement, in full or in part, of especially high and naturally unforeseeable expenditure on medical care, or the free provision of such care (subject to any cost-sharing) in circumstances of high-cost illness.

Community rating
Averaging out all risks among the community, or risk-sharing.

Compulsory health insurance (mandatory, statutory)
A health insurance programme in which legislation defines the population and benefits covered, the conditions of eligibility, and the sources of funds of the scheme. Health insurance is a measure of *social security*.

Contingency reserve
Funds, deriving from contributions or other sources, which are set aside by the scheme to meet unforeseen income or expenditure deviations.

Contribution ceiling
The maximum amount of earnings per week, month or year which is subject to social security contributions. Earnings up to this ceiling are therefore termed insurable earnings.

Contributions
Monies paid regularly by and/or on behalf of insured persons to ensure entitlement to benefits covered by the scheme.

Eligibility conditions
Conditions that protected persons must meet in order to be entitled to the benefits of the scheme.
Such as:

Maximum duration of benefits
The maximum period of time during which a protected person may receive benefits.
Qualifying period
Minimum period of contributions before insured person or dependants can qualify for the provision of benefits.
Waiting period
The period an insured person has to wait before qualifying for and receiving specific benefits.
Free choice of provider
Choice of health care provider by protected person without restriction.
Free rider problem
If persons can benefit from a scheme without contributing to the scheme.
Insured persons (contributors)
Persons paying regular contributions or on behalf of whom contributions are regularly paid.
Moral hazard
Ability of a protected person to exploit benefits unduly to the detriment or disadvantage of others or the scheme as a whole, without having to bear the financial consequences of his or her behaviour in part or in full.
Pay-as-you-go system of financing (assessment premium)
A system of financing an insurance scheme under which the total expenditures for benefits and administration of a given period are met out of the income (from contributions and other sources) of the same period. Pay-as-you-go insurance schemes do not accumulate reserves except for contingency reserves.
Protected persons (beneficiaries, population covered)
The individuals entitled to the benefits of the scheme, including the insured persons and their dependants as defined by the legislation.
Risk rating
Adjusting of individual risk by insurer, usually based on age, pre/existing morbidity.
Universal coverage
Coverage of all the citizens of a country by the scheme.
Voluntary health insurance
A health insurance programme in which affiliation to the scheme is not determined by legislation.

TERMS RELEVANT TO HEALTH CARE DELIVERY SYSTEMS

Acute care
Treatment of an illness or injury in its acute stages, in a general acute care facility, if institutionalisation is needed. Hospital length of stay is generally less than 30 days.
Health care delivery system
Health services system
The prevailing systematic pattern of delivery of health services in a given country or region. The health care system characterises the type, level and

ownership of health care resources, medical practice and referral patterns, as well as the major financing sources.

Health care resources
Infrastructure
Manpower, facilities and equipment involved in the delivery of health care, with availability generally measured in volume per unit population, such as physicians per 100,000 and hospital beds per 1,000 population.

Level of care
Classification of health care into primary, secondary and tertiary care, each with increasing reliance on technology and specialisation.

Long-term care
Long-term care generally refers to institutionalised care over a period of over 30 days, and in a specialised long-term facility, such as a rehabilitation hospital or chronic disease long-term care nursing facility. In most countries the long-term nursing care of patients with chronic illness is excluded under general health insurance programmes, or may be provided under special programmes.

Personal preventive health services
Current concepts differentiate between activities aimed at the promotion of health and primary prevention of disease, secondary prevention (early detection of disease) and tertiary prevention (prevention of progression of disease).

Primary health care
World Health Organization definition: "Primary care is essentially health care based on practical, scientifically sound and socially acceptable methods and technology made universally accessible to individuals and families in the community, through their full participation and at a cost that the community and country can afford to maintain at every stage of their development in the spirit of self-reliance and self-determination. It forms an integral part both of the country's health system, of which it is the central function and the main focus, and of the overall social and economic development of the community."

Secondary care
Health services mainly provided by specialists in medical disciplines, and generally requiring the use of ancillary services for the diagnosis and treatment of illness. The basic secondary care specialities are: internal medicine, surgery, pediatrics, obstetrics- gynaecology, orthopaedics, ophthalmology, urology, dermatology and oto-rhino-laryngology.

Tertiary care
Health services mainly provided by specialists in a broader range of medical disciplines, and generally requiring the use of the range of diagnostic and treatment equipment maintained mainly in university teaching hospitals or regional and national level referral centres.

Type of services
Traditional classification of health services into:
Promotion of health and disease prevention; Curative care; Rehabilitative care; Current concepts accept a unified spectrum of health care with considerable overlap between the traditional types of care.

TERMS RELEVANT TO PAYMENT FOR SERVICES
(Mainly applicable in indirect health insurance schemes)

Cost sharing
User charges
Payments which protected persons have to make at the time of use of health services, in addition to the regular contributions to the scheme paid by the insured persons. These payments generally only cover part of the charges for the services. Differential payments according to income, age or other factors are sometimes applied in social security health insurance schemes, exempting specific vulnerable groups. Cost/sharing can take various forms, such as:

Circumvention fee
Fixed fee which is due if a protected person contacts directly a provider on a higher level of care than on the designated entry level of the health care delivery system, as for example, when a person contacts a specialist without seeing a general practitioner first and being referred to the specialist.

Co-insurance (In French: *ticket modérateur*)
Payment of a fixed percentage of the charge of all or a defined range of services (as well as amounts above the agreed fees in the schedule).

Co-payment
Payment of a fixed flat-rate fee for every kind of a defined list of services.

Exclusion of benefits
Charges for a defined range of services not covered by the scheme and borne in full by the patient.

Fee schedule (schedule of agreed fees and tariffs)
List defining the items and fees negotiated between the scheme and the providers of health services. The fee schedule is updated by periodic negotiations regarding both items and fees.

Over-billing
Additional charge made by the provider over and above the charge listed in the fee schedule. This additional amount is borne by the patient.

Reimbursement
Payment by the scheme to the provider of health care, or to the protected persons as a refund, for all or part of fees for health services.

Third-party payer
The agency which reimburses or refunds all or part of the charges for health services incurred by a defined group of protected persons. The agency may be an integral part of the scheme.

Annex I

TERMS RELEVANT TO THE PAYMENT OF HEALTH CARE PROVIDERS

Capitation

Providers are regularly paid a stipulated fee per protected person for whom they provide services as needed during a defined period of time (quarter, year).

Fee-for-service

Providers are paid for every defined item of service. The different items and their fees are usually listed in a fee schedule.

Salary

Health care providers are employed by the scheme or an agency contracting with the scheme as salaried employees.

ANNEX II

MEDICAL CARE: EXTRACTS FROM PROVISIONS OF ILO RECOMMENDATIONS AND CONVENTIONS

I. FORMS OF MEDICAL CARE SERVICES

Recommendation No. 69

5. Medical care should be provided either through a social insurance medical care service with supplementary provision by way of social assistance to meet the requirements of needy persons not yet covered by social insurance, or through a public medical care service.

9. Where the service is limited to a section of the population or to a specified area, or where the contributory mechanism already exists for other branches of social insurance and it is possible ultimately to bring under the insurance scheme the whole or the majority of the population, social insurance may be appropriate.

10. Where the whole of the population is to be covered by the service and it is desired to integrate medical care with general health services, a public service may be appropriate.

Convention No. 102
(Minimum Standards)

Article 71

1. The cost of the benefits provided in compliance with this Convention and the cost of the administration of such benefits shall be borne collectively by way of insurance contributions or taxation or both in a manner which avoids hardship to persons of small means and takes into account the economic situation of the Member and of the classes of persons protected.

3. The Member shall accept general responsibility for the due provision of the benefits provided in compliance with this Convention, and shall take all measures required for this purpose; it shall ensure, where appropriate, that the necessary actuarial studies and calculations concerning financial equilibrium are made periodically and, in any event, prior to any change in benefits, the rate of insurance contributions, or the taxes allocated to covering the contingencies in question.

Article 72

2. The Member shall accept general responsibility for the proper administration of the institutions and services concerned in the application of the Convention.

Article 6

For the purpose of compliance... a Member may take account of protection effected by means of insurance which, although not made compulsory by national laws or regulations for the persons to be protected:

(a) is supervised by the public authorities or administered, in accordance with prescribed standards, by joint operation of employers and workers;

(b) covers a substantial part of the persons whose earnings do not exceed those of the skilled manual male employee; and

(c) complies, in conjunction with other forms of protection, where appropriate, with the relevant provisions of the Convention.

Recommendation No. 134

No provision.

Convention No. 130

Article 30

1. Each Member shall accept general responsibility for the due provision of the benefits provided in compliance with this Convention and shall take all measures required for this purpose.

2. Each Member shall accept general responsibility for the proper administration of the institutions and services concerned in the application of this Convention.

Article 6

[Provision similar to that in Article 6 of Convention No. 102, above.]

II. ESSENTIAL FEATURES AND OBJECTIVES OF MEDICAL CARE

Recommendation No. 69

1. A medical care service should meet the need of the individual for care by members of the medical and allied professions and for such other facilities as are provided at medical institutions:
   (a) with a view to restoring the individual's health, preventing the further development of disease and alleviating suffering, when he is afflicted by ill health (curative care); and
   (b) with a view to protecting and improving his health (preventive care).

2. The nature and extent of the care provided by the service should be defined by law.

46. The medical care service should aim at providing the highest possible standard of care, due regard being paid to the importance of the doctor-patient relationship and the professional and personal responsibility of the doctor, while safeguarding both the interests of the beneficiaries and those of the professions participating.

Convention No. 102 (Minimum Standards)

Article 7

Each Member... shall secure to the persons protected the provision of benefit in respect of a condition requiring medical care of a preventive or curative nature...

Article 8

The contingencies covered shall include any morbid condition, whatever its cause, and pregnancy and confinement and their consequences.

Article 10

3. The benefit provided... shall be afforded with a view to maintaining, restoring or improving the health of the person protected and his ability to work and to attend to his personal needs.

Recommendation No. 134

No provision.

Convention No. 130

Article 7

The contingencies covered shall include:
(a) need for medical care of a curative nature and, under prescribed conditions, need for medical care of a preventive nature.

Article 8

Each Member shall secure to the persons protected, subject to prescribed conditions, the provision of medical care of a curative or preventive nature...

Article 9

The medical care...shall be afforded with a view to maintaining, restoring or improving the health of the person protected and his ability to work and to attend to his personal needs.

III. PERSONS COVERED BY THE MEDICAL CARE SERVICES

Recommendation No. 69

8. The medical care service should cover all members of the community, whether or not they are gainfully occupied.

6. Where medical care is provided through a social insurance medical care service:

(a) every insured contributor, the dependent wife or husband and dependent children of every such contributor, such other dependants as may be prescribed by national laws or regulations, and every other person insured by virtue of contributions paid on his behalf, should be entitled to all care provided by the service.

11. Where medical care is provided through a social insurance medical care service, all members of the community should have the right to care as insured persons or, pending their inclusion in the scope of insurance, should have the right to receive care at the expense of the competent authority

Convention No. 102 (Minimum Standards) [1]

Article 9

The persons protected shall comprise:
(a) prescribed classes of employees, constituting not less than 50 per cent of all employees, and also their wives and children; or
(b) prescribed classes of the economically active population, constituting not less than 20 per cent of all residents, and also their wives and children; or
(c) prescribed classes of residents, constituting not less than 50 per cent of all residents; or

---
[1] Article 3 of Convention No. 102 and Article 2 of Convention No. 130 contain provisions for temporary exceptions, applicable to Members whose economy and medical facilities are insufficiently developed.

when unable to provide it for themselves.

7. Where medical care is provided through a public medical care service:

(a) every member of the community should be entitled to all care provided by the service.

(d) where a declaration made in virtue of Article 3 is in force, prescribed classes of employees constituting not less than 50 per cent of all employees in industrial workplaces employing 20 persons or more, and also their wives and children.

Article 68

1. Non-national residents shall have the same rights as national residents: provided that special rules concerning non-nationals and nationals born outside the territory of the Member may be prescribed in respect of benefits or portions of benefits which are payable wholly or mainly out of public funds and in respect of transitional schemes.

2. Under contributory social security schemes which protect employees, the persons protected who are nationals of another Member which has accepted the obligations of the relevant Part of the Convention shall have, under that Part, the same rights as nationals of the Member concerned: provided that the application of this paragraph may be made subject to the existence of a bilateral or multilateral agreement providing for reciprocity.

Recommendation No. 134

2. Members should extend... medical care...by stages, if necessary, and under appropriate conditions:

(a) to persons whose employment is of a casual nature;

(b) to members of the employer's family living in his house, in respect of their work for him;

(c) to all economically active persons;

Convention No. 130 [1]

Article 10

The persons protected...shall comprise:

---

[1] Article 3 of Convention No. 102 and Article 2 of Convention No. 130 contain provisions for temporary exceptions, applicable to Members whose economy and medical facilities are insufficiently developed.

(d) to the wives and children of the persons specified in clauses *(a)* to *(c)* of this paragraph; and

(e) to all residents.

(a) all employees, including apprentices, and the wives and children of such employees; or

(b) prescribed classes of the economically active population, constituting not less than 75 per cent of the whole economically active population, and the wives and children of persons in the said classes; or

(c) prescribed classes of residents constituting not less than 75 per cent of all residents.

Article 5

Any Member whose legislation protects employees may, as necessary, exclude from the application of this Convention:

(a) persons whose employment is of a casual nature;

(b) members of the employer's family living in his house, in respect of their work for him;

(c) other categories of employees, which shall not exceed in number 10 per cent of all employees other than those excluded under subparagraphs *(a)* and *(b)* of this Article.

Article 11

Where a declaration made in virtue of Article 2 is in force, the persons protected in respect of the contingency referred to in subparagraph *(a)* of Article 7 shall comprise:

(a) prescribed classes of employees, constituting not less than 25 per cent of all employees, and the wives and children of employees in the said classes; or

(b) prescribed classes of employees in industrial undertakings, constituting not less than 50 per cent of all employees in industrial undertakings, and the wives and children of employees in the said classes.

Article 12

Persons who are in receipt of a social security benefit for invalidity, old age, death of the breadwinner or unemployment, and, where appropriate, the wives and children of such persons, shall continue to be protected, under prescribed conditions...

Article 32

Each Member shall, within its territory, assure to non-nationals who normally reside or work there, equality of treatment with its own nationals as regards the right to the benefits provided for in this Convention.

IV. NATURE AND EXTENT OF MEDICAL CARE

1. RANGE OF SERVICES

Recommendation No. 69

21. The care afforded should comprise both general practitioner and specialist out- and in-patient care, including domiciliary visiting; dental care; nursing care at home or in hospital or other medical institutions; the care given by qualified midwives and other maternity services at home or in hospital; maintenance in hospitals, convalescent homes, sanatoria or other medical institutions; so far as possible, the requisite dental, pharmaceutical and other medical or surgical supplies, including artificial limbs; and the care furnished by such other professions as may at any time be legally recognised as belonging to the allied professions.

Convention No. 102 (Minimum Standards) [1]

Article 10

1. The benefits shall include at least:
(a) in case of a morbid condition:
　(i) general practitioner care, including domiciliary visiting;
　(ii) specialist care at hospitals for in-patients and out-patients, and such specialist care as may be available outside hospitals;
　(iii) the essential pharmaceutical supplies as prescribed by

---
[1] Article 3 of Convention No. 102 and Article 2 of Convention No. 130 contain provisions for temporary exceptions, applicable to Members whose economy and medical facilities are insufficiently developed.

Recommendation No. 134

3. The medical care...should include:
(a) the supply of medical aids, such as eyeglasses; and
(b) services for convalescents.

Convention No. 130 [1]

medical or other qualified practitioners; and
(iv) hospitalisation where necessary; and
(b) in case of pregnancy and confinement and their consequences:
(i) pre-natal, confinement and post-natal care either by medical practitioners or by qualified midwives; and
(ii) hospitalisation where necessary.

The medical care... shall comprise at least:
(a) general practitioner care, including domiciliary visiting;
(b) specialist care at hospitals for in-patients and out-patients, and such specialist care as may be available outside hospitals;
(c) the necessary pharmaceutical supplies on prescription by medical or other qualified practitioners;
(d) hospitalisation where necessary;
(e) dental care, as prescribed; and
(f) medical rehabilitation, including the supply, maintenance and renewal of prosthetic and orthopaedic appliances, as prescribed.

---

[1] Article 3 of Convention No. 102 and Article 2 of Convention No. 130 contain provisions for temporary exceptions, applicable to Members whose economy and medical facilities are insufficiently developed.

Annex II

Article 14

Where a declaration made in virtue of Article 2 is in force, the medical care referred to in Article 8 shall comprise at least:

(a) general practitioner care, including, wherever possible, domiciliary visiting;

(b) specialist care at hospitals for in-patients and out-patients, and, wherever possible, such specialist care as may be available outside hospitals;

(c) the necessary pharmaceutical supplies on prescription by medical or other qualified practitioners; and

(d) hospitalisation where necessary.

2. DURATION OF MEDICAL CARE

Recommendation No. 69

22. All care and supplies should be available at any time and without time limit, when and as long as they are needed, subject only to the doctor's judgement and to such reasonable limitations as may be imposed by the technical organisation of the service.

Convention No. 102 (Minimum Standards) [1]

Article 12

1. The benefit...shall be granted throughout the contingency covered, except that, in case of a morbid condition, its duration may be limited to 26 weeks in each case, but benefit shall not be suspended while a sickness benefit continues to be paid, and provision shall be made to enable the limit to be extended for prescribed diseases recognised as entailing prolonged care.

---

[1] Article 3 of Convention No. 102 and Article 2 of Convention No. 130 contain provisions for temporary exceptions, applicable to Members whose economy and medical facilities are insufficiently developed.

2. Where a declaration made in virtue of Article 3 is in force, the duration of the benefit may be limited to 13 weeks in each case.

Recommendation No. 134

5. Where a beneficiary ceases to belong to the categories of persons protected, the medical care...should be provided throughout the contingency for a case of sickness which started while he belonged to the said categories.

Convention No. 130

Article 16

1. The medical care...shall be provided throughout the contingency.

2. Where a beneficiary ceases to belong to the categories of persons protected, further entitlement to medical care for a case of sickness which started while he belonged to the said categories may be limited to a prescribed period which shall not be less than 26 weeks: provided that the medical care shall not cease while the beneficiary continues to receive a sickness benefit.

3. Notwithstanding the provisions of paragraph 2 of this Article, the duration of medical care shall be extended for prescribed diseases recognised as entailing prolonged care.

V. CONDITIONS FOR ENTITLEMENT TO MEDICAL CARE

Recommendation No. 69

20. Complete preventive and curative care should be available at any time and place to all members of the community covered by the service, on the same conditions, without any hindrance or barrier of an administrative, financial or political nature, or otherwise unrelated to their health.

18. Where medical care is provided through a public medical care service, the provision of care should

Convention No. 102 (Minimum Standards)

Article 11

The benefit...shall, in a contingency covered, be secured at least to a person protected who has completed, or whose breadwinner has completed, such qualifying period as may be considered necessary to preclude abuse.

not depend on any qualifying conditions, such as payment of taxes or compliance with a means test, and all beneficiaries should have an equal right to the care provided.

23. Beneficiaries should be able to obtain care at the centres or offices provided, wherever they happen to be when the need arises, whether at their place of residence or elsewhere within the total area in which the service is available, irrespective of their membership in any particular insurance institution, arrears in contributions or of other factors unrelated to health.

Recommendation No. 134

4. The right to the medical care... should not be made subject to a qualifying period.

Convention No. 130

Article 15

Where the legislation of a Member makes the right to the medical care... conditional upon the fulfilment of a qualifying period by the person protected or by his breadwinner, the conditions governing the qualifying period shall be such as not to deprive of the right to benefit persons who normally belong to the categories of persons protected.

VI. FINANCING OF MEDICAL CARE SERVICES

Recommendation No. 69

4. The cost of the service should be met collectively by regular periodical payments which may take the form of social insurance contributions or of taxes, or of both.

6. Where medical care is provided through a social insurance medical care service:

Convention No. 102
(Minimum Standards)

Article 71

1. The cost of the benefits provided in compliance with this Convention and the cost of the administration of such benefits shall be borne collectively by way of insurance contributions or taxation or both in a

(c) the service should be financed by contributions from insured persons, from their employers, and by subsidies from public funds.

12. All adult members of the community...should be required to pay insurance contributions if their income is not below the subsistence level. The dependent wife or husband of a contributor should be insured in virtue of the contribution of her or his breadwinner, without any addition on that account.

76. The contribution paid by an insured person should be such part of the maximum contribution as can be borne without hardship.

77. Employers should be required to pay part of the maximum contribution on behalf of persons employed by them.

78. Persons whose income does not exceed the subsistence level should not be required to pay an insurance contribution. Equitable contributions should be paid by the public authority on their behalf: provided that in the case of employed persons, such contributions may be paid wholly or partly by their employers.

79. The cost of the medical care service not covered by contributions should be borne by taxpayers.

7. Where medical care is provided through a public medical care service:

(b) the service should be financed out of funds raised either by a progressive tax specifically imposed for the purpose of financing the medical care service or of financing all health services, or from general revenue.

91. In addition to providing the normal resources for financing the medical care service, measures should manner which avoids hardship to persons of small means and takes into account the economic situation of the Member and of the classes of persons protected.

2. The total of the insurance contributions borne by the employees protected shall not exceed 50 per cent of the total of the financial resources allocated to the protection of employees and their wives and children. For the purpose of ascertaining whether this condition is fulfilled, all the benefits provided by the Member in compliance with this Convention, except family benefit and, if provided by a special branch, employment injury benefit, may be taken together.

3. The Member shall accept general responsibility for the due provision of the benefits provided in compliance with this Convention, and shall take all measures required for this purpose; it shall ensure, where appropriate, that the necessary actuarial studies and calculations concerning financial equilibrium are made periodically and, in any event, prior to any change in benefits, the rate of insurance contributions, or the taxes allocated to covering the contingencies in question.

be taken to utilise the assets of social insurance institutions, or funds raised by other means, for financing the extraordinary expenditure necessitated by the extension and improvement of the service, more particularly by the building or equipment of hospitals and medical centres.

Recommendation No. 134

No provision.

Convention No. 130

No provision.

VII. COST-SHARING BY PERSONS RECEIVING MEDICAL CARE

Recommendation No. 69

No provision.

Convention No. 102
(Minimum Standards)

Article 10

2. The beneficiary or his breadwinner may be required to share in the cost of the medical care the beneficiary receives in respect of a morbid condition; the rules concerning such cost-sharing shall be so designed as to avoid hardship.

Recommendation No. 134

7. A beneficiary or, where appropriate, his breadwinner should not be required to share in the cost of the medical care...
(a) if his means do not exceed prescribed amounts;
(b) in respect of diseases recognised as entailing prolonged care.

Convention No. 130

Article 17

Where the legislation of a Member requires the beneficiary or his breadwinner to share in the cost of the medical care ... the rules concerning such cost-sharing shall be so designed as to avoid hardship and not to prejudice the effectiveness of medical and social protection.

VIII. ORGANISATION AND CO-ORDINATION OF MEDICAL CARE SERVICES

Recommendation No. 69

19. Complete preventive and curative care should be constantly available, rationally organised and, so far as possible, co-ordinated with general health services.

27. The optimum of medical care should be made readily available through an organisation that ensures the greatest possible economy and efficiency by the pooling of knowledge, staff, equipment and other resources and by close contact and collaboration among all participating members of the medical and allied professions and agencies.

3. The authorities or bodies responsible for the administration of the service should provide medical care for its beneficiaries by securing the services of members of the medical and allied professions and by arranging for hospital and other institutional services.

28. The wholehearted participation of the greatest possible number of members of the medical and allied professions is essential for the success of any national medical care service. The numbers of general practitioners, specialists, dentists, nurses and members of other professions within the service should be adapted to the distribution and the needs of the beneficiaries.

26. Arrangements should be made by the administration of the service for securing adequate hospital and other residential accommodation and care, either by contracts with existing public and approved private institutions, or by the establishment and maintenance of appropriate institutions.

Convention No. 102 (Minimum Standards)

Article 10

4. The institutions or government departments administering the benefit shall, by such means as may be deemed appropriate, encourage the persons protected to avail themselves of the general health services placed at their disposal by the public authorities or by other bodies recognised by the public authorities.

25. Where the medical care service covers only a section of the population or is at present administered by different types of insurance institutions and authorities, the institutions and authorities concerned should provide care for their beneficiaries by securing collectively the services of members of the medical and allied professions, and by the joint establishment or maintenance of health centres and other medical institutions, pending the regional and national unification of the services.

33. Where the medical care service covers the majority of the population, medical or health centres may appropriately be built, equipped and operated by the authority administering the service in the health area ...

37. Where the medical care service does not cover the majority of the population but has a substantial number of beneficiaries, and existing hospital and other medical facilities are inadequate, the insurance institution, insurance institutions jointly, should establish a system of medical or health centres which affords all care, including hospital accommodation at the main centres, and, so far as possible, transport arrangements; such centres may be required more particularly in sparsely settled areas with a scattered insured population.

42. There should be available to the beneficiaries of the medical care service all general health services, being services providing means for the whole community and/or groups of individuals to promote and protect their health while it is not yet threatened or known to be threatened, whether such services be given by members of the medical and allied professions or otherwise.

43. The medical care service should be provided in close co-ordination with general health services,

either by means of close collaboration of the social insurance institutions providing medical care and the authorities administering the general health services, or by combing medical care and general health services in one public service.

44. Local co-ordination of medical care and general health services should be aimed at either by establishing medical care centres in proximity to the headquarters for general health services, or by establishing common centres as headquarters for all or most health services.

45. The members of the medical and allied professions participating in the medical care service and working at health centres may appropriately undertake such general health care as can with advantage be given by the same staff, including immunisation, examination of school children and other groups, advice to expectant mothers and mothers with infants, and other care of a like nature.

Recommendation No. 134

No provision.

Convention No. 130

No provision.

IX. STANDARDS OF PROFESSIONAL SKILL AND KNOWLEDGE

Recommendation No. 69

66. The highest possible standard of skill and knowledge should be achieved and maintained for the professions participating both by requiring high standards of education, training and licensing and by keeping up to

Convention No. 102
(Minimum Standards)

No provision.

date and developing the skill and knowledge of those engaged in the service.

67. Doctors participating in the service should be required to have an adequate training in social medicine.

71. Doctors and dentists participating should be required periodically to attend post-graduate courses organised or approved for this purpose.

73. Adequate facilities for teaching and research should be made available at the hospitals administered by or working with the medical care service.

74. Professional education and research should be promoted with the financial and legal support of the State.

Recommendation No. 134

No provision.

Convention No. 130

No provision.

X. ADMINISTRATION OF MEDICAL CARE SERVICES

I. CENTRAL, LOCAL AND UNIT ADMINISTRATION

Recommendation No. 69

24. The administration of the medical care service should be unified for appropriate health areas sufficiently large for a self-contained and well-balanced service, and should be centrally supervised.

93. A central authority, representative of the community, should be responsible for formulating the health policy or policies and for supervising all medical care and general health services, subject to consultation of, and collaboration with, the medical and allied professions on all professional

Convention No. 102 (Minimum Standards)

Article 72

1. Where the administration is not entrusted to an institution regulated by the public authorities or to a government department responsible to a legislature, representatives of the persons protected shall participate in the management, or be associated therewith in a consultative capacity, under prescribed conditions; national laws or regulations may likewise decide as to the participation of representatives of

matters, and to consultation of the beneficiaries on matters of policy and administration affecting the medical care service.

94. Where the medical care service covers the whole or the majority of the population and a central government agency supervises or administers all medical care and general health services, beneficiaries may appropriately be deemed to be represented by the head of the agency.

95. The central government agency should keep in touch with the beneficiaries through advisory bodies comprising representatives of organisations of the different sections of the population, such as trade unions, employers' associations, chambers of commerce, farmers' associations, women's associations and child protection societies.

96. Where the medical care service covers only a section of the population, and a central government agency supervises all medical care and general health services, representatives of the insured persons should participate in the supervision, preferably through advisory committees, as regards all matters of policy affecting the medical care service.

97. The central government agency should consult the representatives of the medical and allied professions, preferably through advisory committees, on all questions relating to the working conditions of the members of the professions participating, and on all other matters primarily of a professional nature, more particularly on the preparation of laws and regulations concerning the nature, extent and provision of the care furnished under the service.

98. Where the medical care service covers the whole or the majority of the employers and of the public authorities.

2. The Member shall accept general responsibility for the proper administration of the institutions and services concerned in the application of the Convention.

Annex II

population and a representative body supervises or administers all medical care and general health services, beneficiaries should be represented on such body, either directly or indirectly.

99. In this event, the medical and allied professions should be represented on the representative body, preferably in numbers equal to those of the beneficiaries or the government as the case may be; the professional members should be elected by the profession concerned, or nominated by their representatives and appointed by the central Government.

104. Local administration of medical care and general health services should be unified or co-ordinated within areas ... and the medical care service in the area should be administered by or with the advice of bodies representative of the beneficiaries and partly composed of, or assisted by, representatives of the medical and allied professions, so as to safeguard the interests of the beneficiaries and the professions, and secure the technical efficiency of the service and the professional freedom of the participating doctors.

105. Where the medical care service covers the whole or the majority of the population in the health area, all medical care and general health services may appropriately be administered by one area authority.

110. Where the social insurance medical care service covers only a section of the population, administration of that service may appropriately be entrusted to a representative executive body responsible to the Government, and comprising representatives of the beneficiaries, of the medical and allied professions participating in the service and of the employers.

111. Health units owned and operated by the medical care service, such as medical or health centres or hospitals, should be administered under democratic control with adequate provisions for the participation of the medical profession, or wholly or predominantly by doctors elected by, or appointed after consultation of, the members of the medical and allied professions participating in the medical care service, in co-operation with all the doctors working at the unit.

Recommendation No. 134

No provision.

Convention No. 130

Article 30

1. Each Member shall accept general responsibility for the due provision of the benefits provided in compliance with this Convention and shall take all measures required for this purpose.

2. Each Member shall accept general responsibility for the proper administration of the institutions and services concerned in the application of this Convention.

Article 31

Where the administration is not entrusted to an institution regulated by the public authorities or to a government department responsible to a legislature:

(a) representatives of the persons protected shall participate in the management under prescribed conditions;

(b) national legislation shall, where appropriate, provide for the participation of representatives of employers;

(c) national legislation may likewise decide as to the participation of representatives of the public authorities.

2. RIGHT OF APPEAL

Recommendation No. 69

63. Provision should be made for the submission of complaints by beneficiaries concerning the care received, and by members of the medical or allied professions concerning their relations with the administration of the service, to appropriate arbitration bodies under conditions affording adequate guarantees to all parties concerned.

112. Beneficiaries or members of the medical or allied professions who have submitted complaints to the arbitration body ... should have a right of appeal from the decisions of such body to an independent tribunal.

Recommendation No. 134

No provision.

Convention No. 102
(Minimum Standards)

Article 70

1. Every claimant shall have a right of appeal in case of refusal of the benefit or complaint as to its quality or quantity.

2. Where in the application of this Convention a government department responsible to a legislature is entrusted with the administration of medical care, the right of appeal provided for in paragraph 1 of this Article may be replaced by a right to have a complaint concerning the refusal of medical care or the quality of the care received investigated by the appropriate authority.

3. Where a claim is settled by a special tribunal established to deal with social security questions and on which the persons protected are represented, no right of appeal shall be required.

Convention No. 130

Article 29

1. Every claimant shall have a right of appeal in the case of refusal of the benefit or complaint as to its quality or quantity.

2. Where in the application of this Convention a government department responsible to a legislature is entrusted with the administration of medical care, the right of appeal provided for in paragraph 1 of this Article may be replaced by a right to have a complaint concerning the refusal of medical care or the quality of the care received investigated by the appropriate authority.

ANNEX III

SUGGESTIONS FOR FURTHER READING

Abel-Smith, B.: "Health policy and social security", in ISSA: *Round table meeting on the extension of medical care programmes under social security*, Social Security Documentation: Asian Series, No. 8 (New Delhi, ISSA Regional Office for Asia and Oceania), 1983, pp. 11-18.

Anderson, O.W.: "Government health insurance and privatisation: An examination of the concept and of equity", in *International Journal of Health Planning and Management*, 1988, Vol. 3, pp. 35-43.

Ball, R.M.: "National health insurance: Comments on selected issues", in *Science*, 1978, Vol. 200, pp. 864-870.

Beck, R.G.: "The effect of copayment on the poor", in *Journal of Human Resources*, 1974, Vol. 9, pp. 129-142.

Blanpain, J., Delesie, L.; Nys, H.: *National health insurance and health resources*. Cambridge, Massachusetts, Harvard University Press, 1978.

Brook, R.H. et al.: "Does free care improve adult health? Results from a controlled clinical trial", in *New England Journal of Medicine*, 1983, Vol. 309, pp. 1426-1434.

Cornely, P., et al.: "History of the health care system in Chile", in *Journal of the American Public Health Association*, 1977, Vol. 67, pp. 31-36.

Cutting, C.C.: "A comprehensive medical care delivery system born in industry", in *Journal of Occupational Medicine*, 1971, Vol. 13, pp. 411-414.

Detwiller, L.: "National health insurance: Can the US learn from Canada?", in *Hospital Progress*, Sep. 1974, pp. 48-53.

Donabedian, A.: "Issues in national health insurance", in *American Journal of Public Health*, 1976, No. 4, pp. 345-350.

Doron, H.R.; Ron, A.: "The organisation of primary care in Israel", in H.P. Gleason (ed.): *Getting better*. Cambridge, Massachusetts, Oelgeschlager, Gunn and Hain, Publishers, 1981, pp. 85-102.

———; ———: "Primary care promotion to control costs in social security medical care systems", in *ISSR*, 1984, No. 2, pp. 150-157.

Glaser, W. A.: *Paying the doctor*. The Johns Hopkins Press, 1970.

———: *Paying the hospitals*. San Francisco and London, Jossey-Bass, 1987.

Fein, R.: "The case for national health insurance", in *Saturday Review*, 1970, Vol. 53, pp. 27-29 and 65.

Hatcher, G.: "Canadian approaches to health policy decisions: National health insurance", in *American Journal of Public Health*, 1978, Vol. 68, pp. 881-889.

Hu, Teh-Wei: "Issues of health care in the People's Republic of China", in *Social Science and Medicine*, 1981, Vol. 15C, pp. 233-237.

Mitchell, B. M.: "The financing of national health insurance", in *Science*, 1976.

Newhouse, J.; Taylor, V.: "Financing health care: Here's a fresh solution", in *Medical Economics*, 1971, pp. 244-257.

Noumi, K.: "Financing of social security medical care schemes and the containment of costs: The Japanese experience", in *ISSR*, 1973, No. 2, pp. 180-206.

Patag, F.: "Experiences of the social security medical care system in the Philippines", in ISSA: *Round table meeting on the extension of medical care*, op. cit., pp. 49-57.

Roemer, M. I.; Axelrod, S. J.: "A national health service and social security", in *American Journal of Public Health*, 1977, No. 5, pp. 462-465.

Ron, A. "Sharing in the financing of health care: Government, insurance and the patient", in *Health Policy*, 1986, Vol. 6, pp. 87-101.

———: "Government participation in social security health insurance budgets", in *ISSR*, 1986, No. 1, pp. 52-63.

———: "The public-private mix in health care, report on a conference", in *Health Policy*, 1987, Vol. 8, pp. 24-26.

Singh, H. M.: "National strategies for the extension of the coverage of medical care programmes under social security", in ISSA: *Round table meeting on the extension of medical care*, op. cit., pp. 67-81.

Sloan, F. A.: "The role of health insurance in the physicians' services market", in *Inquiry*, Vol. XII, pp. 275-299.

Tamburi, G.: *The International Labour Organisation and the development of social insurance*. Geneva, ILO, 1981; mimeographed.

Van de Ven, W. P. P. M.: "The key role of health insurance in a cost-effective health care system", in *Health Policy*, 1987, Vol. 7, pp. 253-272.